THE TEACHINGS OF MR P.

The Teachings
of Mr P.

Delilah Sullivan

Published by: Delilah Sullivan
For information: www.DelilahSullivan.com

The author of this book does not dispense medical advice or prescribe the use of any ideas, techniques or suggestions in this book as a form of treatment for physical or medical problems. The reader should consult with his/her doctor in matters relating to his/her health. The intent of the author is only to offer information of a general nature in the promotion of well-being and is not a substitute for medical or professional advice. In the event you use any of the information in this book for yourself, the author and/or publisher assumes no responsibility for your actions.

ISBN-13: 9780995578708
ISBN-10: 0995578702

"To all those who seek a greater understanding to what enables a joyful and exuberant experience of the life we are gifted.

To all of us, for we mean more than life to each other, we give each other life."

MR P.

CONTENTS

MAN: an individual human of either sex; the human race.

INTRODUCTION

It is with the greatest pleasure I introduce you to this book, a book written through me, not by me.

In 2013 I discovered I was able to hear Spirit, namely my spiritual guides. In doing what felt so natural – writing, by hand, the words being spoken to me – I began the most fascinating and life-changing journey. In the process, came this book.

It is a journey which has also been challenging, as my inquisitiveness and deep resonance with what was being shared challenged my opposing need to belong to the world I knew. But as each doubt and question met with the truth of what was emerging, of a connection and sense of wonder which was rooted in the purest of love, support and quest for the best of and for me, I slowly began the integration.

The words, downloads as I call them, flow effortlessly and reassuringly. The hour or so I spend, usually in a favourite coffee shop, penning the conversations and passages offered is often the most fulfilling, grounding and meaningful hour of my day. For in this act of channelling from Spirit via the physical, I sense the connectedness and wonder of our existence and purpose, individually and collectively.

Life has not always been as such, but took a sudden leap into the unknown when I was diagnosed with an illness, aged 41. Overnight I became aware of the significance of the life I had been given, but had not taken ownership of. In the gift of awareness of my mortality, I slowly came to life. The passages in this book, and the process of writing them, anchored my sense of belonging within this unfolding. I hope the reading of it might do the same for you.

The Teachings of Mr P. is Mr P's book. His words, unedited, transcribed by me, as I hear them. An aspect I have had to consider is how to introduce him as an energy-body, to the world. Naturally, when told of his provenance as Plato, this was initially a lot to take in and to make sense of (I had heard of Plato, but knew very little of him or his philosophies, and as yet, have read just one of his books, *The Symposium*). But since, I have realized that we are all philosophers, all travellers-in-arms, spiritually and physically, in this experience we call life. Our only endeavour, to be the best we can be: the fullest, most joyful expression of love and intelligence; physically, mentally, emotionally and energetically.

The communication from Mr P, whilst intended for you, the reader, has been delivered to support my understanding of concepts and aspects of reality beyond my own. As such, it has been given to me in a language – and with a choice of words – which I can convey, whilst still allowing for expanded expression and meaning: for I am aware of hidden gems in the passages, words with double or triple meanings and clues for those interested in the metaphysical. It is a book which keeps unfolding.

The passages, which can be read individually, making it a wonderful companion of a book to be dipped into at random, if read sequentially, layer the learning and experience of a co-creative exploration. There is a power in its delivery, in the non-religious inclusiveness, in the order we are asked to question and reflect – a method, I sense, below the narrative. Above all, it is a book with which we can each create our personal connection, to use as a backdrop to inspire, to question not ourselves, but our interpretations of love, beauty and meaning. For the more we understand ourselves, the more we can connect with the world around us.

It has been a privilege and honour to bring this body of work into form. For me, it has an energy of practicality and expansiveness which both thrills me to be part of, and which pulls to be released. I am fascinated to see where it might go, and grateful to be part of it.

With love,

Delilah
London, November 8th 2016

1

An Offering of Randomness

MON 2ND JUNE 2014, LONDON AT 11.40AM, SESSION 1

Mr P: Randomness is the start of all creation. So this strikes as an appropriate place to begin this discussion. My intention with this series of discussions is to raise awareness within the reader. Nothing more. What you, the reader, does with the awareness will be your individual creationism. For herein lies the parable, that we – you, the reader, your neighbour, and indeed I – are the creators of 'all-that-is'.

Randomness creates mini-equivalents of what is described as the Big Bang. Let me explain. Mr Einstein espoused the theory of energy being constant: that matter turns into mass, and mass into matter. It is all energy. If we picture logs collected and placed to form a campfire, the energy within the logs sits within the energy of the air, on the energy of the ground. All are present, but it takes the spark to create the flame and the heat; and the resulting cinders. The 'spark' is Randomness, and Randomness is the spark of life.

So, if Randomness creates, what creates Randomness? This is the question I hope you, the reader, will feel confident answering by the end of this book. For whilst there is nothing as valuable as inquisitive thought, the nature of existence is that there are no 'right answers'. There are answers which make one feel good, safe; and answers which create discomfort and unease. But the answers which leave even more questions are the ones of growth and learning.

It is through Randomness you, dear reader, are reading these words, so let me explain a little of my-self, for a 'discussion' necessitates some foundations. These words are channelled through Delilah, a skill she has acquired some twelve months ago. They are variations of energy which she *interprets* onto paper. She is acting as a messenger, or funnel for the energy and the words. Randomness brought Delilah and I together; for this work, amongst other work. It is very exciting to be in communication and our partnership works extremely well.

It did not take Delilah long to realise that I had not been completely open with my provenance. Her inquisitiveness around philosophy and Socrates necessitated my disclosure of being Plato in a former 'life', though not my most recent life as a human. The realisation soon happened for her that our work, should she choose it, includes enabling this discussion, this book of words and thoughts. I am very grateful for her assistance with this.

Naturally Delilah had some questions and initial fears around sharing this work. Questions such as "Why now?" and fears such as ridicule: from people questioning the 'reality' of Plato in spirit form. Strangely, she never questioned her ability to enable the work, just the readers' ability to accept the work as genuine. And this is where the emphasis will be placed: on personal authenticity. For in truth, it matters not if one considers these words from Plato, Delilah, or elsewhere; what matters, what truly matters, is that the reader can relate to the message, and form his or her own thoughts. So my request from you, dear reader, is to hear the content and to play with it, give it authenticity in the spirit it is delivered and play a part in creating an energy of inquisitiveness – in whatever form that takes.

TUES 3RD JUNE 2014, LONDON AT 14.40PM, SESSION 2

Mr P: So, we begin with Randomness. Let me explain more. Some subjects require analysis – of the subject, of oneself, of others maybe – but Randomness requires none of these, purely action. Now the action is not physical action per se, but active thought; which may be followed, perhaps swiftly, by physical action. It is the thought, the permissive thought, which enables the Randomness to 'strike'.

To explain, I would like to paint a picture. Imagine a sea, a vast sea. This sea rests within our planet called Earth. It may touch land, or it may merge into other seas or oceans. We may name it sea, ocean, a wave, a stream, a lake, but it is all water. It all has the compound of water. It moves, flows, trickles, evaporates up and rains down. It is always on the move, yet it never leaves this planet. If scientists and ecologists were able to calculate the volume of water held in one form or another within the ecology we call planet Earth, they would record a constant 'whole'. It is not possible to calculate the sum of frozen water to evaporated mist, but it is all water; contained within a pressurised container called gravity.

I will revisit our planet Earth at a later point, but for now, let's picture this sea. However, let's imagine it to now be a sea of Randomness. It is *there* but we do not pay too much attention. Unless it *strikes*. And even when it strikes, it needs to be in our awareness for us to notice it. Once noticed, however, we cannot remove the imprint within us. Like the sea, Randomness is all around – perpetually. It by-passes awareness, causes no effect, and effects no cause until it creates awareness within the individual.

Just as awareness is either 'there, or not there' so too are the strikes of Randomness. Such as with water: some swim in Randomness, use it for enjoyment, a livelihood; others fear it, move from it, or do not enjoy the taste of it. But like water, we are all made of it. Randomness is the sea which creates our growth.

Picture a child. They are born from water, via the embryonic sac, and are comprised mostly of water. Likewise, a random act fertilised this child into life. Once born, our child – until of an age he can make choices for himself – is at the mercy of Randomness. Whilst indeed he, or she, will be co-creators in their growth, it is the progression of random strikes which will determine the *direction* the child will move in. It is not a case of whether the child will progress or not, but which direction that will take; for there can only be progression, nothing 'stands still'.

Our child, as he develops awareness, will begin to take ownership of the Randomness he creates. As children of all ages, we do not know what we do not know. Once we know something we cannot remove that knowledge. Likewise, we cannot undo something we have done. Randomness is therefore the creator of 'time', as it is known. The flow of time, of a past, present and future, is the effect of incessant causes of Randomness creating a 'before' and 'after'.

It is the awareness of *something* which creates the something. Before the awareness, the 'something' was there – in actuality or as a potential – but it is only in the combination of the something and the awareness that it is created.

WED 4TH JUNE 2014, LONDON AT 11.20AM, SESSION 3

Mr P: The creation of the awareness is not in itself random. Because awareness comes from within, it is always controlled and monitored by the individual. An occurrence will happen and the degree to which each individual's awareness will spark will vary, person to person. A tsunami in one part of the planet will create differing degrees of awareness depending on each person's proximity to the event - both physically and emotionally. Equally, depending on the individual, this awareness will create action; either in thought via mental action or in the physical via a need to 'do something'.

Awareness therefore can only be considered a choice. One choses to notice, or not notice. The wonderful thing about awareness is: there is no correct awareness, or incorrect awareness. The awareness itself is wholly non-judgemental. It is the additional choice to place an emotion to the awareness that creates a 'thought'. For a thought 'comes from somewhere'. Awareness *is*. Coming full circle, we can see that we have the choice to 'come from somewhere' or to be in awareness of 'what-is'.

Now the relevance of this little paragon to the topic of Randomness? To identify within the individual their moment-to-moment 'placement' within the field of Randomness. Is one coming from a 'history' of emotional need, or is one lightly within 'what-is'? For these two energy streams create very different outcomes by way of future experiences. And herein lies the question most commonly asked: *"How can I get what I want?"*

A desire to create using a holographic template of one's past (whether 'good' or 'bad') will result in a different experience to a desire to create using one's 'present'. Neither are wrong, and both are right, for both enable creationism. Yet, why would one desire more of what one had? Unless one wished to be back here, back here in the present. Surely, a more economical strategy is to relinquish the effort and *be* in the present? Without the 'history' pulling one back, forward movement is inevitable. It *just happens*.

So, we begin with the thought. Let us spend some time pondering on the thoughts of a thought. Impossible to capture, no? It is gone before we can grasp it, followed by a torrent of cascading thought patterns! Tantalisingly frustrating. And hence the human instinct to 'capture' elements of the thought – in words, pictures, sounds and more. But what if we could subside thought, calm the tempestuous sea? What would we experience then?

THURS 5TH JUNE 2014, LONDON AT 10.00AM, SESSION 4

Mr P: Love. Love is what we would experience in a world of no thought. But, *"Get realistic!"* I hear. For yes, thought is inevitable; but not in itself a requirement for decision-making. Action can happen impulsively, without thought. Indeed a breath is usually just that. Action can also happen 'by itself' as a result of one's subconscious thought. And there is a profound difference between the conscious and the subconscious thought.

In our field of Randomness, strikes will occur as a result of both subconscious and conscious thought. For as with thought, awareness also happens both consciously and subconsciously. It is the disparity between the conscious strike and the subconscious awareness which creates emotional turbulence. For when the conscious 'event' is in alignment with the subconscious awareness no turbulence will be felt, merely peace and tranquillity.

It is the repetitive strikes of Randomness against incongruent subconscious energy which causes distress and disharmony to the individual. For many, the 'coping mechanism' is to *alter* the subconscious to an extent that they can experience some relief as the strikes keep coming. For others, those with sufficient awareness of what is happening, the adjustment will be to the conscious strikes, via a change in lifestyle or priorities. But for most, the strategy is to accept and 'deal with' the disharmony – at the cost of joy.

Allow me to explain how this may play out. Let's gather together a 'typical' family: man, woman, and some children. They live in a house, the parents work and the children attend school. Randomness has brought them individually to this point. Let's assume that 60% of the family's income is spent maintaining the household and 30% is spent maintaining the family's 'lifestyle'. 10% is spare. What do they do with this 10%?

The majority of families will pin all their happiness, and expectation, on the outcome of this 10%. The parents will work, sometimes to excessive hours, in order to produce a surplus: *"So they have something to show for their 'hard work'."* They may also economise, cut back – often on items or experiences which bring them great pleasure – in order to accumulate 'an excess'. They will *go without* in order to *go somewhere*. In the process, they will remind their children of the sacrifices they are making – of their daily unhappiness – so that they can 'get somewhere'. When things 'go wrong' the feelings of failure create even greater disharmony and in-congruency. And the children learn that hard work is 'not enough'.

As human souls, one can rely on common ingredients: a need for safety, a need for shelter and sustenance, and a need for love. But when one is 'missing' a vital ingredient, the mix does not gel. When an individual – or a family – sacrifices one of these ingredients, disharmony is felt. These needs are needed in the *here and now*. Sacrifice today for a desire for the future, extenuates the impact of the *feel good* aspect of creativity. For when one creates more of something one does not appreciate, in order to appreciate at a future date, the experience is diminished in potential.

Our family, with 90% of its income allocated to 'household and lifestyle' has the means to enable safety, shelter and sustenance, and, if conditions enable it, love. It 'lacks' nothing, and it *needs* nothing. It is in the detail that the incongruent thoughts – and as a result, actions – are made. For how easy it is to think of all the 'necessary items' it takes to meet each day! It is these 'additional items' one's conscious mind decides are required which can sit in disharmony with the subconscious.

For a family, the decision on what is of value is compounded by the individual needs of each member of the unit. For what fuels one person's desire for expression will frustrate another's. But when each member is given the space to fully express and explore their subconscious awareness, decisions in line with these deeper needs become more fluid and free-flowing. As each member expresses joy at the strikes of Randomness which fuel their creativity, they begin the chain of creating more strikes. As their 'time' becomes filled with congruent action and intention, the '10% issue' falls away.

So how to encourage congruent action and awareness? By slowing the thoughts and quietening the mind. For when the mind quietens, the subconscious can be heard. It is the resistance to stillness which creates the storm, and it is the storm which evokes the emotions – and the ongoing random strikes, which are created from the preceding thought and degree of awareness. For in choosing to enter stillness and consciously place our awareness in the direction which feels most congruent, one automatically enters alignment with 'what-is'.

SAT 7TH JUNE 2014, LONDON AT 12.30PM, SESSION 5

Mr P: The awareness of 'what-is' places one in the strongest and most powerful of positions. It is the standing in nothingness yet *everything'ness* which, through counter-balancing contrast, creates the avenue for flow. Human beings are conductors, electromagnetically and orchestrally. They write the music, assemble the orchestra and synthesise the sound. What they don't do is *create* the sound. 'It' is already created.

An orchestral conductor has one role: to be able to handle and enable each musician's energy, for the combined benefit of the audience. He, or she, takes what is before him, coalesces the combination into an output which is harmonious and uplifting to the observer. Likewise with observation of one's thought. In observing 'what-is' – either without or within – we, as conductor, coalesce a response. It may be conscious, subconscious, rooted in physical action or thought-form. Whichever is evoked, it defines itself – by the nature of evolvement from non-awareness to awareness – into form.

And herein lies the challenge of the thought-filled mind: What to do with all this form?

An electromagnetic conductor ceases to work efficiently when input exceeds output. It blows a fuse; literally. Likewise with human-beings. What makes humans believe they can increase their input and continue in harmonious flow without altering their output? Something, by the very essence of counter-balance, has to give way; and often this will be by nature of 'collapse'. In the case of our concert the result would be disjointed and disharmonious sound as the orchestra 'falls apart', an ineffective conductor, and a retiring audience.

In the individual the excess is not to be found in output, as commonly thought, but in input. All input is filtered through the mind, whether kinaesthetic, visual, verbal or otherwise. It is all sensory energy which transmutes into a mind-aware diagnostic. The mind, by way of delicate processes, diagnoses an appropriate response; which may, or may not, call on cascading emotions. Either way, the physical body is instructed to elicit a response to the diagnosis. All this is happening internally before any external reaction is evoked. Before one even has a chance to respond via thought or physical action, an inner debit and credit, ever-fluctuating, balancing act is occurring in response to the input. When one is rooted in stillness, the subsequent response is both more efficient and more accurate in intention, for the subconscious can be heard.

When the mind is over-loaded it has two choices: defer or detect. If the awareness is deferred, it is put aside – for a later time, or to build in magnitude, for like attracts like. If the awareness is detected, a response will be diagnosed. But the *state* of the energy of the individual will determine what is detected in the awareness. Low energy will detect a low-value response. High energy will detect a high-value response. A conductor however, requires medial flow for maximum output.

TUES 10TH JUNE 2014, LONDON AT 14.10PM, SESSION 6

Mr P: Conductors are efficient, yet 'strange' in their composition. For how can something so 'simple' process so much? It is this very sense of simplicity which in fact enables the flow of the current. And I say 'sense' because at all times magnetic current, or electric current (via the processing of surplus electrons) is *sensory.* It creates and leaves a residual 'hum'. For humans, as in electromagnetic conductors too, it is this hum which 'interferes' with one's environment. Human beings are no different to electric pylons – just more powerful. For yes, the 'wattage' of a human is considerably more in potential than 'manufactured' electricity which is constant and regulated in voltage.

But like 'real' electricity (and yes, you may by now be detecting the playful side of my 'personality') humans manufacture it according to demand. It is the wise amongst you who realise the supply is available at all times; without effort.

Let's return to the example of our family. When one subscribes to an energy provider, one's intention is to 'buy' energy in order to light and heat one's house, and enable the running and flow of the household. It is the most basic of requirements.

And for this you will gladly pay a premium. But here begins the descent into a *need* for external energy. *"But what are the alternatives?"* I hear you say. *"Heat, light, energy, is a necessity!"* Yes, of course one must be practical, but it is the source of where this energy is originated that I wish to be considered. For many, though not all, the 'ties' to an external supply of energy are already mentally entrenched: energy, and the source of one's life is located *without* – and to get that energy, one must give of oneself, via personal energy and money.

The alternative that I wish you to consider, is that all energy – and I mean *all* – is created from within humans. Your 'energy providers' are merely selling back to you, what you, us collectively, have sourced and created. As creators of 'what-is', all humans, and indeed all living species, past and present, have brought planet Earth collectively to where it is today. That is if we consider it as an 'entity' within itself. For as creators of the world we collectively live in, are we not also intrinsically connected to its entity?

WED 11ᵀᴴ JUNE 2014, LONDON AT 11.55AM, SESSION 7

Mr P: So Randomness, being the creation un-manifested, requires some consideration. For what is it?

In an attempt to not sound overly cryptic, let me describe it as a sea of all possibilities. It is the same 'sea' of ancient times, and like rolling waves, it *just keeps coming*. To explain a little further, 'it' is connected via extrinsic forces to other 'realities'.

Our planetary universe is a vast macrocosm of energy within a vortex of gravity; created by the very forward-movement of Randomness. The more planet Earth creates, the more counter-balanced by corresponding levels of gravity to 'hold' the space it becomes.

The 'space' planet Earth occupies is part of a greater extrinsic space, where many realities 'overlap'. Randomness is a quality shared by them all, but like drops of oil in water, they behave differently – in colour and size. We are only concerned with planet Earth, so no thought is necessary for realities one cannot observe.

Let us imagine an unbounded sea, and let's picture an island. The island is Earth. The sea is Randomness. As the island and its inhabitants create and develop, it takes from the sea: food; supplies by way of items for habitat; and as a means of transport: to discover new territories. It enlarges, claims land from the sea, creates bridges, and grows. The sea encases the island, it is always *there*.

As the population grows, it finds new ways to support itself and it begins to question what is 'out there'. It sends brave men on explorations and it discovers 'new lands'. Communication begins with the new awareness of the other realities, separate to one's island of 'home'. Emphasis is placed on territories, on claiming one's land, pitching a fork in the soil. For if there are 'others' out there: *"Will they claim my territory?"*

As the energies settle and the demarcations are honoured, the inhabitants of our island begin to question and search intrinsically. *"Where do I come from?" "How did we evolve as a species?"* This is the point in time that planet Earth is now at: these are the fundamental questions being asked and investigated by the physicists, the explorers, the common man and woman. And like our island, we emerged from the sea of Randomness.

The desire to understand where we came from, how we behave and why we behave as we do (socially and physiologically), is now greater than at any time in history. Man is searching for answers, and in the nature of Randomness, answers will emerge. For the desire is great. But there is a proviso in order to find the answers one seeks, and that is: all the answers lie within.

Everything one learns has been experienced – in varying degrees. There is 'after awareness' and there was 'before awareness'. The seeker therefore is not seeking answers, but seeking experience. And herein lies the tangle. For if one is not prepared to change one's experiences, then one will not experience change. Without change there are no answers. With change, comes experience. With experience come answers, via awareness.

It is to be remembered that all learning comes from within by the awareness created within. Ten people can be in a room at once, and all will have different awarenesses; and as a result, learning or cascading emotions. Awareness is neutral; it is the attached emotions which create thought feedback, and further emotions. It is for these qualities one chooses a nation's explorers: considered thought, reduced emotions and raised awareness. These are also the qualities of scientists and physicists – planet Earth's explorers. Yet the same proviso applies: the search for without begins within. As the saying goes: "How far down the rabbit hole do you wish to go?"

THURS 12ᵀᴴ JUNE 2014, LONDON AT 15.20PM, SESSION 8

Mr P: To begin this paragraph, one must collect one's thoughts; for it is the drawing on all one's abilities which enables conscious awareness. Many have their thoughts scattered like autumnal leaves on a path in heavy wind. But it is the person with a collected mind that is most useful in awareness. For yes, there is a certain 'quality' of awareness one does well to practise.

It is the application of continual considered awareness which creates prolonged feedback via the physical triggers in the body. A hobby, for example, enjoyed on a regular basis will not only create results by way of actual 'achievement' but also results within the body – for what happens without indeed affects the within. A regular experience of relaxation, or indeed frustration, will create regular responses of relaxation or frustration *within* the body.

Now this sounds obvious, and what most people know, but they are often not able to practise displays of considered, regular relaxation. 'Something' takes over and usurps the endeavour – despite all best intentions. And this is because of a lack of *collection of the mind*; the intention is of a scattered leaf, as is the endeavour, the will and the process.

Marginalised members of society will often attract discrimination by socially comfortable 'institutionalised' founders. Yet it is the members on the outskirts who more often possess collection of the mind. Lack of inclusion creates a state of 'alert', so very subtle, yet pervasive. Those comfortable at the core, by the nature of their scattered attention amongst the majority, will display common signs of inattention.

Often, it is a reverse belief which is profligated by mindless believers of institutionalised collectives. One may question why mindful application be of such high value amongst a society of processes, automation and *requirement to comply*? But without the conscious collection of the mind, one begins to subtly 'lose' one's ability to formulate desired responses. One begins to respond on autopilot, as the energy of the masses grasps with a resounding hold all attempt to think for oneself. For what can be more personal or individual than one's own thoughts?

MON 16TH JUNE 2014, LONDON AT 11.40AM, SESSION 9

Mr P: Strangely, one often fails to consider the reactive impact of *non-awareness*. It is easier to 'not notice' as one falls into lazy habit. *"Oh, that's the way it's done"*. But in fact there is no such element as a decision to do 'nothing'. Once the awareness is there, it is there. And so the decision to 'ignore' creates a double-effect response as the initial response of 'doing nothing' (and remember, a thought is as much an action as the physical) is compounded by the suppression of the desired response had one had full autonomy and freedom.

Let's take an example, of a child misbehaving. After a length of time of the parent or carer 'not-noticing', all of a sudden the secondary impact surfaces: either anger which can no longer be suppressed, or dismissal of the Self as the child is allowed to continue the behaviour. Had the awareness been dealt with at first instance, peaceful flow would have been the alternative.

Now the practicalities of actioning one's awareness are two-fold. There is the awareness *without*, and the awareness *within*. When one addresses, in the first instance the awareness within, one finds the awareness of the without change and diminish in intensity. By contrast, when one goes straight to the awareness of the without, there follows inner turmoil and conflict. Let me explain.

As the child misbehaves he, or she, creates an effect to balance a previous cause – and a new cause creating an effect in his or her 'without'. Our child has intrinsically 'satisfied', by the nature of effect, the preceding cause. Our child is, in nature, neutral. The new cause created, has all potential of effect.

It is the observer's decision as to the effect the cause of the child will have. Contrary to belief, it is not the child's. Let's assume our child is 'misbehaving' even more and runs out into the road. We know not the cause which intrinsically caused the child to run out, it matters not at this point. The only concern is to grab the child and lead it to safety. This, as observer, was the effect created within us. We are now neutral. But if we reacted to external awareness, a secondary effect will happen as we admonish or comfort the child. We have created a new cause. By alternative, if we react to internal awareness, we find less need to create a new cause. It is what it is, the child has been led to safety, and the day continues.

The *'driver'* of the secondary effect (and resulting new cause) is always emotional. As our child is considered *safe*, cascading emotions arise as to 'what could have happened', although it didn't. Most will choose either to admonish the child and 'dig up' a raft of historical examples to validate the admonishment, or self-admonish through their perceived 'lack of care and attention'. They will re-create all sorts of scenarios and imagine their distress at each.

However, the person who gently leads the child to safety and takes time for quiet inner reflection, encouraging the child to do the same, will be able to use the new awareness to make informed and sound movements forward. The 'reaction', if any, will come from internal awareness as opposed to a fantasised version of what may have been. The child, by the effect of not having emotional pressure and need for regret to satisfy the adult's fears and insecurities is also of a place to reflect internally; for despite what one thinks, all children reflect consciously and subconsciously on all reactions and actions they take. It is 'human nature'.

TUES 17TH JUNE 2014, LONDON AT 11.40AM, SESSION 10

Mr P: One wonders why the need for self-admonishment? Why for the parent, and why for the child? It is a need which is 'transferred' generation to generation, despite a desire for the opposite. How many teenagers decry parental expectations, yet behave in the most similar of ways as adults with their own off-spring? For if one is sitting in awareness of 'what-is' our teenager who feels rebellious by way of his or her own thoughts cannot be 'wrong'. What makes a child waver between acquiescing to and rebelling against what is being imposed upon him or her? The rebellious toddler, the acquiescing ten year old, the rebellious teenager, the acquiescing young adult and then, one is *expected* to conform, ultimately to relinquish the desire to grow. An 'adult' conforms to society, this is the expectation. To not, labels the person *different*, 'without responsibility', a 'free spirit'. And how wonderful that sounds!

It is fear which contains one in the energy of conformity. In a desensitised institutionalised society, it is those who conform to external admonishment who either lose collection of mind or experience inner rebelliousness to their conscious actions. The more this rebelliousness is suppressed, the greater the 'explosion' will be. It is the nature of counter-balance.

It is those 'without responsibility', those of 'free spirit' who currently remain at the fringes of what is acceptable. Yet it is these very people who possess the greatest collection of the mind. For even those labelled with 'mental illness' possess a focus and attention to the internal many a guru would respect.

It is a result of non-conformity that the outlier believes he or she to be 'excluded' energetically by the masses, but in truth, it is their connection within which creates the strength of being, and of character, which enables them to support the masses. Indeed, it is the masses who are acquiescing to the outliers, for in creating a 'system' to 'deal with them', they by default create 'safety' within their perceived inner circle. Take away the fringes of society and 'collapse' would ensue. An interesting thought, no? For it is in the observation of 'what-is' that one creates one's awareness. Sitting in one's comfortable society, the awareness of the diminished and desultory 'out there' creates the contrast to 'raise' the perception of the 'in here'. Remove the 'out there' and what does one have without the contrast? For this would mean the removal of ego – and that dear reader, is the driver of existence.

WED 18TH JUNE 2014, LONDON AT 10.15AM, SESSION 11

Mr P: Few consciously play with their ego; for it is the most available of playmates. But to 'play' with one's ego, one must step outside of it. It takes two to play.

Most are either not aware they are sitting and operating in the midst of their ego, or are too trepidatious to entertain it. For entertain it one must if one wishes to live in harmony. There was a time, before the current evolution of man, when the ego was more of an on/off switch. The lion came, the switch went on. But times have changed, 'progress' has happened, and the result of this progress – or shall we say adaptive creationism – is a presence of ego. It is *there* as much as the mind is 'there'.

To attempt to turn off the ego is futile, and why would we want to? The purveyors of peace who seek testament via past scriptures are quite simply delusional – delusional within ego themselves. *"In here, we practice the chosen way, out there you defer to materialism."* But to uphold past ideals from an era bygone is not presence of mind. It is subservience to past illusion. By contrast, to question past scriptures, to investigate with curiosity application to the present moment is an altogether different method of gaining wisdom. It is ego adapted to forward movement, and greater wisdom.

Within the field of Randomness, our awareness strikes a chord. The chord struck today is so very different from the chord struck many centuries ago; or even yesterday. To sit within 'what-*is*' one must accept presence of ego: its limitations and its potential.

Ego is counter-balanced by soul spirit. When one is suppressed, the other rears up. It is just as undesirable to have suppressed ego as it is suppressed soul spirit. For with suppressed ego the soul cannot survive, and it certainly cannot thrive.

It is the defamation of ego which creates the very exposure to the external which compounds the contrast to soul spirit. As a result we observe the divide and duality of man. From this place rears good versus bad, the angel versus the devil, right versus wrong and the most destructive: me versus you.

Should man chose to embrace his ego – and by embrace I mean surrender in the fullest – he would experience divine bliss. This is indeed one's experience of physical death. Yet for most, the fear of this surrender petrifies until one's last breath, which is a shame when it is available at every waking moment.

THURS 19TH JUNE 2014, LONDON AT 10.00AM, SESSION 12

Mr P: It is the understanding of one's ego which brings freedom. Nothing more, yet greatly no less. For indeed it is a challenge. It is not for the faint hearted the walk to freedom. Yet it affords such joy.

One's price to pay in not breaking free of the perceptual chains one-sided ego-feed brings, is a life 'out of kilter'. One is left with a feeling that *something* is missing. That 'something' is the corresponding ego of the soul. For yes, the soul has ego too. How could it survive, and indeed flourish, without that *drive to exist*?

So we have the ego of the self (NOTE lower case 's' to denote the part of the greater Self, upper case 'S' used for the 'whole' of the individual) and the ego of the soul. The former desires growth of the 'I', the 'me', in the world of others. The latter desires growth of the soul, the collective soul of humanity. One cannot exist without the other, and contrary to espoused belief, the soul is not 'superior' to the self. Only those seeking juxtaposed containment would voice it so.

Humanity rides the wave of the movement between soul and self. Indeed, each person is a collection of soul, self, energy and movement. The psyche is the interaction of this whole in the individual. And the individual is the interaction of the Self within humanity's 'whole'. As each person fluctuates between expression of self and expression of soul, so moves global humanity. A blade of grass in a field of reaction.

Humanity's struggle has been to not honour the soul and inner conflict of the self. It has had one-sided attention as the energy of conflict drowns out the whispers of soul voice. But the soul is not passive, oh no! Suppress it too long and it will make itself heard! It is this encounter with oneself which creates the awakening experience; for one-by-one dormant souls are awakening.

The challenge one faces, upon sudden awakening of a suppressed and dormant soul, is the ego of the self is still very much alive and kicking. Now we have two contestants in the ring and the human body and mind as the location of the battle. For in a world of duality the inner conflict is: *"Which path do I choose? Which voice do I obey?"* It is at such points one dies or thrives, for the choice can only be integration of the two as the parts become whole. It is happening on individual levels and it is happening on global levels. Yes, indeed. And this is the 'work' of humanity.

WED 25TH JUNE 2014, LONDON AT 10.55AM, SESSION 13

Mr P: Let's return to the beginning, to creationism. What do I mean by purporting this suggestion? Well, there is lots of meaning to be had, depending on your point of viewing. The world population broadly falls into two camps: those who believe they create their world, and those who believe their world creates them. Actually neither are wrong, for even in the latter creationism is present. The point of difference is in accepting control of one's creation, as opposed to being at the mercy of what happens next and what has happened in one's past. This can make for a very uncomfortable ride!

We cannot talk of creationism without including *acceptance*. For it is when one is unable to accept an event, emotion, outlook or vista that one defaults to *blaming circumstances*. I use the word 'default' with caution here, for all action is performed by an 'owner' of the action, but when an individual (or a collection of individuals) is operating on emotional auto-pilot the boundaries of consciousness become blurred. Indeed, it is this energy of auto-pilot which has until recent times caused humanity to 'default'.

Now this default is not negative; it is what it is, is part of the journey of mankind, and has indeed created much appreciation for the intricacies of one's existence. But it has without doubt caused an energy of global distress. It is now time for this distress to be transmuted to differing energies. We have the scientific know-how to explain matter; it is time for this to be combined with the humanistic inner know-how to start applying this combination to ease distress and increase inner joy and wellbeing. For surely, one can appreciate there comes a limit to how much 'external' an individual can process on an hourly and daily basis?

The lack of belief, or disdain for the creationism of one's own existence, stems from a feeling of powerlessness. If one feels powerless, one is not compelled to *accept*. If one does not accept, one will not effect any changes in line with his or her values. If one is not living to one's own values, one is by default living to someone else's – and hence the belief our world creates us.

It is the difficulty and intricacies in this very combination of acceptance and powerfulness which has caused the myriads of 'ego-trips' we can witness in everyday life. The range is breath-taking, and has created both the exquisiteness of beautiful moments and the despair of exquisite pain.

THURS 26TH JUNE 2014, LONDON AT 17.00PM, SESSION 14

Mr P: Exquisite pain is tantamount to 'life'. The very *height* to which it takes one is what opens the doorway to a new world – whether labour of the mothering woman or the pain as the sheath of a blade cuts through flesh and organs. These are 'pure' experiences of pain as new energy pours forth. But it is the pain of emotions which creates the altogether different experience of despair. And yet emotions are wholly avoidable in duration, if not depth.

Emotions serve a purpose. They guide the ship on the stormy seas. The captain will assist by using the weather to propel in the chosen direction, but it is the wind who is in control. The captain is merely working with the motions.

You may note I describe wind in the humanistic form by the pronoun 'who'. For indeed, like the planet's weather system, a person's emotional system has ultimate control. *"But how can that be?"* you may ask. *"Does that not contradict every-thing you have stated so far?"*

Well…yes…and no. Yes, like planet Earth can 'control' most things except the weather and 'movement' of the said planets' terrain, people can control most things except their emotions and the movement of their inner bodies. This is what most of you believe. "Illness strikes, without control." "Death happens, without control." "Unprotected intercourse creates babies, without control." Humanity's conscious minds believe this…so this is what is created. But "as within, so without" is understood as a maxim, is it not? What is happening on the inside is visible on the outside. So one *sees* and experiences these weather patterns and so the external reinforces the internal. The captain sets sail expecting stormy seas, prepared for all eventualities. Likewise the person expects emotions, and has his or her precautions to manage them.

But…and this is the deeper layer of observation one needs, to appreciate the complexities: what if 'emotions' as they are known today were in fact a 'developed product'? Something man has created over the millennia and packaged and marketed so cleverly on the consumer shelf? Indeed, mankind has done a succinct job in both creating a product – a whole range of products in fact – and developing an inner client. For mankind has created a very prevalent 'emotional body'. There is no other species on the planet yet with such a layer – although it strikes me as not long before your pets will by default develop one too.

This layer of emotional triggers and reactions is 'in charge' whilst it is there being supported and fed by the psyche. It has evolved as a result of the split of the Self into the self and the soul and it is fed by the egos – both of them. For the ego of the soul affects the emotional body in similar ways to the ego of the self.

Now one might be forgiven for wondering: *"Well, what next? Now what?"* And this is where the fun begins. For if we can learn to play with the egos, we can also learn how to play with the emotions. And emotions can create much fun and joy. And that dear reader, is what everyone wants more of.

FRI 27ᵗʰ JUNE 2014, LONDON AT 12.45PM, SESSION 15

Mr P: Why, oh why, has man made 'fun' such a dirty word? For even children are being denied it, it seems. If humanity could get its placement of fun 'front of house' on our shelf of emotional products, what a change that would make to the planet! To even suggest this confounds the minds of most. For most have led a life of completely the opposite. The 80/20 rule cannot even be applied for most adults – and this 'rule' is indeed a *law of nature.*

Currently, the western hemisphere is 'operating' on 20% fun – over their lifetime. Can you imagine such a farce? Typically, this 'lifetime' of fun will include early childhood, sections of later childhood, late teens and early adult years, the odd 'night out', maybe a vacation or two, and if one is fortunate, some of the later years.

Now let me elaborate on what 'fun' is. Fun is not: 'a good time'; 'satisfaction'; a 'job well done'; doing anything *for others* – including one's children; being 'up-straight'; a 'promotion'; celebrating *someone else's* achievements; or acquiring possessions. It is none of these. Nor is it 'drowning one's sorrows'; action in whatever form as 'a distraction'; or compensatory 'self-indulgence'. When many state: *"Let's have some fun"* they pick from the above selection.

Fun is indeed an altogether different experience. It is the most wonderful of emotions – a true gift; one we would wish the whole of humanity to be experiencing 80% of their life in this space/time. For this is most achievable, and indeed experienced by those at the leading edge – for it does not take much to realise the children are the leading edge of your society. Give them fun, for it is an investment in your future!

Fun is that feeling when one is taken over by complete lightness in spirit. The mind is elevated to a higher consciousness and it feels like one's body is half its normal weight. Fun enables a presence in the moment which has the qualities of both non-moving and action. It is imperceptible as to where the energy comes from – neither within, nor without. It encompasses freedom, creativity, expression and stillness. And it is healing.

The problem with society's perception – on the whole – of fun, is that it must be 'purchased off the shelf'; that 'a price must be paid' before one can have fun. And if the child is having fun, the adult 'picks up the tab'. And anyone who is perceived to have more fun than most, than their allowed 'quota', is seen as 'irresponsible', 'naughty' or 'greedy'. For the judgements are cast by those who won't allow themselves – or no longer know how – to have fun.

In truth, it is possible to harness the feeling of fun so it sits with one most of the time – in all tasks, endeavours and moments of solitude. It is an emotion derived from the soul and is pure in intention. It is open, welcoming, curious yet unchallenging in action or intent. It enables soul growth and expansion – and heals the within and the without. It is the soothing compress to the heat of rage and the path to unfolding enlightenment. It is on offer for all.

TUES 1ST JULY 2014, LONDON AT 10.30AM, SESSION 16

Mr P: So how to have fun? For most have lost the ability to employ a reasonable approach; it is 'all or nothing'. Rather a lack of balance, no?

Life is like a balance sheet: the debit and credit must balance. And like a new business, attention must be given to the cash-flow – and supply and demand. Too much investment in productivity will result in not enough investment in outsourcing. A business needs both customers *and* product or service. Likewise humans need both work and play. One needs to spend a little of what one earns to create more desire to earn. The golden question though: *"What is the purpose of my earning?"*

Rarely does one hear: *"I would like to earn more money so I can experience more fun and joy."* And what a shame this is. If humanity – and I refer in this instance to those with the basics of safety and sustenance at their disposal – if humanity were to place this question at the leading edge of daily life decisions, oh what a different world we would live in!

But this involves *trust*, does it not? And so few trust. Which is a shame, for lack of trust is a purely intrinsic emotion. In truth there *is* no trust, there is 'what-is'. Such as with the sea of Randomness, 'trust' is there in potential or actuality. But un-like random awareness which is 'neutral' or '+1', trust is neu-tral or '-1'. Only 'lack of trust' exists. The same with love. Love is always there – it is just 'lack of love' which creates emotion. It is the fear of lack of trust or lack of love which dictates most people's decision-making. And when one decides to 'trust' or 'love' or indeed the compounded 'trust in love', it is seen as a +1. In fact this is an illusion, for trust and love are base states of neutrality. It is the *lack of* which places one within '-/minus' that creates inner discord.

Now imagine, by contrast, being in 'neutral': a light sense of freedom where trust, love, awareness *just is* – a stillness. Imagine making a decision based on *"What will bring me joy right now?"* and *"What needs doing…and how can I make it as fun as possible?"* Wouldn't that be great?

And to play on the word 'great'…this is the obstacle for most of the people. For it seems too great a challenge to operate from this viewpoint…too *unachievable*. But what if it is indeed wholly achievable? What if one could observe and learn from those who are already enjoying this viewpoint? Would you want to stand within this vista, or would you prefer to observe from the side-lines? For it becomes a matter of choice.

THURS 3ᴿᴰ JULY 2014, LONDON AT 14.00PM, SESSION 17

Mr P: Choice is something people really can't get their heads around on the whole. I mean, does one really think *"there-is-no-choice?"* Because if this thought is so, then: voila! …indication of madness of the mind! For when one is so trapped in a blocked mind-set, the wisest thing to do is to step back and pause, for no good can come when in this energy.

It is when one is overwhelmed with choice that safety is found in perceived lack of choice. The mind and emotions can 'switch off' whilst balance is regained. But often we observe people just continue on, as if by pushing through to the end, they believe they will 'come out the other side'. By definition this is a form of death. Sometimes appropriate, usually not so.

Gaining awareness of one's perceptions in any given moment – including, most importantly, moments of challenge – is the single most powerful action one can take. Now when I talk of awareness, I do not refer to the incessant summation of the mind as it adds woe after woe after stress and obstacle.

No, this is not awareness, it is madness. I refer to the awareness when one pauses, allows the energy and thought to drop to the earth, when one *sinks in*, breathes and questions with openness of spirit. When grounded in awareness without mind chatter, choices naturally arise. Indeed as one becomes more and more grounded in awareness, one comes to realise life is indeed one big playground of choices! Life becomes one big *"Wow"*.

The beauty of awareness of choice is that it by default places one within gratitude. The *choice* to look after one's sick child roots the parent in gratitude for having a child to care for. It can be very tempting to say *"but I don't have a choice!"* Oh, but you do. And whilst you believe you have no choice, you subliminally are 'blaming' your child for your lack of freedom. Much more powerful – for both parent and child – is to discuss openly the choices – for what a wonderful display of love that would be!

Even incarceration involves choice. Initially there was the choice to act in ways which led to the incarceration. Once within the confines, there is the choice to blame, the choice to grow, the choice to repent, the choice to absolve.

The aspect of choice which prohibits in most, is the requirement to be with 'what-is' within awareness. For it is not as simple as it may sound. To be fully in awareness, one must be able to be present with one's emotions; 'good' or 'bad'. And this is where the hurdles lie for most. For if one cannot accept the full gambit of feelings, then how can one make an informed choice?

MON 7TH JULY 2014, LONDON AT 12.25PM, SESSION 18

Mr P: It is the random flow of communication – both inner and outer – which *compromises* one's ability to sit within awareness. I use the word 'compromise' for despite awareness being in 'what-*is*', it is also by default in 'what-is-not-accepted'. As one observes 'stuff' and decides to not action it, it nevertheless *collects* as information. One may choose to not watch the news on television, but one is still aware 'the news', in all its despair and intrigue, is still 'there'.

When one is rocketed by ever-increasing levels of information there is, yes, a choice to ignore or disregard sections of data, but underneath this choice can be conflict. It is this conflict…this "I *should*" which compromises one's stability – and therefore one's power. An electric circuit cannot run on 'shoulds', can it?

When one has the good fortune to run into or know someone who is grounded and 'stable' within themselves, know they have diminished the 'shoulds' in their life. The more shoulds: *"I should be doing so-and-so instead,"* or *"I should be a better mother, lover, earning more money"*…the list is endless, the more 'unstable' both the person and the relationship within the experience, and with the experience.

For evoking the emotion of *should* is the conflict between the two egos: the ego of the soul and the ego of the self. In an act to defer the conflict, the 'cause' is projected outwards, with 'blame' towards others: one's boss, one's partner, child or parent maybe. But actually, it is not *"them creating a pull on me"* but wholly an inner conflict between one's own parts. There *is* no 'out there' with choice, there is only the decision *within.*

When one reaches the realisation that *all* choice is made within, one's life becomes transformed. Daylight and clarity floods in as all destructive emotional ties one by one become released. It is the greatest "ah-ha" moment one can experience in relation to *being* within the flow of consciousness. For as one becomes released from the push and pull of the outer, the wisdom and knowingness of the inner can rise. And this is self-realisation.

When one reaches the wonderful stage of realisation of the Self, one instantly becomes aware of the parts of the psyche. As one sits *within* oneself, introduction to, and communication with, one's parts begins. For a while – which may be years, decades or lifetimes – this inner communication will take precedence; for how can we communicate with others if we cannot communicate with oneself? For when one is used to 'speaking within the mind' or mind-chatter, it takes diligence and contrition to begin the conversations within the bodies and heart. For conscious awareness is one step, but thinking and communicating from a place of no-mind is the route of conscious evolution.

TUES 8TH JULY 2014, LONDON AT 16.00PM, SESSION 19

Mr P: In 'today's world' all thought hinges on the Self; namely the placement of the 'I' within the context of everything. Even when discussing aspects of the world 'out there', it is in relation to one's world 'in here'. The observation begins *in here*, it can be no other way. But it does not need to end with 'in here'.

When one can begin an observation 'in here', correspond it to 'out there', connect it back to 'in here', and then go the added step – managed by few – of gently placing it back 'out there'…and leaving it out there, then one becomes free. For there *is* no placement left within. It is the triggers to the thought-filled emotions which create reactive response. By contrast, when the awareness remains outside and separate to the 'I', there is no trigger.

So how does this look? Let's imagine you are walking down the street. You see, in a shop window, a most beautiful scarf. It is just like the scarf your mother used to wear. You want it, and decide to purchase it tomorrow. As you return home, you 'carry' the thought of the scarf, of your mother, your memory of her, and the intention to purchase it tomorrow. That is a lot of thought – never mind about what to eat for dinner! Thoughts from the past, the present and the future. As you wake the next day, the mind is full and one becomes a little less aware of what is present in one's surroundings. As requests are made on you, reaction comes from this place of mean.

Using the double-placement awareness creates a very different response – namely no response. Let's imagine walking past the same shop, noticing the same scarf, absorbing the awareness of the beauty of it, of the recollection of your mother. You pause and take in the whole experience in totality in that moment. The awareness floods your whole body and aura; for there are no blockages, no place 'out-of-bounds'. As you fill, in the moment, you release the experience back to the moment: the scarf, your mother, and whatever new emotion arises. You leave the experience in totality, having experienced it in totality. It rests 'out there', you walk away 'free'. There is no 'need'.

Operating at this level of double-placement enables the person to walk unhindered through life's experiences. It does not prevent acquisition such as a purchase, but it ensures a purchase is 'balanced' in exchange. For example, one might purchase an item through necessity, practical reasons, or as a gift, but when the awareness is not a double-placement awareness, know it is a purchase to fill a void or complete an inner transaction of energy.

After spending time observing one's thought-flow, it becomes easier to recognise transactional acquisitions and movements. For modern society has become a swathe of increasing transactional energy – expressed through global acquisition and speed. And this increase in unbalanced transactions, this ever-growing increase, is what can be observed as gravity.

FRI 11TH JULY 2014, LONDON AT 8.00AM, SESSION 20

Mr P: Gravity. The word of the moment, the challenge to master. For whoever 'solves' the mystery of gravitational pull opens the planet to untold opportunities. Or so the thought goes…

But no. It is not so. For gravity is an ever-moving, ever swaying mass of energy controlled by *you*, dear reader. It is the culmination of the combined expressive energy of *all matter*, but not mass, within the container of planet Earth. It is 'linked', a loose term I use, to other realities but specific in its characteristics.

Gravity is not 'solvable' by equation or observation. Nor is it quantifiable in content or measure. Try measuring the *energy* of the oceans or the jungles with all its variables. But it *is* 'controllable' – by combined output.

The search to extrapolate energy from the gravitational field will not offer desired results – because it is not a 'field'. It is not 'something out there' which keeps you 'down here' on planet Earth. No. It is far superior to that. It is the yin to the planet's yang, the counterbalance to your expression and creationism. The more one 'creates', the more counterbalance the universe provides to enable stability. As you grow, your environment grows with you. As you contract, your environment contracts with you too. A law of nature, supported by physics, mathematics and pure *common sense,* no?

The reason the universe is recognised as infinite is because man's vision is infinite. One *sees* either potential or despair. And one will recognise aspects and indications to support either direction (+1 for potential, -1 for despair). Your planet's scientists and explorers of the infinite see indications that this is indeed 'true' in potential. Yet *all* is true in potential, is it not?

'Gravity' will keep increasing in line with man's growth in creationism. Should man, as in collective humanity, express less creationism, pull-back on unbalanced acquisitions to support – and feed – emotional triggers and unbalance, and generally achieve *inner* equanimity and stability, then your scientists would observe a slowing down of gravitational speed. Do not be misled to believing war and 'man's evils' contract the energies, no. For they produce more 'creationism' than anything. Out of all 'tragedy' love unfolds. But what *would* slow down gravitational speed would be the ability to 'sit in love' rather than 'prove existence of love'. For this is what the planet is attempting to do.

SUN 13TH JULY 2014, ALTEA AT 10.05AM, SESSION 21

Mr P: Randomness strikes in – and for – love at fluctuating intensities both during one's life and one's evolving lifetimes. For this is where negligence of the 'master-time' creates confusion in one.

Within every person are two main time-lines. I say main, for of course there are many, of which you will be aware. There are the time-lines of each day, each job, each object of study, each child and relationship to oneself – all are time-lines. But 'holding' these hundreds and thousands of time-lines are two main ones. There is the time-line of this physical lifetime, and the master time-line.

The master time-line is the one which affords the most interest in terms of 'life's lessons' and 'life's loves'. For it is both infinite yet wholly within one's reality at any given moment. It is the blueprint of one's past and the template of one's future combined in the present. Yet it is unknown. Is this not fascinating?

As a person becomes more enlightened, he or she begins to operate more and more from the master time-line. Other time-lines become less important within themselves, yet offer the 'television screen' of what is happening on, to, and with the master time-line. One becomes the observer and conscious creator of experiences which serve the necessary learning and experience required by the master time-line. We begin operating 'for' oneself as opposed to 'as' oneself. Very different.

The master time-line acts as a sounding-board for one's experiences, yet is also the 'reality'. Imagine a line in the sand. The master time-line is on the right, this physical lifetime on the left. When one is placed on the left our experiences reflect off and back to us in this lifetime. We are in the reality of 'oneself' but limited of expansion whilst having a sense of the greater 'out there'. By contrast, if one is placed on the right, within the master time-line, our experiences of daily life and interactions are reflected back to us, becoming 'the illusion' of this lifetime. Placed within the master time-line, one can observe without attachment the activity of oneself – and others. A 'lightness' becomes present as we realise the impact of our physical life resounds with a softness and gentleness against the beat of the master drum. Events contain less importance, yet become more meaningful and…tasteful. Life becomes rich as we realise it is indeed endless.

It is when matters of the heart strike that we can get pulled into present day lifetime perspective – with the perspective that one can only 'lose'. *"To love means to lose"*…and so we experience fear as we love; fear that we will have our loved one taken away or that we will be taken away from them. Now some would say this is a duality, the contrast needed *to love*: a form of appreciation. But I would differ in opinion, and suggest that whilst operating from the place of this physical lifetime, one cannot in fact be experiencing pure love at all. For the 'I' is forever present. *"I love you"* is centred not around 'you' but 'I'. Love, as an emotion, which in the context of relational expression it can only be, is always an observational transaction. And transactions require a 'return' gesture for fluid movement. Therefore, expressions of love can only be considered acquisitional transactions from the emotional body.

Love as an object cannot exist, for it is not quantifiable; mathematically or scientifically. Atoms may be mathematically quantified; thoughts may be scientifically observed but the 'flavour' of the atoms or thoughts cannot in themselves be captured, other than within the 'I'.

However, when one is placed within the master time-line, a different experience in relation to 'love' arises, as it is experienced as an energy within the master time-line *and* as observational within the physical lifetime. Placed on the right of the line one experiences both aspects of love. Whilst on the left, one experiences love in the context of the 'I'…yet we know somewhere within our DNA that it 'contains' so much more.

It is this search for love, this desire to abate what we don't quite understand but feel at an atomic level, which drives creationism in mankind. It is the urge and the release; the giver and the taker; the master and the slave. It is a four letter word which underpins every movement of our existence...yet one is unable to capture it. So what is it?

MON 19TH JULY 2014, ALTEA AT 14.35PM, SESSION 22

Mr P: Love is actually very tangible...when on the side of one's master time-line. Until such time it remains elusive. Now this may sound elitist and highly condescending but it is so.

When one dies, and passes over as you say, the Self – of the soul, the self and the heart-energy – moves back into the master time-line in totality. When in this place, one experiences love absolute. It is the air, the earth, the wind, the sea. It is each other. It is pure energy known as love. It is unquestionable; like the air you breathe.

Yet the air you breathe on planet Earth is not the air of love. It is neutral. Love, by contrast, is not neutral. It has a different composition, and a different depth and weight. It is also 'reflective' – which I will explain in more detail later.

When one, whilst in the physical lifetime, sits within the master time-line, a 'taste' of this love is experienced. To experience it is to know it. It is joy unbound – as there *is* no 'I'. One's '*what-is*' becomes both one's place of being and one's place of viewing as all realities collide in the moment. At these times one is at their most powerful.

Those who know of my work as Plato, will know my 'greatest' work was on the subject of love – love in all forms. Yet what I have learnt in the space/time since then leaves me desperate to share on this, the greatest of topics of discussion. I use the word 'desperate' with trepidation of interpretation for the meaning I apply is of eagerness and conviction of purpose.

My journey since Plato has involved much learning and with hindsight, 'research' on the matter. I have had four human time-lines since Plato: as a woman in the 1200's; a woman in the 1600's; and as a man of great wealth in the 17th century. My final physical time-line, and the one of my greatest learning and culmination, was as a monk, in the 18th century. My 'experiences' of love in all cases revolved around the greater lessons regarding sexual desire. For the two, love and sexual desire, are inextricably connected…yet not entwined.

As this piece of work evolves, I will address and share my revised and updated thoughts on love. It gives me great pleasure to be able to do so. Yet it will not be all I will cover. Aspects of metaphysics, laws of nature and universal truths will be included, as will observational 'discussions' on matters of a practical nature. For within my thoughts lie two arenas. And this must be carefully and clearly understood by the reader. There is the arena of my personal master time-line and all I wish to share of my discoveries and learnings, and also the greater arena of all-that-is, which we are all discovering collectively. I hold no 'God-like' powers and do not have 'all the answers'. I only know what I know, which is through experience and inquisitive exploration. My observations and sharings are not for all tastes – and indeed that would be undesirable for our collective evolvement – but my reason and purpose for this piece of work has been most carefully assessed and prepared for this space/time. I am judged ready to share and this readership judged ready to participate in what I anticipate being a both dynamic and rich experience for us all.

From this point forth the layout and formula of the work will alter as I address the different topics and subjects. The book is intended as one which can be absorbed in sections and at random; indeed to operate within Randomness whilst reading and questioning these words would enable the greatest participation possible – and to enable Randomness all one has to do is listen to the whispers, observe oneself and act on them in the faith of all-that-is. Let's begin…

2

A Story to Warm the Heart

A little story to warm the heart. Of trust and innocence of the gentlest kind:

> She whispered in the midnight breeze, *"Are you there my love? I can't see you."* A soft rustle in the growth, barely discernible save to one of expectant heart, told her he was coming to her. She smiled inwardly, the remnants of uncertainty fading, her lips softening in the peaceful pleasure of knowing they would be together again, that he was safe. She stood, still as a hummingbird as the silence descended on her, her hearing sharpened to his approaching scent. She could taste the tension of the moment as the undergrowth spoke of his desire to be with her, his breathing barely concealed in his wish to move

without trace yet with intent. With all her senses she awaited him, with all his being he wanted her.

It is moments like these that touch the soul, that enable our world to come alive as all our senses interplay to create an alertness and presence of being that surpasses the mundane of ordinariness. Life, in such moments, becomes enthused with a desire one recognises as 'of man' yet elusive to man save in the company of mutual desire. For when the exchange is wholly participatory 'holiness' abounds.

It is this sense of unification which confuses man. For how can something so intangible, so against the doctrine of patronage, yet so animalistically and physically pleasurable, be 'right'?

Is it the crashing and cascading of boundaries as desire fuels intermittent possession and surrender as relinquishment turns to power? Or is it the 'silence' as for just one moment in this lifetime, one quietens the ancestral voices of past and present and becomes what and who one is?

Perhaps the unification creates the very 'completeness' only surrender and intention can provide. For in the moment of utter vulnerability, power can be both deceptive and divine.

THURS 17TH JULY 2014, ALTEA AT 12.20PM, SESSION 24

She waited not for love's descent, but for the totalness of the infusion of completeness the moment was bringing to her. She was in control, yet incapable of diversion to either left or right as he appeared

in the moonlight of the midnight air. Within her vision was the masculine she desired, incumbent upon her senses as fortification to her courage. For what if they were found? The risk was great, yet participatory in the encounter, a necessary adversary propelling desires' liberation. He paused briefly as he saw her beneath the tree, his eyes betraying fear within accomplishment. She raised a finger to her lips silencing the moment, capturing his attention as she held his gaze. He was powerless within her embrace, though distance separated them.

As a voyeur to another's affair of the heart, one experiences 'differ or detect' as we judge from our point of standing. Have we, in reading this prose, witnessed an escape to safety, an entrapment of deceit or a random encounter? Do we sense fear, impending betrayal, love's birth, or sensual compassion? Is she fearless, or fearful; is he trapped or now free?

We will each have differing observations, suggesting differing emotions within us. But it is the 'quality' of the arising thoughts which create movement within our observation. Do we possess a quality of distrust, of envy, of longing, of empathy? Or perhaps of dismissal and disdain as our hurt and wounds create barriers to feelings and recognition of shared moments. For we will each have experienced moments like this, if not within such a context. For desire of something is in actuality desire of everything, harnessed into objective retaliation within a certain form. It is both the problem and the solution.

Now the Buddha, as an example, advocates through manuscripts deployment of one's suffering to abate desire. But how can one unveil one's entrapments without experiencing one's panacea? And if the answer, the solution, is within one's being, surely *the obstacle is the path* as the saying goes? Denial of desire is, I suggest, denial of humanity's ability to heal itself of its encroaching apathy to self-creationism and increasing lack of courage in the face of wanton joy. For perhaps our story is purely of joy, for joy's sake and joy's pleasure?

TUES 22ND JULY 2014, LONDON AT 12.55PM, SESSION 25

As he slowly moved towards her, the bracken and leaves quietly crunching underfoot, his dampened skin glistened with the perspiration of the chase. *"Yet why am I still panting?"* he asked himself. *"What is driving me now I am here?"* He stopped, both feet planted firmly on a ground which pertained to the moment yet belonged to no-one as stillness engulfed him, bringing an air of desolation with it. He had done it, done it all, everything he had said he would. But he had never asked himself *"Why?"* The reality of his actions confronted him; the weapon of desire revealing the blood of revenge: a scalding blade piercing his heart as he stood before her beauty, forlorn in the knowledge now flooding him...the knowledge that he would never see this mother again.

Maternal love. For many a love of the deepest kind, a love which knows no bounds. Yet does one ever question the validity of such expression? For how much freedom can exist in an energy as engulfing as a woodland fire on a summer's day? Just how 'reasonable' can such emotion be? For both the mother, and the child.

Society hides behind the word 'love'. More distress is caused as a result of over-use, misuse and misunderstanding of both the word and the emotion – for they are two very different things – than any other in our language. 'Love' as a word is used to capture a moment, to define a transaction between two people, whether that be in a story, a song, in a card, a letter, or vocalised through speech. It is 'something' we place *out-there* in an attempt to explain and capture what we feel *in here*. But within, there are no words, purely emotion, so how can they be one and the same?

'Love' as an emotion is all-powerful, all-destructive and all-encompassing. One's earliest example of love – being our mother's love in knowing no bounds – enthuses us with the belief that 'love' is almighty and omnipresent; and in ownership of maternal – and paternal – love, our forebears, through such expression entrap a child's freedom. A child is reared to need such love and to fear lack of love: "*Without love a child has nothing.*" Oh what a shame society impedes its growth in this way!

A child does not *need* love, a child *is* love. A child *needs* freedom to express itself and explore itself within an environment of safety; to discover the love that it *is*, that we all are.

A mother's love can be a beautiful thing...when it is directed at the mother. A mother's love, when directed at the child can be suffocating, destabilising and harmful to all. A mother, just as she is, is a beautiful expression of life and joy. Without the entrapment of 'love', a mother will feel no fear, no loss, no denial. She can be a vessel for growth, freedom and joy – and that is a wonderful thing.

WED 23RD JULY 2014, LONDON AT 9.30AM, SESSION 26

Still rooted to the spot, she saw the wounds appear in him as he convulsed within emotion. Instinct told her to go to him, yet she refrained. For what reason, she did not know. But she knew one thing. That she loved him with all her heart, would do anything for him – if he would permit it. And in that moment she understood; that no matter how much she tried, the permission was not there, was held by another. A helplessness descended upon her as she watched the cloud of ancestry catch up with him, engulf him from behind. He had broken free, escaped; yet before he could even catch his breath it had regained control – of him, of them. Its power rendered the situation powerless. And it had taken control by snatching the very essence of their flight: Desire.

To watch manifestation is to watch life in motion. The normal view is of another: the person. We watch what they do, hear what they say, interpret *the other* through our filters of inner experience. But far more interesting, more revealing, is to watch not the person, but the energy of manifestation – what appears and sits 'around' the person, the interactions people have and the effects the surrounding manifested energy and mass creates in another…or in many.

In 'watching' this prose, this story, we can focus on the woman, the man, or the energy manifesting between them. To focus on the energy as a first point of reference utterly changes one's perspective as the watcher, as we observe not the completed transaction of the person but the more alive, more vivid and current motion of energy fluctuating in response to matter. For humans are matter held within energy. The taken concept of "everything is energy" is both true and not true. Yes, ultimately all is energy, yet not all energy is equal. Matter is contracted density as a result of 'doing'. Mass holds both this energy and the energy of Being. But it is the formless energy – the potential of Randomness which is the most powerful of energy.

When one observes the formless between forms, one begins to see the 'life' being created. And it is at such times one can also observe the emotions triggering the conversion of formless into form. One gains, as observer, a view of the whole picture, not just the completed parts.

Desire is both the formless wishing to come into form and the form – the human emotion – wishing to express and become formless. It is a balanced transaction and often a healing transaction as the matter within the mass of the body softens and replaces with 'newer' matter; an updating of one's software if you will…

It is the lack of flow of desire which creates energetic blocks in people and their physical bodies. And the biggest, most challenging handle on these blocks? One's past.

<u>THURS 24TH JULY 2014, LONDON AT 10.55AM, SESSION 27</u>

"But…," **she uttered, knowing there was no use; the words would not be heard. Her shoulders slumped as the anger rose in her.** *"But I love you,"* **she shouted.** *"I love you!"* **Her eyes glistened, wide, portraying a frustration which could not be contained, which drove into the air around her. A wild energy poured out of her, from where she knew not. It was deeper than her heart, by-passed her heart in fact. It had no beginning and no end. She was not in control, she was not out of control, she was, in that moment, utterly nothing filled with a despair belonging to everything. She was paralysed, static in every way. Except one: if only he would look at her, raise his eyes to hers, then she could respond. For respond was all she could do.**

Today, as we sit within our reality observing the world we have chosen, we might ask ourselves: *"How much of this have I made happen? And how much of it has happened to me?"* For indeed it has been 'chosen'.

There are three main types of choice. Firstly, there is the conscious choice when instinct, intuition and the soul drive a choice which feels *right* on all levels. A second type of choice encompasses the subconscious choices we make as we travel along our path – the path which includes our physical lifetime and master time-line. We can choose to resist and resent our master time-line path or we can chose to work with it, learn from it, alter it. And the way to alter it, our reality, the world we have made happen, is to *choose* to learn and grow *through* the experience – and hence change our reality. It is all choice. It is all thought.

The third type of choice is reactionary choice, in response to inner blockages on an emotional level. They seem powerful, loaded, vivid choices but they are deceptive, for they are indeed not 'choices' at all. For someone else is in control. In our story, the power is with the man. His lack of response, a powerful hold on the woman's 'future'. Where is the weakness? And who holds the strength? What does the interplay of energy between them tell us? What is our perception?

Freedom is the dropping of reactionary energy. Period. Enlightenment is the dropping of reactionary energy within and without, enabling conscious, clear, crisp choices and action. Freedom enables enlightenment. Enlightenment creates greater freedom. Love becomes present as movement towards the master time-line enables conscious awareness. Yet conscious awareness is the starting place for conscious choice. Perpetual movement allows the contrast, the contrast creates the desire. The desire moves us towards love. Pure love.

FRI 25TH JULY 2014, LONDON AT 9.45AM, SESSION 28

"Just once," he said. *"It only happened…just once."* Still he would not look at her, would not raise his bowed head, yet his clenched fists displayed his conflict within. He felt torn apart – a three-way split taking limbs, flesh, oxygen and heart. *"What just happened?"* he silently screamed. *"One minute I am free, at last tasting the freedom I so yearned for, the next I am paralysed, destroyed. And nothing 'happened'…until…I saw her."* Slowly he observed his mind placing the parts together, finding the links. He became detached from himself, was able to observe himself from above it seemed. He shook his head – but he felt nothing – the connection to his body was fading, altering. He was aware of his senses, yet they were different, intangible. He saw himself raising his head and looking at her. He saw the two of them, face to face, motionless, captured within something he could no longer understand. *"What is happening?"* A thought but no longer a scream, as a softness and understanding touched him. Finally he understood…

It is the lack of understanding which creates the understanding. As confusion *without* increases, wisdom *within* appears. Unless…we are strangled by emotions and energetic ties.

Man's experience of freedom is centred around physical freedom: lack of internment, ability to move, see, touch. Desire is channelled into experiencing the physical, acquiring the physical and destroying the physical. Yet the physical is just a reflection, a mirroring of the internal; a 'casing' if you will. A light-bulb will not shine without a glass casing – the bulb contains the light.

Within man are other freedoms: emotional freedom, energetic freedom, mental freedom and conscious freedom. Ignorance of these come at the peril of dissatisfaction, for no amount of physical acquisition or deployment will alleviate the need for these gifts – gifts which are pertained to the Self. These gifts, we can only give to ourselves.

WED 30TH JULY 2014, LONDON AT 10.00AM, SESSION 29

His gaze landed back on her face. He took in, soaked up, every seed of being he could from her; for he knew he would be turning away, leaving her too. He felt no emotion, was experiencing a detachment which raised no questions, yet he knew he would miss her…and the dreams they had conceived yet not given birth to. *"Oh how he would miss her!"* He knew that. Yet he knew even deeper in his soul that the time had come. An unspoken agreement – where from he knew not – was calling him into

action. One moment he had been slumbering, the next, alert to a presence which afforded safety and a stream of certainty as it beckoned him forward. As he moved, hypnotised by its lure, his thoughts gathered around her. His heart swelled, hurt almost in physical expansion as he saw her swallow her needs and courageously stand aside to allow him to pass. Neither had moved yet everything had changed. Her courage would be hers, his freedom would be his.

It is energetic freedom which is the most powerful, the most dramatic in resonance. For all affects energy and is tied by energy.

When one becomes aware of the presence of energy, one's world alters inextricably, as the connectedness of 'life' in all its forms can be accessed and felt. A door opens to a dimension pertaining to all levels of awareness: for past, present and future become one's everyday play times. As one becomes comfortable within the tangible presence of divine and earthly energies, one can relax and enjoy the sensations. This is when life becomes fun! For with choice, come the pleasures often denied those without the ability to choose within awareness. To consciously choose an energy of lightness and pleasure is to choose one's soul.

Let me not mislead though…for such a path is not an easy path to take. It requires walking into the unknown, dropping attachment, and discovering oneself. And this last requirement is by far the most challenging of the three. Indeed…for it requires honesty of Self and of one's placement as reality is viewed both from the position of 'I' and the position of 'not I', the position of detachment. It is the art of viewing in duality; and it is very powerful.

Let me explain. To view (oneself and others) from duality creates neutral awareness, as the viewing from within and without counter-balance each other. All healing and conscious awareness comes from neutrality (neutrality is a topic I will cover in-depth in this book). As an object or situation is viewed from duality, from the 'I' and the 'not I', the neutrality enables the 'excess' – the awareness – to rise. The 'object' of attention becomes not the object or situation in itself, but the arising awareness: whether this be a thought, feeling or sensation. The interaction is then with the 'surplus', the awareness, the 'creation'. And because this new creation is free of attachment, one can interact with it with freedom and ease. This is the beginning of conscious evolution.

THURS 31ST JULY 2014, LONDON AT 10.25AM, SESSION 30

He never looked back. He didn't need to, didn't want to dilute the intensity of what he was experiencing. He knew this moment – the power of it – would carry him through the times to come, would support him in what would present itself before him. For he understood now, that there was no more running, fleeing or regret. Everything, *everything*, had shifted in that instant. As he walked, he felt

**strength return to his legs; became aware of his
heart beating, *"Yes! It was still there...functioning!"*
and he took a breath. The night air now tasted
cooler, quieter, crisper. He became aware of his
presence, his strides, his comfortable urgency. He
kept walking, although he had nowhere to go.**

A sense of belonging is what drives mankind. Yes, and with
a vigour and intensity which rarely diminishes with time. In
fact, quite the opposite. As one approaches ones end of physical life (perceived or actual) the drive to establish resonance
with those occupying planet Earth, one's co-habitants, increases. It is a tangible desire to remain in the present...forever.
Immortality in one's pocket. Control in one's pocket. A legacy...something to show for all one's 'hard work' whilst denial
ruled the show. The greater the denial, the greater the desire
for immortality. This is the experience of those sitting within
one's physical lifetime – hence man's need to procreate.

But when one steps into one's master time-line, one steps
into immortality – and denial disappears, to be replaced with
a sense of belonging. It is a sense of belonging which takes
some understanding and some connection with: *"For how
could such uncertainty create such a sense of peace?"* It is the journey of worth, of searching for one's place within mankind and
'what-is' which creates both the template for one's life and the
contrast needed to execute that template...to put the *life* into
the life-time.

MON 4TH AUG 2014, LONDON AT 10.50AM, SESSION 31

Strangely he knew which direction to head in. Like an animal following a trail, the scent of another, he instinctively followed the invisible path in front of him. He could not see it with his vision, but he was *seeing* it with his senses, his inner compass guiding him forward. He felt a pang of hunger and realised he had not eaten since daybreak. He needed water, some bread and, yes, a rest. Yes, he needed to rest. At last he could rest.

The universe is a moving, contracting, expanding wave – within the container of perception. Nothing stands still, yet nothing changes in its method of movement. Such as man has many time-lines, he also has many 'equations of movement' in action at any one time – until one's physical death and beyond.

Man – and woman, though I use the term 'man' to include both the sexes as a generic – man, is an ocean of waves, from tempestuous storms to calm waters; all formation of an ocean in motion. As one wave dispels, another builds; as a storm passes, stillness appears. The movement of man's ocean is a beautiful thing – in all its temperatures – for the stillness cannot come until the storm has passed and abated in totality. Yet man abhors the flow of emotions, of the unknown and unexpected. He tries to control, avoid, deny the very energies which give him life. It is this suppression, this trying to tame the ocean which creates the despair: despair of 'what-is' counterbalanced by external control mechanisms, which creates the inner conflict.

Man needs to rest. Mankind needs to rest, in order to flow with its creationism. But it does not allow for this, the most basic of requirements: one half of the 'equation of movement'. Mankind lives in fear of resting: *"What am I missing whilst I sleep? Whilst I turn away? Whilst I turn off just momentarily from the noise?"* Man is not inclined to let another over-take, take the lead, be 'better than'. He, or she, feels the need to 'earn' a rest, *earn* self-care, *earn* one's place in humanity – even to earn love and worth. Man is addicted to 'doing' and mankind is addicted to the fear of missing out.

If one does not allow the rest – the true rest, at a cellular level – then 'nature' will provide it; through illness, circumstances and enforced solitude. It is the way of enforced equanimity; to provide the space for recalibration and balance – to create a *deep breath*.

There is not just one type of rest: I talk not of purely physical rest. For indeed one can be physically very active yet fully rested. I talk of emotional rest, mental rest and energetic rest.

All these 'affect' one's cellular constituency. And like we may need to 'rest' our arms, or legs, or head or heart, we at times need to rest our country, our land, our imagination. They all flow in waves.

Our man in the tale needs rest; rest from his life so far, rest to absorb the change – the loss and the gain – rest to his physical, mental and emotional bodies. We can understand his need to rest, yet why can man not understand his or her individual need too?

TUES 5TH AUG 2014, LONDON AT 9.15AM, SESSION 32

The food nourished him, but the sleep nourished him more. He had not much sleep, but he awakened refreshed and eager. He took out what coins he had, paid for the hospitality and entered into the sunshine, inwardly thanking the white stucco building for the roof it had given him for the night. His host handed him some provisions wrapped in paper – something for lunch – and he smiled his gratitude. He nodded – as much to himself as the elderly couple – and set on his way. He had no money, no-where to go – but he had food for the journey, energy within and his freedom.

"Forsaking all others." My, what a doctrine man imposes upon himself! 'Conditional living' from the outset, as boy and girl are raised in anticipation of marriage to another, to forsake all others, to continue the tradition of matrimony. Preservation of the species, but at what cost?

To "forsake all others" as an energetic vow creates conflict within, as the hand of God, of ancestral ways, dictates through expectation one's future. How can one *know* one's future and how one will feel and behave? To enforce behaviour is no less than a form of imprisonment – imprisonment of the soul, and lack of trust. To need a vow to create trust? Trust for whom?

As man or woman enters a contract of trust, they subconsciously transfer the power, the trust, from themselves into 'the contract'. And they become compromised within; a freedom has been removed. Every action – thought or physical – is reflected and judged in reflection of the contract, and the contract, the marriage, supersedes the individuals.

To "forsake all others" for another is to forsake oneself in actuality. To live in awareness of the moment is to make conscious choice in the moment: to choose without attachment to reactionary energies. Conscious choice is powerful and is empowering; for the individual and those in its vicinity. When one has 'chosen' another, and contracted to another, choice is diminished – for to honour the contract creates conflict in honouring oneself. To 'trust the contract' is to trust the process – and this leads to expectation.

But to trust oneself and to trust 'what-is' leads to fulfilment and honesty. For how can one trust another if one does not trust oneself? How can one be honest with another if one is not honest with oneself? And if one has trust and honesty of Self, why the need for a contract? To prove to whom?

Man hesitates to trust, and man does not trust honesty. Hence the development of 'the contract'. But what a free life it would be without contracts…without the need to 'prove' one's intention! Imagine the freedom that would create, the opportunity to express one's love, intention and desire in honesty. Imagine the space for love that would be created, and the freedom within each individual, each man and woman to express their authenticity – not because they *should*, not through fear, but through purpose of Being. Yes, that would be most wonderful, no?

SAT 9TH AUG 2014, LONDON AT 11.40AM, SESSION 33

Step led to step, led to step, to step. And so the distance was covered. The afternoon breeze reminded him to take rest, to eat and to keep pondering. For though he walked with a freedom, his mind seeked answers: solutions to his questioning. What the questions were, he did not know, but their presence drove a desire in him. It was a desire which distance was not abating. And it was a desire which knew no language he understood. Yet it was there…so all he could do was keep walking. Afternoon haze joined evening sunset, which gave way to nightfall. Still he had no answers, still he had nowhere to go. Still he kept going.

It is at midnight, that we consider a day turns into another day. Separate within themselves, twenty four hours apiece. Yet one day falls into the next as time carries over. Cumulative mathematics at its highest. For to have 'time' – this time, this day – one must have had all previous time, or more accurately, one *has* all previous time.

As one is born into a physical lifetime, one enters 'what-is'. Yet 'what-is' is comprised of the accumulation of all time. As the random spark of birth creates new life within this sphere of energy, all 'time' is adjusted to accommodate the acquisition. As mass converts to matter, energy is released. It is this energy we call 'life'. It is this energy which binds, and it is this energy we call love.

The scientific understanding is binding energy. Man has not explored this phenomenon in its potential. Binding energy is the field of humanity; it is love, the actual tangible content, and the unknown. Man's search to make the unknowable known can be found in binding energy. Yet man's personal search gives no space for this exploration, so busy is he capturing what he 'knows', what he is taught to have. To discover the unknown, one must walk into the unknown: unaided save for one's desire and belief in that desire. To capture that belief is to kill the belief – for whilst it is the necessary lubricant, a belief cannot be contained – it must grow and develop with the exploration. The journey necessitates intention, yet no required outcome. And this is what man finds hard. For to learn another language, to learn to understand things differently requires letting go of all that time has provided. The mirror shows not the man, but the time. And when the time has 'passed', man's view is not obvious, the landscape is not familiar. It is this journey one must take.

<u>MON 11TH AUG 2014, LONDON AT 9.25AM, SESSION 34</u>

Suddenly he stopped. He observed himself standing dead still. *"Have I died?"* **he thought, so strange was the feeling of nothing. For it was not just a physical pause, but all of him had just…***stopped.* *"How strange,"* **he observed again…watching himself just standing there.** *"What now?"*

"Yes, what now?" **the body answered, communicating directly with him…with his** *awareness* **which was no part of his body. There stood the two parts of him, looking at each other, questioning each other. Yet 'he' was elsewhere: the observer. He looked to the left, to the right, sensing their disparity yet aware that 'he' was separate from them both. He had become…***three?* *"Where did he begin, and where did he end? And what now? He could not just 'stand there'… Who was going to decide?"*

Randomness creates and man destroys. This is what we are told, and hence what we observe. We could substitute Randomness with God, The Almighty, Source, a power from above or the tide of evolution. But because so much 'effort' has been laboured into making this all 'happen' – so many years, and lifetimes, of toil – when it dissipates, a loss is felt. *"All that hard work for nothing."*

The ancestral legacy each generation is burdened with necessitates a reaction of blame at this 'loss'. We have to blame *someone*, for we did not honour our promise to protect the work of the former generations. And if we cannot blame others, worse, we blame ourselves. Man cannot accept.

But as man needs to create, man also needs to dissimilate. And it is this dissimilation process – of *telling a different story* – which 'breaks apart' the old. Thought alone will change how things are in their current form. Change is inevitable, indeed it is desirable; for the old must make way for the new. But it is (the thought of) the new which creates the dissolution of the old. And this must happen.

Man is raised to protect the old…to do things as they have always been done… *"or else all will be lost."* Creativity is encouraged, but only in so far as to 'increase' and 'capitalise' on what one has. But imagine if man was raised to leave the old behind, to go out with freedom and excitement into a world of opportunity and resounding response where it did not matter what he accumulated, or not, but his freedom and sense of connection was exalted.

In order for man to create growth, he must tear apart. It is in the wounds we heal. It is in the wounds new tissue is formed. The deeper the wound, the greater the growth. It is when man breathes his life as the life of the clan, of the ancestral line, that the tear is seen as 'destruction by man'. For to see ourselves as our clan is to 'lose' the clan in the process. Yet this is the work, this is the freedom man is seeking.

Like the man in our tale, one must tear apart the layers superfluous to our innate self. The same for a corporation as the man on the street. It is in the 'space in between' where the answers lie. Always.

TUES 12ᵀᴴ AUG 2014, LONDON AT 12.05PM, SESSION 35

The decision was made for him. He saw himself slump to the ground, kneeling in the dust of the path. A wave of compassion flooded him – flooded him as the observer and flooded him as the body. Now it was the awareness's turn to observe, to see and experience what was happening 'out there', *to him*. The awareness was both of the detachment *and* the compassion. Somehow, the one accentuated the other, made each more powerful. He felt both disconnected, yet utterly connected at the same time. As the tears landed in the dirt, the earth gave him strength…the strength to allow himself to let go.

To let go is nirvana to the soul. For man is so busy 'capturing', he has no time to let go. He is on the treadmill of accumulation. And if he does decide to 'spring clean' or open a closet, it is soon shut, with the merest of attention. Rarely does he delve into the recesses or allow the questioning its destination. It is why the 'letting go' happens *to* man. For when the desire, the inner subconscious desire, for change is so great, the space will be made. As I say, all is in the space in between.

But conscious letting go – of people, supports, emotions, energies and thought patterns – requires courage and strength. It is one thing to display courage as a result of catastrophe and hardship, it is another to voluntarily display and execute through *choice*. But oh, how powerful!

Mankind has a tendency to give accolade to those who experience hardship, and disdain to those who let go through courage of choice. Yet the latter is the more challenging, the most fraught with uncertainty, the more lonely of the two. For it encompasses 'leaving the tribe' to walk into the unknown. Indeed one can spend more effort 'running away' where one stands, trapped in unseen chains, than the man who turns to brighter light. It is in the steps of action that the path opens and it is in the steps of action one lets go.

THURS 14TH AUG 2014, LONDON AT 11.15AM, SESSION 36

The pause which winded him and knocked him to the ground gave way to sobs of relief. His body racked with energies as the waves flowed through him. He did not try to stop them, but went with them; feeling a relief and a contraction at the same time. It was so fast, so fluid, so all-encompassing,

it carried him, as much as his body carried the energies. Wave after wave came and gave way to another. Part of him did not want it to stop, the relief was so deeply felt, and...pleasurable. The angst was pleasurable, the pain was pleasurable: because it was moving. No longer was it stuck, stifled and burning. Like a child during labour, the movement was both excruciating yet wholly satisfying; his purpose and his desire.

It shocks one to know pain is chosen. But it is so. Let me explain. Pain is an emotion. Period. It is an emotion felt by the mind, the heart, the soul or the body. Physical pain is emotion being expressed by the body. When a child is born and reared, as its body grows it does not feel pain – it is effortless. Yet is its body not stretching, growing, adapting? Muscles give way, bones dissolve, extend, adapt. Organs enlarge, move. Yet no physical pain is felt. The child is in a state of growth – and growth, in its pure form is natural, instinctive and hence carries no heavy emotions. With no barriers or emotional blocks our child will keep learning and growing, pain free.

Emotion, if not released, is 'held' in the body – the physical body and the energetic body, controlled by the mental body – the mind. Our bodies 'hold' our life – in Spirit as much as in the physical. Yet our subconscious – our connection to 'what-is' – wants to discard these emotions, to free itself. 'Illness' is the subconscious discarding what it no longer needs. Hence why children are born with illness – they come to heal: of emotions and energies of a previous life. They come to this life to express, dissolve and cure themselves. Their subconscious knows how to do this – they want, at a deep level to *feel* the pain, so they can transition it, move through it, become free of it. The 'pain' is the release of emotion. It is why death can be painful, yet it is 'chosen' – for it gives the freedom, not of the pain, but of the emotion.

Yet emotions are intrinsic, healthy – what gives our existence vitality, interest and diversity. It is through emotions we grow, learn, develop our wisdom and joy. Man comes to this life to experience these very gifts, to experience the contrasts and expansion only possible through emotions. It is the nature of man to both move towards emotion and simultaneously move away. To grow, and to protect. To expand, and to contract. To give, and to receive. This is life.

SAT 16TH AUG 2014, LONDON AT 10.30AM, SESSION 37

It is at this point the story ends. For in the release of his past, he released the stories of his past to the almanac of what-was. In no longer having a hold on him, he was free. Free to begin living as himself. The book was there to reference if he so wished, but he did not need to carry it with him. His hands were free, to do with as he wished. Action would now be conscious; thought, filled with clarity; movement, a response to intuition; and destiny his to have.

Man believes he must strive to achieve: work hard, forego, 'do without', relinquish himself. Oh how misguided! The equation I will refer to in this book to demonstrate man's path to peace begins with: +1 and -1. These are the only two digits one need understand, for all of matter rests on the variations and combinations of these most beautiful of symbols. For symbols they are…carrying the connections of energy and mass (for energy-connection differs from mass-connection) which constructs our reality as we each know it.

So for man to 'strive to achieve', he is operating in the sphere of -1. He has foregone; so in *this* moment his life is 'less than', -1. He may spend many days, months, years in -1 whilst reaching for the +1. One day, when he 'gets there', if he gets there to grasp the +1, he will reach…neutrality. The minus 1, negates the plus 1. The risk though – the fear which will have hovered – is: "What if I don't get there?" And this is when man becomes ruthless.

The alternative seeked by many, lived by many, is to spend one's days in +1. Each day, +1, +1, +1… The -1 is applied to good use (for it must be used, expressed, in *movement* to enable flow) by application to removal of all obstacles which may prevent the daily state of +1. The expression of the -1 energy, which laws of nature deem must be present, is expressed 'intrinsically' in those who seek to reside in the state of +1. One processes, absorbs, adjusts, questions, *learns and grows*. The processing – without damage to others – of the -1's enables the flow within the +1's.

This differs from those abiding to the state of -1. As they rest in this place, the +1's, as they come are pushed away, delayed for another day; life is 'postponed to the day it is deserved' – and one becomes further entrenched within the -1's.

It really is this simple, should one wish to adopt this perspective. In the adoption of the awareness of +1/-1, everything which 'hinders' this flow begins to adjust and soften as one experiences new outlooks. The 'matter' in one's lives may not change, but one's perspectives and sensations relating to them will. One can experience the matter of a job, an illness, a challenge within +1 with a flow of -1, or within -1 with resistance to +1. It matters not on where one currently sits, for the intention determines the outcome.

TUES 19ᵀᴴ AUG 2014, LONDON AT 11.40AM, SESSION 38

So our story told us many things, if we had the perspective of curious questioning. For some, it would have been a love story, for others, a tale of destruction or enlightenment. It may have brought up emotion, recognition, disdain or indifference. It may have seemed touching, sensitive, awkward, illogical. Perhaps nonsense, perhaps truth? For each of us it will have different meaning, or no meaning other than that of dismissal. But it serves a purpose – as do all the stories we tell ourselves and create for pleasure or pain. For there is always a choice, is there not?

But let us for the moment look at the story from a perspective of love. For love is the topic man believes he is searching for – indirectly or directly. Love of money, love of nature, love of a partner, a child, a pet. Love for someone, something. Oneself, perhaps? 'Love' is the topic of most books, the subject of many songs, the *reason* for most people's behaviour. Yet it remains so lacking, so elusive, so fleeting. Here one moment… gone the next! Its very transient nature: its attractiveness and its effectualness. Man's search for love…an occupational hazard when we recognise how obsessed humanity is with this grail deemed holy.

Today the search is the same as one hundred years ago, five hundred years ago, a thousand years ago. Yet it is more 'painful' today, for the reminders of its absence…so vivid in your vistas. All of your 'matter' is presented as a gateway to love: *"Decorate your home if you want a loving family"; "Feed your family this or that if you love them"; "Do so-and-so if you love yourself"; "Get a good job to 'look after' – aka love – your family."* The list is endless and indeed there is not one aspect of the western world that is not 'sold' on love. Even your governments sell themselves via manifestos – purporting how they will 'look after' you, their citizen.

The contrast of this: how love is lacking in one's life. One is aware of…the friends one 'does not have', the wealth one 'does not have', the new car, the physical wellbeing, the adequate pension, the ability to…need I continue? Society looks at what it has, and doesn't have, but it does not question the measure it is measuring. For what is love?

The difference today (I use the term 'today' in the broad sense) is that western society – and global society to a degree worth mentioning – has lost connection to what 'love' is. Your society is tricking you with the very thing you search for; like goldfish in a bowl searching for the way out.

Five hundred years ago, man understood love within a 'smaller' context – yet man *felt* love, knew what it was, appreciated it, respected it. His, or her, only experience of it being through direct experience or story-telling. Man would fight for love, die for love, but rarely dismiss love.

Today, through the advent of electronic communication and visual stimulus, man has images of love thrust before him – but they create no experience other than one of lack. In the awareness of 'what's missing' man begins searching. But what is he searching for?

3

"WHAT IS LOVE?" MR P
AND PLATO DISCUSS

Mr P: This is the part of these works I am most looking forward to, for in the questioning, the most audacious responses can be allowed into fruition. The mere utterance of the word or thought places the energy into 'action'. The thought has been had; it *exists*.

So the question is: *"What is love?"*

Most will answer, *"Well, it's what I have with my loved one, my children, my family and friends. We all know what love is.…"*
    But I beg to differ. For how can one person's interpretation of a lifetime of experience – including hurt, fear, admonishment, courage, fright, joy, wisdom and truth be the same as anyone else's? Who has the gold-standard level we all measure

by? Is it Jesus? Mother Theresa? The Buddha? The Prophet Muhammed? Or perhaps your neighbour?

When searching for 'love', is one searching for this kind of holy love, or just the run-of-the-mill 'standard' love? And if one is content with the standard, everyday version of love, why the chapels, churches, monasteries and temples? Why be wed or interred by a minister? Why not by thy neighbour?

The greatest misnomer is that of another's love. The greatest. If every person on planet Earth relinquished the need to perceive another's love, but expressed what arose within, there would be no war, no pain and no hardship. Society would thrive, children would flourish and resentment would vanish within a generation. But understand, what would arise within would not be 'love', no. It would be purpose. And that purpose, for all mankind, irrespective of creed, colour, profession or nature, would be the expression of truth.

Mankind is fighting not for love, but for one's truth...for what is holy to each and every soul on this planet. It is the perception of mankind's love towards man, woman and child – the words "I love you" – that hinders the process, that creates the wounds. *Love* gets in the way of truth. Much more powerful, more vulnerable, and needing more profundity, are the words: *"I see you, I see you in your truth, and I allow you to see me."*

The exploration of this topic is the basis for this section of works. It is a question humanity is ready to ask, for the answers in themselves will create a wisdom humanity is ready to acknowledge. It is time.

TUES 23RD SEPT 2014, LONDON AT 11.40AM, SESSION 40

Mr P: It is through a process of "question and answer" we can explore – for there are no 'right answers', yet perhaps wise answers. In offering *my* answer, I hope to shed a viewpoint perhaps not offered before, or at least in the context of a discussion such as this.

Love is a topic close to my heart – it has been my downfall, my saviour and my advisor in many lifetimes. Until my last physical lifetime I searched for answers within 'love' itself. I explored, circumnavigated and dissected to find the essence of it. I had moments whence I captured it, or so I thought, for it always remained elusive, temporal and, oh, so transient! Its very nature causing me to nurture answers. But to all avail. For the answers came when I stopped searching. The answers, I share with you now, and if you feel so inclined, draw on your own answers to find your truth, for it is in the combination the richness unfolds.

PLATO: "To feel love, is to know love, is it not?"

Mr P: To feel love is to feel an energy which is present in that moment. When one *feels*, one is open, allowing, and honouring 'what-is'. But that 'what-is'ness' is merely energy – a combination of interrelated forces, namely atomic sub-structure, nuclear dimensions and particles of thought-form.

It could be a feeling of hatred, of envy, of denial – again these would be the same energies of nature at play. It is the same 'method' to feel – like carrying a load. One uses one's hands, arms, shoulders perhaps; whatever the load, it is carried in the same manner. Yet the basket may contain different wares. It is the same with feeling.

Not everyone is adept at feeling. And this is the first distinction to be made. The ability to 'feel' more than one's neighbour, does not mean the person contains more love – but merely the ability to carry a load effectively. But is this a good thing? Perhaps, if the load is joy. Perhaps not, if the load is sorrow.

Carrying one's load is a task. It requires effort and it requires sustainability. This is not love. Carrying one's load encounters the hand of uncertainty, of destination, of purpose. This is not love. Carrying one's load necessitate calculation, balance and movement. This is not love. Yet humanity believes these to be the very components of love.

To *feel* is to be open to the energies which abound. It is man's purpose in physical lifetime. But it is not love. Man comes into this world to explore all senses, be they smell, touch, taste, comfort, sight, empathy, hatred or love. In this context, love, like the others, is a sense. And "to *sense* love, is not to know love, no".

WED 24TH SEPT 2014, LONDON AT 10.00AM, SESSION 41

PLATO: "The love which abounds creates the essence of life itself, does it not?"

Mr P: I suggest it is not love which creates life but the belief in the power of love. The belief in the potential that love can bring, is what drives the desire for love. For the *power* of love can be observed most clearly – unlike 'love' itself. If one reminisces, we can observe what 'love' brought us or did not bring us. Our senses of that experience feed back to our core. And in return, our core – our animalistic instinct, what enables man's survival – desires more of it, for it enables the very survival of itself.

When one observes into one's future, again the wish for the feel-good experience – why would one choose differently? Unless one has been 'hurt' by love. And this is where we can observe this equation more clearly.

The equation I speak of is that of geometric exchange. For there can, by the very laws of nature, be no 'missing particle'. All is *fair* in existence. So the 'absence' of 'love' cannot in itself be a requisite to the 'presence' of love. To feel (note: a sensory aspect) hurt or love or compassion is *outside* of the geometric exchange. It is *within* the person. But the exchange itself, between two people, or a person and an object for instance, is a balanced equation; an exchange, interchangeable in its components and direction of intention. "I can look at you, you can look at me back" – this involves an energetic exchange. Equally, "I can look at the wall, and the wall looks at me back" – involving a likewise exchange.

So, within this viewpoint, "What abounds?" This can only be intention. An intention to *feel* something – whatever that may be. But to *own* one's intention is a courageous act. Most prefer to 'lay blame at the door of another' – and hence the existence of reactionary energy and the desire for 'love' as a panacea.

I therefore suggest, it is not love which creates life, and indeed I would add, not the power of love which creates life (although this has a separate value in itself), but the *intention* which purports to all existence.

There is a difference between intention and potential, and this is when we re-visit Randomness. Intention is the spark within the potential sea of Randomness. Human instinct is to play in that sea, to *experience*, to *feel*, to en-joy. To feel the contrast between the spiritual and the physical – to be able to 'report back' on the physical experience – indeed this is what the inner sensory feedback system is. Love, being a sensory experience is one, just one, of those senses. 'Love' itself does not create a human life, nor feed a hungry mouth. It is an *exchange* which creates the essence of life, and it is the intention to experience more *potential* which drives the instinct.

THURS 25TH SEPT 2014, LONDON AT 10.20AM, SESSION 42

PLATO: "Why is it, when the feeling of love arises, that one experiences a sensation like no other, of profound connection?"

Mr P: My dear Plato, the feeling of love can be a most beautiful experience, why yes. It takes us to highs indescribable in the moment and deep lows one cares not to revisit. But in each experience of love, whatever the context, there is the involvement of another, as a trigger to that feeling – even if the love is experienced *within* oneself for no prescribed 'reason'. The thought, the memory, the connection with another – in whatever form, including community form – is what triggers the sensation of love.

By contrast, when one experiences such effervescent highs *without* another, say whilst observing a sunset in the pure abandoned moment, this is joy. Joy involves no-one but oneself. Joy is unadulterated beauty in the moment, and joy is the connection we seek. It is the connection within, which feeds off the connection with all-that-is.

When one is 'in love', be that with one's partner, one's child, or one's companion, it is the hint of joy within the moment that grabs our reflexes, and creates the sparkle and subconscious knowingness that tells us that we are part of a bigger context; that we are meaningful. It is not *love* itself, but man confuses the emotions with the essence of life itself. Love is not life, it is joy that brings life. Man is seeking joy and he will not find this through love.

Love, as you suggest, has great value – if used wisely. As such with anger, despair and rejection. All, if used for awareness, recalibration and courageous movement enable great exploration into growth and evolvement. But love cannot be used for growth unless it is played with, touched upon lightly and allowed freedom to flow forwards: to circulate, and to be shared. Love is not something to be owned, captured or contained. Indeed, one would not choose despair in such way, would we?

Love is the most overused word in the western hemisphere, and as a result, the most misunderstood. Should man choose to remove this word from his being, a world of sensation, discovery and enlightenment would present before him. For how to describe the feeling one's child or parent brings? One's greatest joy or one's passion? In drawing on the true meaning, one's authenticity would emerge and one's words could do no other than reflect one's true meaning – and *that* dear Plato, becomes meaningful.

MON 29TH SEPT 2014, LONDON AT 9.30AM, SESSION 43

PLATO: "To trust someone involves the aspect of love I feel?"

Mr P: 'Trust' is a complex yet simple association. And I call it 'an association' due to the emergent nature of it. It is something which grows, and despite relapse at times, if allowed, continues to grow. It is complex in that it is different for all, and draws on different 'needs' within the individual or the collective, yet simple in that as trust is reached, that *is it*: one has gained an increased level of trust. Even when someone experiences distressing and profound levels of abuse and harm, once the healing has occurred, trust, in an increased form is realised. For trust requires an acceptance of 'what-*is*'; it cannot be experienced 'in the past' or 'in the future' – purely in the now.

By contrast, love is experienced often 'in the past' or 'in the future'. One can think of an experienced or anticipated situation…and feel love – or more accurately, the sensation of it.

Not so with trust. But there is, I agree, an aspect where the two *collide*, and this is where the association occurs.

Associative feelings are highly complex – for they relate to one's sense of safety and security. A 'link' is present between, let's say, love and trust, or harm and distress. Or perhaps between love and distress, and trust and harm – the combination differs, and can include more than two aspects. But returning to your suggestion, Plato, yes, trust and love are often associated by the individual. *"If I love him, I must trust him"* or *"She doesn't trust me, so she can't love me."*

In fact love and trust are very different and one would do well to keep them 'separate' in one's awareness. By linking aspects, a web is created, and knots soon appear. For indeed it is wholly infeasible to 'expect' another to provide one's trust. As with joy being an *internal* aspect, so is trust. Love, we have discussed, involves others. Trust begins with oneself, yet gradually becomes conditional; a baby 'trusts' itself, until it is told by example that it cannot, that it must earn trust from others, that others 'know better'.

Now an infant of course needs guidance and role models. But when the role models don't trust themselves, they by default display these qualities to their young. And in that search for meaning – that search for safety and security – they look for love. Love I suggest, is an addiction like all others; it is just more subversive and less 'damaging' to the physical body than alcohol or induced highs through substance. But it is a 'high' nevertheless, defined as an addiction for it involves another form, be that a person.

The high of joy, I suggest cannot be deemed an addiction, for it involves no other. Likewise peace, and likewise wisdom.

PLATO: "But trust surely involves others, through no less than connection and practicalities of living?"

Mr P: Ah! And in your question, therein lies the answer. It is in the search for connection that man gives away his power and his trust. For whilst he searches without, he loses within. For those who have mastered the art of searching within, trust abounds and one realises there *is* no without that can 'affect' the within – unless we allow it to do so.

When man is raised to satisfy others, be they elders, peers or society at large, practicalities of living are given priority. The energy is placed there, and in doing so, expectation ensues. And within this expectation are love and trust of others. But when one trusts oneself and 'what-is', the practicalities become separate from *life*; and connection with life itself underpins all interactions. These interactions are from a base of trust, embrueing everything with a sense of safety and security. So I offer that trust involves oneself, the practicalities of living involve others, and connection sits on the boundary between, and underpinning, the two.

TUES 30TH SEPT 2014, LONDON AT 10.10AM, SESSION 44

PLATO: "So tell me, in your view of love as a sensation, what triggers this grounded view of others not needing the 'exchange' of love? The doctrines, and the examples experienced by all, surely advocate 'exchanging love'. What can be more grounded and 'human' than this?"

Mr P: Such a question, rich in annotation, requires an equally deserving answer! The joy of words!

Human instinct is to give oneself to others. A baby, in being held, en-joys this state of vulnerability and empathic energy. Indeed, he or she will thrive in it. Its instinct, when held or comforted by a known or recognised energy, is to 'let go', to allow itself to 'be held'. Within this process, the infant gives itself over to the care of another – and soaks up a sense of security. The linking – the association – of giving oneself to another and the feeling of safety has occurred. Touch is very powerful, and its absence denies rapport for the child. Indeed the 'touch' of aggression can be desired in place of no touch at all. The 'rapport' created between the infant and the giver of safety sets the seed for this human instinct of giving. It can be no other way.

But at this time a dichotomy occurs. The mother or father will feel 'love' for the child, but the child feels only 'safety'. It does not know what 'love' is. The child may feel hungry, tired, agitated, unsafe or safe. It will desire the feeling of contentment, where joy and inquisitiveness can naturally arise. But it will not recognise 'love'; until it is told so, and until it is introduced as a concept.

As the child is told *"I love you,"* it begins to be 'touched' by it. Its absence creates a contrast. And just as with physical touch, 'love' becomes desired – for safety. And often, established forms of safety such as physical touch, a kindly face or energy, become withheld when the child is not complying to the given context of love. So, herein begins one's 'grounding' in love.

As our child grows and adapts his or her behaviours in order to experience safety, so too do the parents and society at large. The 'response' to the expectation of reciprocal love becomes contrasted with the questioning deep within the elders. It is not just *humans* who display a un-ease with the status quo, but society itself expresses this unease through contrast. And this can be seen most clearly within the element of control. As the children grow, the elders 'lose control'. *Love*, the currency of expression, turns its tables for as the children depart the nest, the elders become the seekers of safety. Yet they are stuck and hindered by their very own rules.

As one – child or adult – navigates through time/space, a dance between giver and receiver of safety is performed. Dear Plato, this is what I call human instinct. It is honest, authentic and 'human'. It is both unconditional, in its need for expression, and conditional, in its need for survival. It is what is *needed* whilst walking planet Earth.

The 'exchange' within this dance occurs *within* oneself. As our needs alter and change, so our external adapts and evolves. A dance needs the dancer to connect within, to move. To respond – yes, but in response to external sensations triggered by internal ones. A dancer is grounded within herself, or himself – and indeed *cannot* dance if not within a feeling of safety and abandon. The same abandon our small baby allows in being held.

So I offer 'safety' as more grounded and human than 'love'. But love also holds a place – for it creates exchange. And exchange enables connection; the breath of life.

So far I have painted an unfavourable picture of love, but it holds a dear space in my heart. How could it not? But I have come to see love as an exploratory energy, an energy to carry one to greater heights, through learning and new experiences. There are no answers in love, there never will be. For answers come within – and within we are peace and joy, but not love.

WED 1ST OCT 2014, LONDON AT 9.50AM, SESSION 45

PLATO: "I hear what you are saying, and indeed I find it hard to disagree. But love goes much deeper than interaction or exchange, when it can be felt as a pervading force. Without this force of love as a guiding energy, what would we have?"

Mr P: Perhaps some clarification is needed by me. Love is an energy, yes I agree. All things are. But it carries only the weight of exchange – which may be of past, indeed a long time past. But it is not an energy in its own right. Indeed to allude so would be to bestow the highest of ordinations. Are we saying love supersedes God? Is greater than God? *Is* God? Then this I suggest, is the error. For how can one 'access' what is not 'real'? A feeling is *real*. To feel anything: love, hatred or despair are all *real* to the person experiencing the feeling, but it cannot be 'captured'. As one's God cannot be captured.

In giving oneself over to 'love', in the belief it will ease all tension and woes, creates a reliance on the chosen expression of love – be that a person, a religion or an object. The attachment belies the search for safety.

Nothing within existence can be captured; it can only be *felt*. Human beings exist in order to feel and to evolve. One doesn't evolve by 'having' love or 'gaining' love. No. One evolves by feeling love – and to feel something we must be prepared to also let it go. Feeling is movement, and that movement is created by exchanges of energy – a force which is created by the very exchanges from feeling. It comes full circle – we, every one of us – creates the forces we experience and operate within. They feel nice…or they feel not nice, and then we choose our direction. This is the force one and all operates within. It is not that some operate within love, and some within a different force. And it cannot be that the *chosen* force is love, for love is a reactionary response created from birth.

So without a 'force of love' what do we indeed have? All that we have, is what arises within us. And this needs no labels, no judgement, no criteria. It is the critiquing of one's behaviours that creates inner discord. If one does what *feels* good, feels right within the moment, in the context of 'what-is', harmony and acceptance would ensue. The 'force' is not of *something* but of *oneself*. And this can be an awareness which creates discomfort. For to accept oneself in totality is not what man is programmed to do.

FRI 3ᴿᴰ OCT 2014, LONDON AT 11.20AM, SESSION 46

Mr P: So, my dear Plato, whom I 'know' so well… Here I stand before you: as 'myself' now, viewing my-Self of past. The interaction, the exchange between us is palpable, definitive – yet illusionary to all except Delilah. Many will consider this fiction; and bizarre. For how can someone firstly 'record' from an unknown energy force, and secondly, within the plural from the singular.

But it is quite explainable, is it not? All humans have the ability to 'split their mind'. Indeed most operate with a constant stream of discourse running through their heads. The body, being a reactionary organ, absorbs the mind chatter. This discourse requires the subject and the object – be that a person, an event or definite mass – in order to occur. Man is adept at 'talking to himself'. This discussion we are having is purely a more 'evolved' form of talking to oneself.

Now my purpose in highlighting this ability that all have, is to point out the multi-dimensional qualities within each person – be they in human form or spirit form. Man interprets; full stop. Delilah, in recording this discussion is interpreting our energies and the energy of words between us. It is quite a skill, but one available to many, if not all in potential. And the key ingredient in interpreting – whatever the context, be it a language, an image or a message – is the ability to *feel*. Delilah acquired this rather unique skill *because* of her openness to feel in this dimension. Indeed she is better at feeling in this dimension than the physical dimension. Yet it makes her no more 'special' than anyone else. It is just her natural instinct, and a place where she experiences safety.

All beings – of the human form in particular – have the potential to feel; be that emotionally, physically, intellectually or abstractly. Each person's unique gifts are expressions of feeling. But when 'negative' energies are placed in the way of this act of feeling, the feeling becomes tinged with discolouration and disharmony.

My suggestion is that the misinterpretation of love creates obstacles to man's natural expression of feeling. Each individual is so unique, so delicate in differentiation from the next that the inner dialogue of what is needed for the practicalities of living becomes one's own obstacles. An assumption of a life-long partner, a 'stable' home, children, pets, a steady and safe income, a decent car, some savings... need I go on?

More important and worthwhile is the ability to express one's feelings – however abstract and obscure they may seem. And my suggestion is that they not be 'through love;' but through joy. For then, the expression is complete to the individual, without the constraint of others.

PLATO: "If I understand you correctly dear fellow, you dismiss the expression of love in totality? But is this not therefore a lack of feeling?"

Mr P: In some aspects, quite so. But is not life but a series of decisions on feelings? One chooses to not feel something, or to feel something. That is, when one is conscious enough to understand it is a choice. For many, being entrenched in associative attachments, it is a series of being pulled from one feeling to another – and I suggest this 'framework' has 'love' at its core. My advocation is that love is chosen in momentary fashion – as is hatred or grief, or pleasure. For man *chooses* disharmony or ambivalence as much as he chooses happiness. The trick to be mastered is to be able to move in and out of many, many feelings for this creates both an interesting and fulfilling existence. How boring to pursue the feeling of love in singularity!

<u>MON 6TH OCT 2014, LONDON AT 9.00AM, SESSION 47</u>

PLATO: "It strikes me therefore that you view love as a 'passing moment,' but when something feels so utterly satisfying as love in action does, why would one not choose to experience more of this?"

Mr P: Human instinct is to seek safety. Love is something which can only arise within an energy of safety. So yes, love in action, as you call it, feels most wonderful when one is combined with another within safety. But herein lies the entanglement. For when both are parted, is the yearn for the love or the feeling of safety? I suggest that love only 'works' when the two are present. For instance, during a heated row, the safety may disappear, and then one questions the love. At death, the safety is transferred, so one may question whether 'love' exists as a source – for how could the person one feels so safe with be 'taken'?

Most choose to sit in love and *then* seek the safety – often by trying to change the other, or create something new which entangles one to another: be that a child, a project, a 'problem' or an expectation. The more helpful and more peaceful approach is to sit in safety and then observe for love. Without fail, the latter provides the inner happiness and joy man seeks.

Within this context of observing for love, is the misnomer of desire. And this is where even greater confusion lies. For to separate love and desire requires an honesty qualified by virtue. 'Love in action' can just as often be 'need' as desire. Equally it can be revenge, possessiveness or exploration. If love is a sensation, then the instinct by default must be something else, no?

PLATO: "You speak of virtue, but is love not the greatest of virtues? What could be more virtuous than giving love to another or to one's God?"

Mr P: Ah! And herein is the conundrum. How to give with no expectation of return, yet honouring the law of nature of 'exchange'?

PLATO: "But if love is a sensation within oneself as you suggest, then what is the 'giving' we speak of? I now see your suggestion more clearly for I find myself unable to word the question I wish to ask. But I sense that virtue may lie in the discretion required in the exchange?"

Mr P: Exactly dear Plato. So now we can see love as a sensation, virtue in the decision and an exchange of 'something'. That *something* can only be desire. Let me explain by way of an analogy of a car.

A car needs a driver – this is love. It needs passengers, from time to time, let's call these emotions. It needs direction which we will call virtue, and it needs fuel, which is the desire. Now instantly we see the contradictions to our discussion, but let me explain.

Although 'love' is a sensation, it is also an 'ideal': the 'vision' held by man and hence the *driver* of man's actions and reactions. The fuel or energy needed to drive man forward creates the movement. Yet man, when viewing his car and its performance gives scant attention or recognition to the fuel. It is resented as an expense, taken for granted and 'invisible' when observing the beauty of the vehicle. It is the same in life.

When man operates without virtue or attention to the desires, he drives aimlessly and without confidence or safety. 'Love' is at the wheel and 'love' becomes desperate…and seeking.

By contrast, with a foundation of virtue and desire creating safety and confidence, it matters not what emotion is at the wheel for the intention and the direction is safe in the hands of virtue, and fuelled by constant desire. The road opens up and the destination becomes unimportant for the journey is so much more fun. This is the energy of giving with no expectation, for the 'giving' *is* the journey. The 'exchange' is within oneself.

<u>TUES 7ᵀᴴ OCT 2014, LONDON AT 9.20AM, SESSION 48</u>

PLATO: "So tell me then, without 'love' as a driving force, would not the world of planet Earth be a 'poorer' place? For without the direction of love – whether towards individuals, or the divine – where would attention go? For does not virtue have 'love' at its core?"

Mr P: Indeed planet Earth would look very different in the eyes of the beholder: of each man, woman and child. And the children would benefit the most. For they need not love, but safety and comfort and adventure to express the desires so natural to them. But does a child *know* virtue? No. Not until it has been experienced. I suggest that a child discovers virtue within, as a result of experience of the contrast – which is currently mostly of love. As a child moves through his or her world, her feelings will be in response to sensations of love. *"Does this behaviour increase feelings of love…or whatever is being experienced…or decrease the feelings?"* The *virtue* is the decision-making in the face of a choice: the choice being of a sensation.

So I would advocate that virtue is a barometer – a measure – of action and reaction. A 'virtuous man' would display considered and conscious reaction in the face of aggression. It is not the 'aggression' itself which is virtuous or not, but the response and ensuing movement.

So man's virtue is exercised within a society with love at its core, but it could equally be exercised within a society with survival via discretion or admonishment or individuality as its central 'force'. A child's expression of virtue in such an environment would, I suggest, be *the same*, yet 'coloured' by the energies. For virtue is not a sensation or feeling, but a degree of consciousness and courage.

PLATO: "Ah! But courage is invoked by love I feel. Yes, the *decision* to act I can see as virtuous, but the courage to take the action, if not for love, then what for?"

Mr P: My suggestion, the 'conclusion' I have come to, is that *virtue* is divine, and one's guiding force. The uniqueness of each person's virtue, creates the richness and beauty of life. Man feels more comfortable, at ease and peaceful when he is acting with virtue. There is no discrimination in virtue, for each man's expression is authentic to him, or her. But when one's response is to 'love', virtue is often relinquished in favour of love.

PLATO: "My thoughts about virtue have been extensive; and centred around the cultivation of virtue – by man and society. So in this I have accord. But the disassociation of virtue and love, whilst comprehensible in example, creates a 'distance' I struggle to fill.

Mr P: Yes, Plato. I see your point of viewing, and I sense the 'distance' you talk of. Man feels uncomfortable with distance and space – the inclination is to fill it. But perhaps it is this urge to act and to respond that has filled this 'space'?

Man is not keen to leave stones unturned, to ponder and reflect. He prefers to conquer and build. And to facilitate this desire, he needs man-power. It is not a solitary act. Man does not like 'working alone'. And why should he? Yet the cultivation of a work-force, of the safety of numbers, necessitates an incentive. And what better incentive than 'love' and camaraderie? "Cultivation of" is not an expression of virtue, for virtue is in response to 'what-is'. The expression of virtue creates the direction, but the desire to cultivate is what fuels the vehicle. The distance dear Plato, is the journey of 'life'.

MON 13TH OCT 2014, LONDON AT 11.05AM, SESSION 49

PLATO: "Reasonable though it is to suggest virtue is of the highest order, I question man's success in having executed virtue, and therefore perhaps it is not deemed as important or worthy, as love?"

Mr P: Quite dear Plato. But man would not be in existence today if it were not for a collective exchange and expression of virtue, would it? One might consider *love* sufficient to withstand the tempestuous seas of life, but I question in return whether 'love' played a part in the *execution* of humanity. No doubt, on a practical level, love aids reproduction, but only as a sensation, for desire fuels the act of reproduction – or love-in-action as you so honourably phrase it! So if desire fuels reproduction of mankind, love can only be present as a sensation within desire – which we have established can be one of many.

So we are led to other aspects of man's evolvement. We have criminal and justice evolution, community and societal evolution and parliamentary and governmental. Medical evolution too – these are all aspects of mankind's evolvement – and all spearheaded by, and balanced within *virtue*. Man may 'love' his job or role within these aspects of expression but his actions will always be quantified ultimately by virtue.

Virtue decides whether a worker should keep his job, or whether care via an operation is given. Virtue decides if one should be incarcerated – no amount of love will override this if he or she has acted 'without virtue'.

So I suggest that man *feels* love, but acts with virtue and when this is out of balance, so is the resulting effect.

PLATO: "But dear fellow! How can one *feel* love if there is no avenue for expression: if that avenue is occupied by virtue? Love needs to be 'played out' to be enjoyed."

Mr P: Ah, and here you show your hand! For I frustrate you. And this, I sense is man's Achilles' heel. The 'frustration' causes the despair; and the search for quick answers.

The dilemma is between 'doing the right thing' (virtue) and 'doing what feels right' (love). Because of man's 'colouration' in this lifetime, one's perceptions – of what is love and what is virtue, and what is right and what is wrong, and what feels nice and what doesn't feel nice – become confused and 'messy'. But messy is good; when one realises one is in a mess. For then the untangling can commence.

Have you not considered dear Plato, how little *love* and *virtue* are discussed at school? Why it should be included every day! For how can society expect to raise grounded, balanced members of society otherwise? Let the child decide if he or she wishes to pursue education via religion, but don't deny the child the knowledge of wisdom and choice! Why the fear in educating the young to think and evaluate their situation in life? Can you call this...love?

When virtue is placed with proper dialect into the mind, love by default arises and comes in to play. But always virtue must come first. This is where the emphasis must be, and this is where the exploration into the *makings* of humanity abide.

TUES 14TH OCT 2014, LONDON AT 9.05AM, SESSION 50

PLATO: "This discussion is veering towards society; the external. But with love being a sensation – and I accept your proposal on this fair point – surely it can only be an *inner* experience? Is the connection of love not with another, but with *the* other, one's God? If society believes and trusts in a God, then surely this love supersedes all other? If 'God *is* love', then why would man be mistaken in believing that love is primary?"

Mr P: You raise a lot of questions and I propose therein the ultimate of questions: "Is God love?"

This is a question each man, woman and child must answer for themselves, for wherever the belief is, the love lay. And here we have 'the truth' – it can only be one's perception and belief which creates one's answers. Belief arises through virtue and knowledge – knowledge being experience. Man is always applying his 'best virtue', given his knowledge to-date. A man of more knowledge is a man of more experience – and not necessarily the most esteemed or 'wealthy' in society. But that is how it is often judged.

So if man *knows* God as love, then this *is* his truth – and whom dare deride this should question *his* virtue. But many also do not see God as love, or see God and separately see love. Many see equanimity and peace, and God in holiness. Many see no God, but a Universal Consciousness and Oneness within all of humanity. Some see nothing, and the nothing makes them question.

But what is love, what is one's truth, but the searching for answers? Could the pursuit of knowledge through experience be the very love we endear ourselves to experience? Could this be the circle of life? The experience to experience?

If this were so dear Plato, then perhaps man could lay down his armour and get on with the business of experiencing. For in the effort to *get there*, man builds armour to prevent disappointment and distraction. But where is he going? How can he *know* what he hasn't experienced, to know where he's going? The only answer can be to 'join one's God', although all actions may be to defer death. So between the detection of 'God' and the deference of 'death' we have a 'distance' – and this, as we know, can be frustrating. And this is when one seeks safety and connection. Some may call this distance 'life', but I would suggest, that when the distance is being travelled through fear, it is more a case of *living*. 'Life' is a case of growth and joyful expectation of the unknown as it arises. 'Living' is reactionary and in response to where one does not want to be.

So within this, where is love and where is one's truth? The answer can only be 'everywhere' can it not? For each has a unique feeling-perspective that is the truth in absolute for that person: for that soul on this collective journey of ours.

Let us discuss now, not the subject of love, but the intricacies of the nature of this universe of ours. For in the exploration of the science and laws of nature, fascinating reflections on love and one's God or truth can be seen. Let us revisit this most wondrous of topics with the hindsight of new awareness this evolving discussion will bring.

PLATO: "Of course dear fellow. I look forward to, and will enjoy, the awareness you will no doubt bring and relish my part in the exploration. For this is surely the 'making of mankind'."

4

MR P AND PLATO DISCUSS THE METAPHYSICS OF HUMANITY

THURS 16TH OCT 2014, LONDON AT 9.30AM, SESSION 51

Mr P: Let's begin this part of the journey by looking at the substructure of atomic energy. I say substructure, for man has not delved too far in this arena; just touched the surface.

The 'workings' of an atom have been discovered, yet the 'workings of the workings' have not. As yet. It will not be long before this basic make-up is unveiled of another layer. For the discovery of atomic 'sub'-structure will go hand-in-hand with creative 'growth'. As attainment is reached, depth discovered, and so the cycle goes. It all happens in perfect time.

Yet it is the 'space' between, the void between the sub and the plus, where the answers lay. The answers are always in the equation. Is that not so, Plato?

PLATO: "Indeed, the geometrical assimilation of data un-
covers many answers: from lunar activity to crop growth and
formation; from the most complex of sums to basic arithmetic;
from the circle of life to the circle of cellular activity. Yes, it
seems so indeed."

Mr P: The equation which underpins all assumed mathematical data to date, is that 1 + 1 = 2, and that 1 − 1 = 0.
This is the foundation that society is built on, from one
brick upon another to the computerised programs which
run all systems from air traffic control to bank balances.
But it is not as 'simple' as 1 + 1 = 2. No. For in all exchanges
lie equations. And indeed, in all equations lie exchanges:
many.

Geometry, the study of the mass of an equation, is the
closest man has got to the realisation that all is not as it seems.
Until recently. For now the scientists, mathematicians and explorers of the universe are beginning to touch on the 'depth'
of an equation.

Within the next ten years, a new form of mathematics will
become unveiled. It is here now, yet it needs embedding and to
have a useful role in order to be deemed 'accepted'.

One could consider it the 'shadow' of basic arithmetic, the
background equation to the surface sum. Let me demonstrate
via a simple scale.

$$-3 \qquad -2 \qquad -1 \qquad +1 \qquad +2 \qquad +3$$

You will notice there is no zero in this scale, and for good reason: there *is* no zero. There cannot be, in any formation or equation. This will become clearer over this discussion.

So, using the scale above, on the surface it looks 'clean' yet it is supported by a greater scale. Using the 'void' between -1 and +1, it could look like this:

$$1 ---- \ --- + \ --++ \ (-+++ \ ---+) \ --++ \ -+++ \ ++++1$$

Again, this is a very simple depiction of -1/+1, and this more detailed scale could be broken down again into greater depth. And so it goes.

But not only does the depth go 'backwards', it also goes 'forward', into all potential outcomes. It does not move side to side – this is a different aspect all-together – but the backwards and forwards *motion* of the +1's/-1's is what creates 'movement'. And from each 'point' on the scale cascades *its* ascents and descents of scale. *This* is the void in which mankind is made and resides. It is atomic, yes, but it is quantum also. In fact, it is *more* than quantum, it is quantum-equation exchange, supported by movement of the mass. And for this reason, 'life' is unexplainable.

Plato, let us explore over the subsequent days how this equation of matter infiltrates and affects life on planet Earth. 'Times are changing', as they always are, but now is a time of calculative expansion, and this deserves the awareness and respect of exploration.

MON 20TH OCT 2014, LONDON AT 10.00AM, SESSION 52

Mr P: So when a typical family of two adults and two or three children 'exchange' energies, there are a lot more outcomes available than one might expect. But the *direction* of the exchanges is supported not by the undercurrent of potentiality but by the beliefs of the unit.

This 'unit' is, whilst operating as one, an adjusting, breathing 'calculation'. All its members, bringing with them their -1/+1's, contributing to a sum total which is comprised of, and by, the unit. As different members of the unit rise in prominence and subside in flow, the unit *breathes* and moves. And as new members join, and others leave, it adapts and evolves. But the laws of nature *allow* for a constant unit calculation.

The beliefs that pervade and trigger the unit into directions and action (through movement forwards in action or backwards in reaction), cause the resulting situations and 'living conditions'.

Plato, does it not strike you how definitive man is about being in or out of the unit? When a unit observes a member walk away, they close the door – and this is to preserve the calculation I feel. In the closing of the door, the lone wanderer, for he is abandoned as a member, begins his own new calculation. He will create new exchanges and a new unit. The old unit will adjust and merge, but very quickly regain its original strength. Is this not the workings of an atomic cell? Does an electron not behave accordingly around a nucleus? What 'keeps' the nucleus attractive in its totality? What draws an electron from one atomic exchange to another? These are some of the questions which relate directly to mankind's behaviour. For is man not a collection of cells? And importantly, what *keeps* this collection of cells together? I suggest that the answers provide more than the question demands.

PLATO: "It is true that man is comprised of atomic matter, and the movement of the planets and stars *affects* life on planet Earth and hence its inhabitants, yet the *direction* man chooses is surely definitive in its assumptions? Mankind chooses his or her direction, and is able to function most efficiently without the knowledge of how that comes to be. For what purpose are you suggesting these answers will provide?"

Mr P: Mankind, Plato, is confused. And for the most part, unhappy. Expressions of joy are declining in favour of stimulation of senses not touched by physical experience. The planet is numbing and losing its 'sensitivity' – and this is reflected in its inhabitants. But the soul of the universe feels this sensitivity still – and this causes questioning within. For man is seeking that balance, *knows* it is out-of-kilter, but does not know how to *get there*.

And the answer, as to all these things, is within. And this appears so daunting and so unobtainable when the attachments without constrain so. But what if this can be explained with numbers? What if we can show that it is a very simple *exchange* of -1/+1, that all one *can* do, is decide to move towards +1 or -1?

PLATO: "Yet you speak of a depth to the numbers, that all is not as it seems? How is man to interpret this for his use and knowledge?"

Mr P: Man is clever, Plato. Indeed, one of man's unique qualities is the ability to hear, to assimilate and to take what resonates. Man *reasons*. And this 'act of reasoning' draws on the very essence of what it *means* to be alive. It is the core dynamic in exchanging 'what-is' with 'what-can-be'.

Now man may also ignore this inner reasoning, but at some point – and I sense this time is now approaching – man will allow this reason to the fore, will allow it to emerge, and breathe into the unit. So he need not *understand* all he hears, but he will *know* what is reason. And this will edge direction to what feels more *appropriate*. One does not need be a scientist to *know* the sciences 'exist' in everything one does or sees. One does not need read great works to know they exist. Likewise man does not need know how great he is to know his greatness. But the awareness of new information attracts movement towards it – and this, like atomic energy, enables creationism. It is our job, dear Plato, to provide the awareness, it is man's job, however, to reason its worth.

WED 22ND OCT 2014, LONDON AT 12.30PM, SESSION 53

PLATO: "The *decision* man makes as a result of his or her reasoning is often not the one the 'reason' would advocate though. How is this reflected in atomic movement, for surely the electron moves to what attracts it?"

Mr P: Indeed. Man has many options as a result of his reasoning yet only one can be taken and actioned. As one steps into action, all the variables, all the equations of -1/+1, support and *breathe* into the movement. But vast though the equations are in their calculation, the action is very definitive. Liken it to walking in a pool of water. The mass of the water remains the same, but the movement of the body constantly fluctuates the placement of the water. But man *decides* his direction within the water – whether it be definitive strokes or floating on the surface.

Now the decision he makes, yes, affects the experience, but it does not, such as in the instance of a man in a pool, permanently change the outcome of the pool – unless he exits the equation. Let me explain…

Whilst man is 'moving towards', it matters not if the equations are -1's or +1's, as long as he is moving in the general 'direction' of his reasoning. He may *reason* that 45 degrees to the north-east is his direction, but in the journey, he may step 70 degrees to the south-west followed by 60 degrees to the north-west. But he is always aiming for the north-east. Indeed a 'detour' can be very illuminating and enjoyable – especially if humour and curiosity are allowed into play.

So the equation our man formulates as he goes is always supporting his vision: the 'illumination' of his reasoning. This is why man has, and needs dreams; both the conscious vision and the subconscious 'sleeping' dreams.

But when man loses his vision, this is when he steps out of the equation, when he is servant to others' equations and the turbulence – and surviving the turbulence takes superiority. He is drowning in the sea of possibility and raging calculations. He is out of control.

Now the behaviour of an electron *mimics* this behaviour of man. As above, as below... The 'vision' held by man is illuminated to the molecular make-up of man. The cells *see* the vision and indeed 'understand' the reasoning along the way. The body – the physical body I talk of now – adapts and allows, indeed often *enjoys* the states and flows of the -1's. It can *see* the bigger picture. It knows, more intelligently than man consciously knows, the allowance of ebb and flow, of stillness and restraint, of *allowing* the flow yet partaking wholly in that flow. *It* knows when to rise into +1's and when to lead. It is a constant adaptive harbouring and expressing of energy. The electron therefore *knows* that it needs to join 'over here', so it can get 'over there'. Such is the intelligence of life-form.

But what *frustrates* an electron, is when it is prevented from the desired movement. And this is when tension is felt in the human body. The mind-body link is the electromagnetic flow of ease and tension between the vision, the direction and the flow. Such as with the analogy of the car, the flow fuels the vehicle: creates the energy so the driver (the vision) can take direction (through reasoning, or virtue).

The *release* of tension is so very powerful, for the electrons can then move again in the body. The *distance* between the vision and the movement of the electron now becomes non-existent; without the obstacles, the electromagnetic wave from the mind instantly impacts the electron – hence why, if believed, instant feel-good and instant healing can occur. Likewise, instant dissatisfaction and instant tension. The electron never loses sight of the vision, hence why it is so vital this is upheld. When man refuses to *believe* in better things, the molecular structure is not permitted to behave towards 'better things'. It really is that simple.

PLATO: "We talk of *frustration*, and surely this will always be present in potential if one is *set* on a 'vision'. How is man to uphold the vision, of something in the future which does not, as yet, exist in this time/space, whilst remaining wholly within 'what-is?'"

Mr P: Ah! A wise observation, and one which requires the simplest of answers, for despite an obvious plethora of possible answers, there is, but one: the *vision exists for today*. Everything else is but an obstacle.

Man is *deluded* by space/time. When sitting in 'what-is', the vision 'exists'. Yet man, through denial and fear, places a space/time between him and the vision. In that space/time is the journey, and the frustrations via *obstacles*, and the euphoria upon release of the tension, as the energy flows forth.

Yet the *vision* is *here*, in the now. Space/time is a perceptual factor, influenced by the degree in which man relies on others to 'achieve' his vision. When man drops this attachment to others, and to, I suggest, the vision of 'love' as the destination, he is free to experience and *live* his vision in the here and now. And this, dear Plato, is when man experiences ultimate wellbeing and joy, for the molecular structure of the physical influences the euphoric states of the emotional, mental and energy bodies. Man then *knows* what joy is and can but express this within his moving ebb and flow.

SUN 26TH OCT 2014, DORSET AT 10.00AM, SESSION 54

PLATO: "Within the *feeling* of movement, there is such a thing as stillness. It can be quite tangible, quite apparent to observe – in oneself, and others. How is this explained?"

Mr P: Stillness is, I suggest, a quality, not an actuality. It is a way of being within 'what-is'. The cellular components do not 'still' – even in death. In death, the breath is *transferred* from the physical to the wholly energetic, but it remains. Such as with the degree of the memory – the thought of a 'deceased' one lingers – so does the reflection of the *breath*. The physical body decomposes: this is cellular movement. It is never ending.

I suggest, that because man believes it 'ends' at the end of the physical timeline, he believes *stillness* to be undesirable. Yet the quality of stillness is a wonderful precursor to movement of the whole. It is the ebb within the flow, and the pause between one breath and another. Cultivating stillness *creates* time, for it slows the space/time awareness. The trick, is to *be* within both stillness *and* movement for this creates a depth, a richness, to the cultivated time/space experience. And yes, it does indeed influence the cellular activity within the bodies; all four bodies of the physical, mental, emotional and energetic.

As the neutron attract the protons, it emits a 'signal'. This signal is 'empty' in its stillness. The, how shall I say, 'minus' of the neutron and surrounding protons attracts the 'plus' of the electrons. The stillness attracts the movement, and when activated, the exchange is made: the *connection* is made. Yet the neutron acquires this stillness from the movement of the 'whole': within the exchange lies the equation, and vice-versa. So when the whole encompasses the quality of stillness, the neutrons do too. And this gives the neutrons and protons *choice*. 'Space' is literally created within the body. Tension passes, awareness increases and movement is enabled. The feeling and actuality of space gives a freedom and an inquisitiveness which delights the soul. And best of all, this space is created across all levels, for the emotions are freed, the mind clears and the energies lighten. As the physical effects compound, so do the effects on the other bodies and now a chain reaction is activated. It is this chain reaction which then in-stills greater calm and desire, for the two are linked.

TUES 28ᵀᴴ OCT 2014, LONDON AT 11.20AM, SESSION 55

PLATO: "The chain reaction you talk of is, as I understand it, a purely energetic one, for you talk of the 'pluses' and 'minuses' within their energy context, not their *given* properties. The sum total of an elemental reaction – a 'portion' if you will – of the chain must contain therefore its equation within? Yet if the exchange is but part of a larger chain of exchanges, how is the equation both formulated, and understood?"

Mr P: Ah, well explained, for you have answered the question, by posing the very question; with the same 'method' which can be applied to our topic.

Any exchange is both unique in its individuality and part of the whole. Likewise man and woman. Each person or creature to walk planet Earth is a unique bundle of energy yet equally, a part of a chain: a *portion* of 'what-is'. Every single person is connected to others via chains of exchanges. No man, woman or child are otherwise. Yet just as each person makes a unique contribution to the energy chains – whether in the midst of a gathering or alone on a hilltop – he or she is reacting to the 'whole'. In choosing to sit alone on a hilltop, one is reacting to the crowd. In choosing to be within a crowd, one is reacting to solitude. There is no *getting away* from the concept of inter-cellular energy exchange.

On a 'smaller' scale, a cancer cell for instance, is unique and individual, yet needs the 'whole' of the body to 'react' against. A cancer cell amongst other cancer cells, whilst just as *powerful*, is not dramatic – it needs the contrast of the non-cancer cells to become unique, yet in the combination creates a chain reaction in the direction of growth. If one choses to dis-arm and render powerless a cancer cell, one must bring the 'opposing' energy to *meet* the energy driving the cancer. The two energies, in their merging, dis-arm and disable the contrast. This Plato, is a law of nature: *The sum of two halves is greater than the whole.*

Indeed it is so profound a law of nature that it is visible in every exchange – whether an exchange *towards* or *apart* – and in all movement and decision making on the planet: from how cities are formed, wars fought, healing achieved and life experienced.

But returning to your question, it is such a case on the cellular level too. We can take a portion of any energy exchange and we will see two elements occurring. If the exchange is 'bringing together' we will see the ensuing chain reaction funnel and attract support of other elements also attracted to the exchange for their own 'reasons'. By contrast, if the exchange is 'pulling apart' we will see the exchange open up and seek supply of, and be attracted to, alternative sources of energy.

So the formulation is, in basic terms, elemental movement within the whole. The effect occurs on a cellular level of microscopic scale through to movement of galaxies. It is the contraction and expansion, the yin and yang, the in-breath and the out-breath, the rise and fall. It is unavoidable and utterly desirable for it *is* movement. But the secret dear Plato is in understanding the movement, for when one understands that we are just a link in the chain, that we are all linked, that we are all the chain, we can't help but choose a different perspective. And when the individual exchanges merge and fall away with this awareness, the chain both remains intact and grows in strength. It is the law of nature – that the sum of two halves is greater than the whole – which feeds man's search for creativity. For in *creating*, man both protects and frees.

THURS 30TH OCT 2014, LONDON AT 12.05PM, SESSION 56

Mr P: This discussion, whilst interesting in its formulation of ideas and concepts, does not offer *solution* to man's disharmony. For man seeks solution though there is no 'problem'. Plato, does it not astound you to see man so confused and *trapped*? Man has mastered the art of flying, of lunar exploration no less, of having every conceivable luxury at his fingertips, yet carrying a deeper unhappiness than ever known before. The internal turmoil no more sated than at any time in history. Does this not intrigue you?

PLATO: "Indeed it does, but for differing reasons. I observe two worlds on planet Earth: the 'haves' and the 'have nots' as is commonly described. Such disparity amongst one population. Yet the 'haves', the ones who consider themselves so fortunate are the poorer in spirit and wonder – the *dispirited* of the two. The half without every luxury available to them emanate an energy of much lighter vibration and purity in sound.

And as I sit here and observe this contradiction between what the halves believe about themselves and unconsciously display about, and of, themselves, I ponder your words. For here we have an example of two halves and surely therefore the law of disparity, as I will refer to it, of the two halves being greater in sum than the whole. It begs the question of, for what benefit such a split, and for what purpose a 'solution' if man cannot see his reflection?"

Mr P: Quite. A perfect example – on a larger scale – of the *turmoil* which happens within man. And the key word you use here, as you well know, is *reflection*. For what we observe in others is a reflection of what we see within. It is the man who seeks his answers – his solutions – *within*, who sees his or her true self. The same for the 'First World' or 'Third World.' Likewise for the eastern hemisphere and western hemisphere. Man is all things, all emotions, all states of being – he just cannot easily see this, for he doesn't *believe* it.

The split of the 'haves' and 'have nots' is unavoidable within this current state of observation, for whilst man focuses on the external vista, he will see the full contrast. He – or she – may *believe* they are firmly rooted in one 'camp', may believe they would be 'better off' in the other, but this is mere illusion. As the First World consumes more and grows both physically and materialistically he will by default observe the Third World decrease in size and stature – until such a time as the integration happens within. As man allows the meeting within of wealth and poverty, satiation and hunger, harmony and dis-harmony, he will see it meet and merge in the external too.

The 'reflection' is both a mirror and an image. As one stares at the reflection, if this is not seen as desirable, it is seen as unworthy. But one is judging oneself in this instance. And whilst one judges another, be it *in person* or a reflection of a belief, dissatisfaction is felt within. Turmoil is created and fuelled.

The *solution* – via the integration within of the 'meeting' contrasts – is the exchange within the equation. The contrast affords the equation for without the parts, there is no sum. As men and women slowly integrate within, the two halves, in their merging, create a 'whole'. And in this joining, energy is released; the *excess* if you will, or the 'resulting effect' as an-other method of explanation. This resulting effect is felt as joy and visible within the equation. For what creates the equation, the equation creates. Joy enables more joy.

SAT 1ST NOV 2014, LONDON AT 15.50PM, SESSION 57

PLATO: "The equation however, in being *affected* by the surrounding cascading links and vibrations, cannot be 'pure' in itself? So explain, if you will, how an equation can give a 'result' within this co-dependent environment?"

Mr P: Indeed, it is somewhat difficult to envision. Each equation has within it, an element of the surrounding 'atmo-sphere'. Somewhat like paint colours blending and merging in a palette. So the calculation may be primarily red and white, but will include some pink, some neutral and some positive. I see your ears prick and your eyes raise at the mention of neutral and positive! Perhaps we could describe it as the addition of water and a paintbrush?

Within *every* equation is an element of neutrality and 'positive charge' – always. Yes, the 'equivalent' of the stabilising neutron and charged proton. The corresponding element of 'negative charge' is the electromagnetic connection; in grander terms, known as the electromagnetic field. It is the combination of these 'elements' within the calculation – combined with the 'static forces' of the atomic matter (be it mass, matter or form) which *results* in the creation, the birth, of existential growth – be it form, thought-form or form-less.

The 'static-forces' of 'atomic matter' are what is currently perceived as dark matter but is indeed gravitational force. 'Gravity' is tangible, for it is *created* by man's existential output. Man makes gravity occur: by thought. As with all things. Fish, for example, do not have – as yet – the thought ability of man. Hence a world of lesser gravity. This is just one example. Gravity is a double-impact element, in that the *reflection* is what man observes. He does not witness the image in static form; this is the *hidden* part of the calculation – the mathematical 'depth' if you like…

So, dear fellow, in answer to your question, the equation is affected by so much more than the merging of the two contrasts – and *this* is why the halves are greater than the whole. For when the two halves merge, the gravitational element is released – and suspended in static form – awaiting further connection and *activation*. For this reason, 'gravity' cannot be harnessed as an energy: for it is the effect of a *release* of energy. When man stops 'creating', he will see gravity – and universal forces supporting this current expansion – reduce and contract. It is cyclical and desirable. But the release of the gravity – in the 'decline' of creationism – will not be harness-able to planet Earth, no. Its 'power', transferable to a new vision only. For this is what occurred at the time of 'the Big Bang'. Vision made man, and man holds the vision.

The equation which underpins all which I speak of is:

$$V > pos + neg\ alignment > neutral\ acquisition\ by\\ attracting\ forces$$

The vision creates the positive and negative alignment which creates the neutral acquisition by attracting forces.

The 'neutral acquisition' is the *space* in which the connection happens and the gravitational forces are released. These released forces are counter-balanced by attracting forces, and so the equation is *balanced* within its creationism. The whole equation is 'held' by the vision, and *involves* surrounding links and cascades. Like the cell *sees* the vision, so mankind sees his 'results'.

PLATO: "A thorough if somewhat complex depiction of creativity, but tell me, where does 'joy' – or any other state or emotion – feature in the equation?"

Mr P: Joy is in the neutral acquisition. As is every 'feeling' and sensation to man. It is in the space between the -1's and +1's. The neutral acquisition, in being *neutral*, creates the contrast when divergence to one side – to minus 1 or plus 1 – occurs. When within neutral – also known as the state of gratitude – the contrast has *merged*. The 'attracting forces' supply more of the resulting feeling; and so the cycle goes as the vision is upheld, attracting yet more fluctuation and yet more forces. As man's emotions and feelings adjust to the ever-fluctuating state of 'what-is', his 'placement' fluctuates from the -1's through neutrality, to the +1's. But it is in the state of neutrality that the contrasts merge and joy is expressed.

SUN 2ND NOV 2014, LONDON AT 15.05PM, SESSION 58

PLATO: "Your explanation of how the scale between the -1's and the +1's affects human sensation and feeling likens to a thermometer or barometer of cause and effect. I understand how this would cause ever-fluctuating movements, how nothing can 'stand still,' but tell me, how does one equate for *external* events which affect one's 'supply' of the current attracting forces? If I am standing here, quite pleasantly satisfied within myself with my 'what-is', how do I comprehend a tsunami of catastrophe which may hit, unbeknownst to my expected outlook?"

Mr P: I understand your question, and this is a somewhat difficult one to answer, for the implication is one of lack of control or influence over one's destiny – which we know to not be the case.

The prevailing *attracting forces* operate on many levels, including the level of 'divine will'. The reason for difficulty, is in the explanation of divine will: for this differs for each man, woman and child. But for the purposes of this explanation, I will describe it as the collective union of combined energy – purely for this discussion. Divine will prevails 'above' all other wills, yet, as with all things, is also part of the equation. Divine will resounds through spirit worlds as much as through the physical world, and *is* the vision which holds all energetic matter and mass.

The influence of divine will is the effect of the cause of the collective energetic neutral acquisition of planet Earth and its inhabitants. Man forgets that he is not the sole inhabitant of planet Earth. Look around and you will observe an animal kingdom far greater in diversity than man. Dare one consider this animal kingdom has no influence on the prevailing 'status' of the planet? Likewise man cannot *see* – in the most part – the inhabitants of a spiritual, non-physical nature, but dare he oversee this influence? Man accepts a world of near 95% 'dark matter,' as yet unfathomable to the human mind: dare he disregard the possibility of cause and effect within this sphere of evolvement? All this and more *contributes* to the 'what-is' experienced in each moment. But what man cannot *feel,* he discredits.

If man could *feel* his body more attunely, he would either prevent or diagnose dis-ease before it 'strikes'. But he is a careless listener. If he could *feel* his planet – the very ground he walks upon – he would either adjust his impact or *expect* catastrophic effects in temperature and movement. But he is a careless caretaker. If man could *feel* his emotions and the effect it has on his nearest and dearest, he would temper his response and control his desires for manipulated possession. But he is raised to *expect* recompense, and to expect 'results'.

But the *result* of collective energy can be varied. Just as man experiences disaster and destruction, he also experiences joy and wonder. The +1's that resonate outward give as much pleasure and healing to the collective energy as the -1's give despair. So within the collective output 'victims' of the group equation will experience their fluctuation within the substructure linking; by the very nature of the exchange. For the exchange is both uniquely *personal* and generically populace.

The equation, through interference of 'what-is', is held by the vision of each man. Each man's vision contributes to the universal vision; like each inhabitant of a village 'colours' the dynamics and quality of life of the whole. Man is not so likely to notice the quiet, peaceful neighbour, but the noisy fractious one will certainly get attention. But this is a *reflection* of man's level of listening. For we *see* what we wish to see, and hear what we wish to hear.

TUES 4TH NOV 2014, LONDON AT 10.15AM, SESSION 59

PLATO: "The connection between man's inner and outer world is perceived to be understood – yet I hear a resonance in your words: that all is not quite as it may seem?"

Mr P: Indeed, there are some who understand on a subconscious level the intricacies of our wonderfully exquisite universe, but for the most part man considers himself and his tribe the be-all of survival. And whilst man's tribe *is* important, it is no more important than any other tribe. The viewing and prioritising of one's tribe above all others, indicates a narrower perspective within the individual, for yes, the inner perspective creates and is reflective of, the outer. It is not, as commonly perceived, that the outer reflects the inner, but the reverse. For man is *affected* by his environment, yes, but more so by the *combination* of the two.

Man sits on the edge of reason *and* on the edge of believing: at all times; balanced and interacting between the two; one reflecting the other. The edge of reason (the external) 'shapes' the beliefs (the internal). Hence why the external influences to the greater degree. Each person's unique inner calibration will create differing experiences and outcomes, depending on their 'placement' and emotional positioning in each moment – and a lifetime can equally be 'a moment'. But the external vista is the same for all of humanity: a ground to walk upon, skies to dream within and temperature and nature to inspire movement. Every man and woman is born into the same cooking pot of ingredients, but the unique mixture creates the taste.

PLATO: "It will seem somewhat far-fetched to suggest to a man born into 'poverty' and tedious labour that he is of the same experience as his neighbour of wealth and magnitude. For how can this be of *equal* position? What of the child born rosy and of flourishing health compared to the child of sickly disposition? How in this instance does the outer reflect the inner?"

Mr P: Randomness. Randomness *creates* the ensuing vistas within the cellular makeup of man. But it is *always* within a context of 'what-is'. Let me explain. All is energy, this is understood. What is not yet fully understood, is that energy *lives* – it moves and breathes. It lives within one, and is of one. So as random connections are made, energy attaches and detaches itself. Like the electron which moves from one atom to another, so does energetic exchange on an emotional scale. As above, as below. What man experiences consciously, his cells absorb unconsciously – and vice versa. As man experiences his or her contrast in life – all against a 'neutral' background – his *intention* is carried forwards; and backwards. The 'generations' coloured by the intention held by the thought-instigator. The reflection back to man creates the edge of belief, for what he *sees*, he can reason with, for he recognises it in his cellular make-up. The outer reflects the inner, but the inner is dependent on the outer. A tunnel-vision is created, and the physical body responds accordingly.

Now what upsets the apple-cart so to speak, is the interaction of the heart and soul. For both, uniquely and individually are guiding forces within man, and within the greater mankind.

Man beats as a single heart-beat and has the vision of a single soul, but is not accepting so – yet. For there is more contrast to be experienced before man reaches balance and neutrality. And why not? For the contrast affords much to please man, and to add significance and growth. Mankind is where it needs to be right now, for the awareness of what does not feel good will create the vision and realisation of what does. Man, in physical form, is a sensory barometer of where mankind stands as a collective – and this is why such divergence.

PLATO: "So tell me, how is man not to 'blame' previous generations for his *ill*-fortune, or conversely, live up to expectations when residing in *good*-fortune? For if he played no part in reaching his 'placement' at birth, what is the incentive to change his vista if all he can see is his reflection? Indeed, how does he even become aware of the neutral background we all share?"

Mr P: By *feeling*. When man *feels* where he is, where his feet rest – the body supported by such feet – he begins to *know* himself. When man knows himself – as all infants do upon birth – he recognises himself in all others, and sees the vastness in himself, reflected in all others. As man releases the divergence by *seeing* others, by receiving their energy without resistance, he creates and allows inner neutrality. He *sees* the neutral backdrop of each man, woman and child, and in seeing such a vista, his inner reality creates a new outer reality. Neutrality within supports the backdrop of neutrality without. A new connection has been formed: with the substructure of existence.

WED 5ᵀᴴ NOV 2014, LONDON AT 10.15AM, SESSION 60

Mr P: Today, in the world as it is, the energies which 'started' this universe have grown in diversity and incongruence. The 'quantity' of energy remains as it always was, but in the *spread*, a dilution happens. It is this dilution which creates greater contrast. But it does not feel as *rich* or as *full* as the thicker measure. The aspect of neutrality is that this energy *is* neutral; colourless if you will, yet a rainbow at the same time – within the invisible are all shades and hues. It is a law of nature; that of common diversity.

So as the dilution happens, 'colour' is introduced. Emotions are the colour. For as one 'splits' and fluctuates between the split (-1 to +1), emotions arise. In seeking wholeness, balance, oneness, man is healing this split. And what affects the within also affects the without, and vice versa. This is why not all is equal in perspective, for a person healing through action the 'exterior' is also healing humanity's 'interior', and vice versa. Each man, a place in the equation, for each man *is* the equation.

PLATO: "Understanding this somewhat metaphysical view of humanity does not allow for man's carefree and *easy* interaction. For you talk of *feeling* but what I sense from this discussion is a sense of 'responsibility', of *careful* interaction. In observing oneself, is one not in danger of losing the very essence of what it is to be human? Should man's virtue not be from the heart as opposed to the mind-based awareness?"

Mr P: I understand your concern, and in using the word concern, I sense in you a reservation in relinquishing the heart as a
driver. For the heart gives man excitement; much *life*-blood, and
feelings of connection. Man is exiting a period of great heart-energy – over many centuries. This driving energy has created wars,
joys, romance, courage, bravery and histories which abound in
stories of conquest and duels. But heart-energy alone does not afford peace or harmony. It is not congruent with balance. And the
world now seeks a period of balance; a time to pause for reflection.

The antidote to the vibrant heart-energy is the soothing
soul-energy – and the way to access this is through the body.
The physical body tells all: it is man's window to the world, his
presentation of what is happening within. It is not of physical
beauty or stamina I talk of, but of the poise, the energy, the
look behind the eyes and the hold of the hands within one's
posture which portrays man's comfort within himself. And no
man can conceal his expression of the physical, and for this
reason, man will always remain centred within his emotions
and given outlook. He will always attract more of this given
outlook – by way of the attracting forces.

But the awareness this discussion affords is able to influence a man's perception of what is occurring in and around
him; should he resonate with it…meaning should it infiltrate
his edge of reason. But this is as far as these words can go, for
it is just awareness of a different perspective. For the man who
has already this perspective, it will increase his edge of belief,
for the awareness reflects what is already within. The mind is
the facilitator of this exchange on the boundary of the two. It

is the filter which both protects and provides. And perhaps it might be said, underused?

PLATO: "The mind, yes, I agree not used fully to its advantage, but man is ruled by his heart, no? Is mankind really ready to shift to matters of the soul or pertaining to the mind when there is so much unresolved conflict within the heart?"

Mr P: My suggestion, is that man's conflict within the heart is *because* of his – or her – dependence on it. 'Love' is attributed to the heart. And whilst man searches for love – for what is a sensation – the heart remains unfulfilled. The search goes on, and I feel, as a singular aspect outlook, will never be satisfied. Man mishears his inner whispers. Scarce attention is placed upon the harmony and expression of the soul. Always the heart!

PLATO: "Man often equates the soul with death or transition. There is a fear harboured in 'listening' for death for many, perhaps?"

Mr P: It is true that the soul comes into prominence at such times, but this is as a *result of* the quietening of the mind following a quietening of the ego. In the face of catastrophe – 'life or death' situations or transition of any type – a 'window' is created and man hears his soul; acknowledges it. But it is always there, just masked by the mind filled with thoughts of the heart: for ego is, for the most part, a need for love.

Whether man identifies with the heart for reasons distilled through the generations in response to lack of love, or whether it is as a response to a fear of the soul, I know not. But man always, always benefits from connection with the soul, and for this reasoning on my part, I advocate exploration of man's soul.

PLATO: "I return to my previous questioning though: for how can man *take on* this exploration when he is not yet healed of the heart?"

Mr P: But how can he not when there is so much to offer? For the soul is as powerful, more powerful I would advocate, than the heart of giants. To operate without attention to the soul is to operate without power, and without meaning and connection. For meaning through another dost not create fulfilment. It is through the reflection of another we realise our meaning, it is through the power of the heart the soul is ignited. But the heart is a facilitator, a provider of senses and feeling. It is not the *recipient* of the meaning; this is the domain of the soul. For mankind's soul is undernourished and left wanting.

PLATO: "Tell me dear friend, if man is 'born' as a soul and 'dies' as a soul, surely he is by default in connection with his soul? If man is in the physical world to experience the physical, would this not constitute a *good use* of one's time?"

Mr P: On the surface, yes, I see your point. And perhaps I am overly optimistic in foreseeing man's relationship with his soul – and the souls of others. But my optimism lies in the face of fear. For does man not bequest the search of love through fear of it not being exercised, or indeed realised? Are not reflections of what could transpire and wreak havoc on man should he forfeit 'love', not visible everywhere he turns? The soul would never speak in such way, would never condemn a man for any action in search of inner connection with his truth. Man has not found his truth in love, but it was always there in his soul. My suggestion is that the soul offers better direction to peace and harmony. And when one is peaceful and harmonious, the feelings related to the underlying drivers for love can be seen and honoured. For is not love an excuse for self-expression? Is it not the case that man – for the most part – needs others to express his inner feelings and desires? Is this not a human instinct to share and exchange, to see oneself reflected in the eyes of another? I believe so.

But the soul offers a part in the equation. For when man observes his reflection, it must resonate within. When it resonates primarily in the heart, it creates movement – for the heart is a moving organ – and the moment passes to another moment. But when it resonates in the soul, it creates stillness and fullness – and man grows in worth and being'ness. The feeling stays and fills what needs filling – its links to others affected by the exchange and much is shared. The connection is *felt* and it is tangible.

PLATO: "And how does the mind interact for optimal connection with the heart and soul?"

Mr P: The mind is a transistor – it assimilates incoming energetic waves and replaces it with adapted outgoing ones. In that order. But other than that, it plays no part. The 'exchange' happens *within* – within the bodies, and for this reason, the body tells all.

FRI 7TH NOV 2014, LONDON AT 9.10AM, SESSION 62

PLATO: "Man does not, I feel, understand the true worth of his body?"

Mr P: Indeed, I would agree. For it is his sensory spaceship on planet Earth. Would one neglect one's 'mother-board' in quite the way man does, if he knew there were no parachutes? For whilst he appreciates it when the moment calls for it, at best man takes his body for granted. It is for this reason illness is so powerful in man; and even then he blames the spaceship, never the captain or the sensory input.

PLATO: "Your reference to the mother-board, a clue within, I am sensing?"

Mr P: You know me well, for yes. A mother-board is an equivalent of an equation. All parts, all circuits, lead back to itself, and should one of the parts, or wirings, be affected in some way – through whatever reason – the circuit as a whole, the mother-board as the sum of the equation, is affected.
    The *reason* man does not fully recognise his body is because he does not *know* his mother-board; or his operating dynamics.

Response is often intermittent, hesitant and from a variety of 'flash-light' parts. One minute the response is from over here, the next from over there, and this causes strain and destruction to the infra-structure. The mother-board becomes reactionary and is placed in constant vigilance and alert. Man recognises this as 'stress' but this only touches on the damage occurring beneath the surface.

When man spends time and interest getting to know his mother-board, transformation happens. Sadly this so often occurs as a result of 'system failure', when the circuits finally overload and self-destruct. But when the *pause* has happened, and when man recognises his ignorance of himself and is will-ing and eager to *hear* himself, reconnection can occur very quickly indeed. For the equational law – of two halves being greater than the whole – aids this process of recapitulation.

PLATO: "How, in such an instance, does man avoid 're-building' himself to the same model and thus repeating behaviours?"

Mr P: When the 'pause' has happened, nothing can ever be the same again, for a shift has occurred and there can only be one of two outcomes: +1 or -1. But man has an ally: his con-sciousness, his connection with his soul. For the soul only ever is directed to fullness and peace. For when the energy quietens and the bodies can subside in their struggle, the soul can be heard. When man connects with his soul, no fear is felt and no *effort* is needed. The process happens *by itself* for the parts of the circuitry are now on the same wave-length. Harmony is restored whilst the bodies (of which I speak of the emotional, mental, energetic and physical) repair and replenish. Whilst man *listens* to himself, he is creating himself in accordance with his truth.

<u>TUES 11ᵀᴴ NOV 2014, LONDON AT 10.30AM, SESSION 63</u>

PLATO: "*Today* man is sensitive in his environment. In times past, the infrastructure created the support needed by man for wellness and 'fitness'. The flow over the years of the development and dynamism of the body was reflective of man's journey through the years – *of* the years. There was a certain fluidity. But to observe today, is to see 'stops and starts', ruminations within energetic entanglement and a cluster of activity with no clear sense of direction. I see 'young' ageing and declining at greater speeds than their elders and mankind 'deteriorating' and recovering at haphazard rates. Mankind is in a state of struggle and flux."

Mr P: Indeed, and it is frustrating to observe when wellbeing is the *desired* state and not the normal state of being. And yet man *ignores* this internal state of affairs in favour of belonging with the crowd. He would rather be accepted than accepting of himself. And the more sensitive he becomes to the imbalance, the more he numbs to himself.

Part of the reasoning lies in man's desire for expansion and connection, and in this he is no fool, but the foolish behaviour is in believing this expansion and connection is the gift of others. Man creates his own expansion and connection – but from the place he is conditioned to not reside: his inner worth and being'ness…somewhere intangible and deemed elusive and therefore, valueless to most. *"Inner fitness does not 'pay the bills', so therefore I will place it bottom of my list of priorities"* – and instead go to the gym or expel his stamina and frustration to the ears of angels, for no-one else hears him, no one hears the silent scream.

PLATO: "Until catastrophe strikes…"

Mr P: Until catastrophe strikes. The gift of the angels, with the solution within the equation, for now there is 'space' for the inner work to begin. Always, the 'catastrophe' enables and creates the space. It is law, for it is the sudden re-adjustment within the alignment of the plus and minus 1's, triggering acquired acquisition of neutrality – the place of healing, and the place of safety within.

From this place of neutrality attraction happens at great force, for the signal is clear and unencumbered. It is the degree to which man maintains this clarity which affects his resulting state of being.

PLATO: "Yet it is not an easy thing to remain unencumbered whilst juggling the turmoils of the bodies? We all know this well."

Mr P: We do. But we also know what wellness *feels* like so it becomes a natural inclination towards which we are drawn and are attracted to. For mankind today, many do not know consciously what this feels like, it is 'forgotten' in infancy. The *blueprint* remains but the method and extracted behaviour prohibits its expression. It is for these souls that inner work can be most powerful for it takes one back to one's core existence, to where 'life' began.

PLATO: "Man could be forgiven for thinking this a 'backward' movement, a state of *failure?*"

Mr P: Man is conditioned to thinking of this acceptance of his or her physical, mental, emotional or energetic state as 'failure' rather than *break-through*. Indeed it is referred to as a 'break-down'. In actuality, it is a state of neutrality enabling the attraction of what is needed for expansion and connection… for *breath*.

PLATO: "The *results* of man's breakdowns do not end favourably for all. I understand this can be attributed to the movement between the minus and plus 1's, and of neutrality and the attracting forces from such 'placements', but how does one explain the *benefit* of such a breakdown, as it is referred to, if the outcome is not guaranteed as favourable?"

Mr P: For man's soul, the outcome is always favourable. For the ego and for the discriminatory aspects of the self, no, a battle will often ensue. But for the soul, the journey continues, for it will always transition into wellness. Always.

TUES 18ᵀᴴ NOV 2014, LONDON AT 12 MIDDAY, SESSION 64

Mr P: It is the elusive aspect of the soul which both intrigues and scares man. For it is so tangible, yet intangible when against a backdrop of conflicting desires. The 'shadow' of one's presence in the world of acquisition creates the reflection man is often not comfortable viewing. He stares at his shadow, puzzled and confused, yet dare not look at himself. Indeed he criticises and critiques his shadow – and the shadows of others – yet dare still not look at himself.

The obvious consequence of this point of viewing is a dislogged sense of belonging as the reflection of the ground he stands on is 'pulled apart'. When the view is in jeopardy the destination becomes untenable.

PLATO: "Many a man or woman is not aware of this 'split' within; of the duality within one's reflection and 'one-Self'."

Mr P: Indeed. A 'reflection' is deemed as something 'tangible' such as a vision in a mirror or a puddle. But this is not the case. A reflection in a mirror or a puddle or the sunlight catching on a building is an 'illumination' of energy. It is tangible for the eyes. But this energy of reflection is 'all-around', in constant movement at all times whether 'seen' or not.

As man grows into toddlerhood, he splits. As the pulls of affection make him question his placement of safety, he begins to *please others* before pleasing himself. He begins to comprehend the mechanics of 'love' in his environment – I say *begin* for it often never ends. A child does not know 'love' when he or she is born, but he soon learns the desired interpretation of love in his community. It is this 'split' which creates the duality – and the shadow. For now there is an inner and an outer. It is natural, and it is desired. For without this split, man would not *experience,* he would just 'feel'. The split creates the need for choice, for the mind and brain to 'trigger' into action. The shadow is visible to the child; but from within the reflection of his parents or loved-for carer. Indeed the child will have within his or her environment all aspects of sexuality: of masculine and feminine; of belonging and separation; and of connection and abandonment. These 'signatures' of sensory adjustments *create* the dynamics of the stimulated being we call a 'human'. The fibres, nerves, sensory pulsations and inner consciousness all create together a unique, functioning person on the planet.

But the undesired effects are the disconnection with *why* this duality exists. Everything is for good reason, but little understood. Man is perpetually trying to 'fix:' himself and others – usually others – by way of *pulling apart* or *bringing together.* But neither are desirable. It is not the requirement for 'oneness' which will heal – this is a fallacy of man. Nor is it the requirement of blending and harmonising with others, of 'giving of oneself'. No. It is the acceptance of the duality, the acceptance that things are meant to trigger and create discord that heals the soul. It is the acceptance of good *and* bad, of his *and* her, of mine *and* yours, of the desired *and* the undesired which heals. This is neutrality and this is the place of peace.

The duality is the very gift of life. It creates the waves, the breath and the energy planet Earth resides in; and it is perfect in itself. What is not perfect, is that man cannot experience this duality within peace, the peace of within. For in truth, there is no *out-there*: it is but a reflection of 'what-is'.

WED 19TH NOV 2014, LONDON AT 11.35AM, SESSION 65

PLATO: "Rather than describe this *illusion* you refer to, that we are intrinsically part of, as 'duality' would it not be accurate to refer to it as *discord*? For when one *accepts* the duality and can see and sense the perfection in all, the split is transcended, no?"

Mr P: In a manner of form, yes, this is so. But…man is comprised of emotions, and the emotions drive the energy. So whilst one can have moments, perhaps extended moments over years of inner peacefulness and acceptance, a time will come when he or she is triggered back into the world of duality. To shift in such a way can indeed be the 'hardest' way to navigate through the physical timeline. For everything as it is understood and *known* becomes 'untrue' – for the emotions rule the ship, despite best efforts. And in such cases man spends his time and effort trying to get 'back to shore,' to *safety*, when in fact he is in the perfect place, experiencing the perfect emotions and being in 'what-is'.

The tussle between feeling good and feeling bad creates the void man is trying to fill; whether through alcohol, drugs, work, enforced 'play' or any form of numbed acquisition. A seeker of spiritual gratification is no less confused or 'hooked' by his own emotions. The discord remains under all action and the thought is influenced by a need to *be in a better place* and to leave behind what does not feel good and which triggers unsavoury emotions. And so the searching and yo-yoing.

It is true that once one 'transcends' it is an inner transcendence of the emotion or the representation of the emotion: until another emotion comes along. It is when the underlying signatures are transcended that the real work happens and true enlightenment is gained: and to transcend one's signatures one will – and must – accept the duality; to the level that the duality is received into the psyche, becomes embroiled in the energy of 'what-is' and 'what-one-is'. It is the very reversal of the driving energy created at birth by the split. It is the full circle. It is the re-birth.

PLATO: "How does man know how far along he is on the journey to his soul? How to know what *work* is to be done?"

Mr P: It is a good question, and one I am happy to answer, for there is nothing more satisfying to witness than a being transcend to full circle; nothing.

It is with great pleasure that I have watched Delilah embark on such a journey. She is not *comfortable* with being used as the 'topic' in this discussion, but it is the nature of our work, and so she is obliging.

Delilah began this journey, as we all do, long before this physical life-time. But in this aspect of her evolution, the trigger came five years ago. She was not aware of her movements, was engrossed in a world of incongruence and subservience to her-Self, but the whispers began voicing to a louder tune. As they became part of her 'what-is', movements encompassing this call showed themselves to her. Some she took, some she didn't. It didn't matter, for when the time came to *decide* she knew her desires. And then the journey-proper started.

Delilah's 'work' was in healing herself of a deeply impactful illness…initially. She experienced great transcendence at this time – was joyful in the extreme as her desires were answered. For many, this place of found wellness and euphoria would be sufficient. But the call kept coming. Her *bravery* was not in 'beating cancer' but in delving into the emotions which created both the expression of illness *and* the desire to be joyful. She does not see this as being a choice, for her memory serves her to believe she had no choice, but indeed she did. She did not at that time have trust, and this fuelled her journey; but the choice was always there. It is a brave soul who enters the lair of the emotional body, for consciously entering is very different to being tossed and thrown by it from a place of denial.

Man will always move at a pace to suit his Self: the total of his parts. He will know when he is ready to edge forward, and when he needs to rest and just enjoy the view. The *speed* of his or her journey is dependent on many factors: from *this* lifetime and the next, for the past bears no aspect of the journey underway; there is here, right now, and a destination.

The arrival at 'full circle' is when the journey stops, when one stands in one's destiny: for there is no more seeking and no more searching; the answers all lie before; both within and without, and in one's duality and the duality of 'what-is'.

It is at this 'place' in time and space that man enters *peace*. 'Life' continues as normal, but it is never 'normal' again, for normality is but an illusion. When man *wakes-up* to his or her uniqueness, the journey beckons and when man accepts his or her uniqueness full circle is attained.

THURS 20TH NOV 2014, LONDON AT 9.05AM, SESSION 66

PLATO: "The question which comes to the fore if I may, is the unquestioning nature of the 'work' as you describe it. Man is encouraged to accept his power, his abilities and his being'ness – yet he is asked to *enter the lair* as you describe it and relinquish his egoic weapons and tools at the gate of reason. For to enter the emotional cave is to enter the world of unquestioning surrender to the unfathomable, I feel?"

Mr P: And a very elegant prose to describe the journey of the warrior! Man's greatest battle will always be with himself, no matter what the circumstance. In honouring the conversation within, man can observe, participate and en-joy the battle. But when man conceals his emotions in order to battle the other – the reflection he observes in others, be it brother, sister, neighbour or continent – he neither observes nor participates, he *fights*.

Entering the cave is akin to the last battle, the last stand; for there can only be one of two outcomes. Illumination of the cave as man declares his benevolence to the forces which fuel him or eternal darkness as man continues the battle within.

So yes, 'unquestioning surrender to the unfathomable' is a wonderful description of the requirement to undertake such a journey. And this is why not all men are ready for this stage of their evolution.

PLATO: "You are, it seems, proposing this wager with one-self is a *requirement* for mankind? But if one's peace is to be found in accepting the 'what-is', what hinders the energy of peace as one sits outside one's cave or continues on by?"

Mr P: *Peace* is a very different state to 'being peaceful'. For many, being peaceful is the destination and yes, in such time/space, acceptance of the cave but no desire to enter is the *peaceful* thing to do. But for some, deep, profound inner peace is the calling: to the 'state of peace'. And this is an energy which *surrounds* and encompasses all of one's being'ness. The desire for inner profound peace will be the throw-back, the re-balancing, of past energies: the movement required to bring one into neutrality. For each soul is on a journey to find neutrality, and this is why each soul's journey is unique. The *requirement* is in accepting the inner calling to one's neutrality, one's place of balance.

'The cave' will always present itself, for man is an emotional being as much as he is a spiritual one. It is the man who enters with his soul on his sleeve as his compass and guide, who gains the favour of the unfathomable. And it is the unfathomable which 'releases' man from his turmoil. But in entering the cave, man has surrendered to the darkness, to the need for outcome, and for the safety which protected. In relinquishing the safety man finds his depth, and answers the call, not from a known place, but from the very unfathomable which beckoned. He at once knows himself and knows he will never know himself, for therein lies the duality which supports all of existence.

FRI 21ST NOV 2014, LONDON AT 13.20PM, SESSION 67

PLATO: "It is understandable to those who have transitioned such an emotional journey, but there are many 'attempts' at vanquishing the *threat* of the unknown before the insight and knowingness of the unknown is felt and understood. In describing man's physical time-line in such a way, are we not prolonging its very 'insurmountability?' For where is the 'helping hand' in such a stance?"

Mr P: Indeed there is a *revealing* of the requirement of man's journey which goes hand-in-hand with an energy of assisting. It is only the man or woman who is ready to hear these words who will hear them – so there is no danger in 'preventing' a soul from transitioning the cave who wishes to. But the man or woman who is ready to, or who has just experienced such a vanquish, will benefit greatly from the awareness words such as these can bring. For many, it is the acknowledgement of how exhausting such a battle can be – and I say can, for it is never the same for all – which allows the very release and acceptance; for to know one is *in* the battle as opposed to facing the battle can be the very panacea to peace. To 'pretend' the emotional lair exists not is to live in suppression – and for many this is the comfortable option. But it is only in the revolt and the resolution that the suppressed rises to first challenge, and then defeat.

The inner battle 'holds' the fight and creates the dynamics which play out in the shadows and reflections of one's physical world; and when this is understood, the energies first shift, and then diffuse. It is the awareness of the diffusion which releases the hold on the innate creativity and energy of man. It is always in the awareness.

PLATO: "To observe a soul exiting the cave is a special moment, in more ways than one. But to observe the *entering* does not seem to qualify for the standing it deserves?"

Mr P: It is a shame, but yes, this is so. For man is fearful of the unknown and will do all in his power to prevent the *spread* of the malignancy – for this is most often how it is seen. In labelling the other as 'bad' or unsavoury he alienates both himself and the object of his fear. It is why the western world has so many 'mental institutions', homes for 'broken' people and cases of dis-function and alienation. As the effects of the lack of acceptance of man's journey, and the 'requirements' of such spread, so too does the stigma and isolation. The very 'spread' of what is merely the unfathomable, is created by those that most fear the cave. And so man is denied the very helping hand society professes to offer. As I have said, it is a brave soul who enters the lair – and a supported one who exits.

PLATO: "You refer to support, but how can this not conflict with the requirement for man to enter alone?"

Mr P: Whilst man must enter the cave alone – be that 'physically', or emotionally at the point of surrender – he never walks alone. Yes, he must turn his back on all that he knows, but all that he knows never leaves him – and it awaits him as he exits, or when illumination occurs. But what he *walks away from* can vary in support and energetic equations. To know that $+1$ equations support and surround you as you take those steps is very different from knowing you are surrounded by -1's. It is those that move from an energy of -1's who both benefit the most but struggle the most, and for this reason such a journey can be challenging. It is the very degree of contrast, the dramatic duality which society resides in which creates both the desire for illumination and its inaccessibility.

PLATO: "But would it not be fair to say that the soul feels not this pain, does not have an awareness of this 'lack?'"

Mr P: Indeed the soul is joyous upon entering the cave, for it knows it will be heard and seen once the emotional body has subsided. It is the guide and the compass, and so it *knows* its direction. And in this, it is never alone.

5

A Discussion on Emotions, Trust, Love and Purpose

MON 24TH NOV 2014, LONDON AT 8.55AM, SESSION 68

Mr P: Today the emphasis is on man's ability to *consume* his emotions, not a desire to express them. It does not serve to reflect on times past, but we can observe if we do for just a moment, the difference in energy flow and expression to millennia ago. The 'tipping point' in this way and means of expression is not of recent times – in the age of technological advancement – but from times prior, when man desired *safety* in extreme measures.

'War' creates both intense *lack* and intense *connection*. War in itself is not, I would suggest, a 'bad' thing for it highlights creativity, contrast and self-empowerment. To 'die' for one's beliefs can be the most rewarding and enlivening of transitions. But to kill is different, a very different energy. And so how to have one without the other?

This is the energy man has been operating in, but in a way which has created physical safety; but at the cost of spiritual safety. The deadliest of wars are those which are fought in the name of 'property'. Ironic that the very thing man fights over is not in fact belonging of him – is not something his soul can take *with him*?

PLATO: "Man has always fought for resolution of 'ground' properties. I would consider it both as a desire to protect for future generations by way of establishing 'rights', and also of confirmation of a 'way of living'. But time moves in continuum, and so the disparity: as the generations desire not what was fought for but what the 'enemy' withholds. Does man really know what he fights for?"

Mr P: It is – has to be – man's lack of spiritual connection which creates the desire to fight and protect a 'way of life'. For when connected within, no desire is greater than expression of oneself within what is presented, *as it is presented*. It is a perfect flow of energy in, and energy out, in the most peaceful yet enlivening of ways. *Life* in and *life* out. No desire for war can exist and safety is not *searched for* but felt; whatever the circumstances.

PLATO: "The trust required to have this peace is somewhat dependent on nature 'providing'. How to balance this need for survival against a lack of desire to seek further 'nourishment?'"

Mr P: The nourishment man seeks is of energy: powerful, en-livening, joyful energy. It has been sought in pastures, in crop-filled lands, in herds of meat, in rivers, in towns, in continents and in the very base offerings of planet Earth: of its natural energies and gases. But no amount of searching and acquiring will satisfy the hungry consumer. For the shopping for ingredients does not make the pie. And it is the pie man believes he needs and seeks.

Man has spent many a millennia trying to make his pie, to keep his pie and to feed his family whilst always 'making more'. But all of this is but a fallacy, an illusion. He *tries* to believe in a God, that all will be provided, but cannot trust to let go of the pie. And so, he is neither spiritual, nor in charge of his destiny. He fears, and so he seeks war and revenge on those who appear to have their pies neatly stacked up and abundant. He knows there are those 'worse off' but he feels no *better off*. Yes, he has 'enough', but it is never enough; and through this intense lack of self-trust, innate trust and dependency on the external illusion, he enters war with himself. He knows he will die for his cause, and in this he accepts his fate – and he knows he need not kill another to win the battle – and so he believes he will go with 'God's grace'. He seeks no evil and delivers no evil, and so he believes he is 'safe'.

But this is not peace. The best that man can hope for in circumstances such as these is a peaceful journey towards one's fate, one's battle with oneself; and maybe – hopefully, he be-lieves – he will meet his master in the next of lifetimes, when all will be taken care of, when he can relinquish the battle.

PLATO: "I hear in your tone an air of incredulity and… disdain?"

Mr P: Perhaps. For it is with great sadness one observes this 'grey-ness' of existence and the suffering man expresses through a desire to nourish, but an inability to access the very ingredients which are so abundant and so full of vitality…and so 'free of charge', yet invisible to many.

The sadness is not 'of me' but within me, held by us all as we offer our own unique 'helping hand'. For no-one can watch and ignore: it is not a possible equation, for in the Randomness of the awareness the spark has been ignited. All of mankind *cares* and so the sadness is both intrinsic and extrinsic. I feel sadness in my soul and I feel anger at man's inability to *see* what he sees but ignores in favour of 'safety' without. The anger and sadness are mine, and fear not, they are more than compensated in my individual equation by joy and humour and knowledge and wonder. But the combination fuels my desire to offer a helping hand, and for this reason my 'spiritual emotions' are perfect within themselves.

PLATO: "I hear acceptance and balance within your words, but what of hope?"

Mr P: Indeed; this is but a collective journey we are on, and so my work is rewarded on a most constant of basis as moment after moment, lightness and enlightenment is triggered into 'what-is'. It is a most joyous of experience and experiential of existences, and one cannot therefore have anything but gratitude and wonder. But hope? No. Hope is a feeling experienced purely on a physical level, for when one is within peace, one *knows*. Hope is not needed for the awareness brings the very safety, belief, and deep, deep inner connection which informs one's soul of the perfection in all-that-is and of what-one-is. Hope is replaced by trust, and in trust one finds the true essence of the energy which supports us all. And so my desire to offer this awareness and offer the idea of trust enables the very balance I and all seek...and come to know.

TUES 25TH NOV 2014, LONDON AT 10.30AM, SESSION 69

PLATO: "It is with regret that I fear that most don't trust, and crucially, do not want to trust, for to do so would open the lid on a tightly closed and full-to-the-brim box of tricks and cacophony of voices – past and present – to alleviate not the fear, but the courage to encounter oneself."

Mr P: And this is why it is so important at this time to share one's personal encounters, with oneself, yes, but also with the state of trust. For whilst man may decline the offer of entering the state, he can still feel the effects and touch lightly should he wish. Moments of trust – of stepping out of an existence of non-trust – can do wonders for the soul and relax one's presence into a much calmer and frankly more beneficial way of being. Even a touch of this helps one's physiology.

The society of current times is ensconced in a state of non-trust: the opposite of trust which is fear. Firstly, let me expand on the word fear, for it is largely misunderstood. 'Fear' is an instinct which grips one by all the senses. It is a 'do not enter' on a circumstance or a 'location'. Fear is a *positive*, a +1, for it is man's gauge of whether to proceed or not. We would always advise man to honour and respect his fear; to ignore is to fool with the known danger ahead. And to ignore one's fear is to play the role of both advisor and judicator, and this is neither necessary, nor wise.

But different to fear, yet often imperceptible in its dichotomy, is the call to courage: an altogether different instinct. The call to courage, also a +1, draws on the very heart-beat of the soul – all that man is – to rise to his own challenge. Man instinctively and intrinsically knows when this call beckons and in his response he is neither fearful, nor careful. He answers, like a bird in song. Until that is, he lets the fears of others impede his way. And then he becomes both fearful, and courageous...and stuck.

At this point, he will either slide into -1's and return to the safety of fear of others or rise into +1's and excel within himself. This choice, presented on a daily, hourly, often constant basis tires and exhausts mankind. It is a battle; *the* battle. And society offers no reprieve.

All that is offered by man fuels the lack of trust, but thankfully, the offers of nature, of planet Earth and of one's inner spirit quell this energy and instead replace it with a balance and an irresistibility to which man is drawn. And one's spirit, of all and all-that-is, supports not only what one sees, but also what one does not see. Hence the growth in the universe, in the galaxies and in the unfathomable.

Man is drawn to the quest for his spirit; to live by and through his spirit: the very essence and complete equation of all that he is, and may become. But this can be hard in a society or community which sees not man's unfathomable but his failures.

Plato, look around and observe the obstacles and defences built by man. The threats abound: of destitution, of loss, of deceit, of abandonment. At every turn man is faced with warnings, with 'advice', with recommendations which lock him ever deeper into the confines of his four walls and inner frets. Before he or she can consider a life well-lived, they must have approval, recognition by others, abundant acquisitions, *proof* of 'stickability', politeness, subservience, acknowledgement of one's unworthiness through enforced displays of incongruent behaviour, not to name financial wealth enough to pay for not just today but all the days of this life of time. Where, oh where is the joy to be found?

PLATO: "Indeed, man considers himself a worthy slave to others."

Mr P: And not just a slave, but an *informed slave*. For he does so willingly and effectively. Yet he believes he is free, or at the very least can earn his freedom if he obeys the 'laws of man'. But what of the laws of Nature and the laws of Spirit…which is what man truly is of?

PLATO: "Man it seems, trusts man above all else. For he is tangible and responds when *prodded*. But Spirit and Nature respond too – just man cannot see this worthy and influential of replies."

Mr P: Indeed, and for this reason we can only but encourage man to listen. For he, or she, must take the learning and the wisdom; we can offer, but we cannot give.

Man, should he wish, is able to experience and feel trust: in himself, in his spirit, and in the spirit of others. It is akin to tuning into a frequency which differs not in volume but in understanding. For to understand trust is present in all-that-is and all-one-is opens the door to a freedom so vast and so 'outside' of man's fearful state that the journey both beckons and inspires. It ignites the very core of what it is to be human and experiencing the wondrous state of life on planet Earth. And it is practical.

PLATO: "Practical, you say?"

Mr P: Of course! For how can one navigate one's day when one knows not what to do, or knows not what one is doing? With trust, clarity abounds, and action becomes both effortless and enjoyable.

PLATO: "It appears to me that one can have trust in one area of one's life – and experience ease and growth and enjoyment – but not in another?"

Mr P: Yes, this is so, but it is only on the arrival at full circle, when one has trust within oneself *and* of all-that-is, that true transcendence and freedom is attained. It is not in the eyes of another we see ourselves, but it is in our eyes we see others.

WED 26TH NOV 2014, LONDON AT 9.00AM, SESSION 70

PLATO: "And in our eyes we see evidence of love, we hope. Or would this equate, via the links of both transcendence and physical presence in the Randomness, a 'view' of trust in love? For if one *trusts*, and therefore *knows*, what does, and can, one know about love?"

Mr P: Ah! And this is why our discussion on the merits of love is not as *simple* as we might think. For how can we *know* love of another if the other is but a reflection of oneself? One's shadow, illuminated into vision.

For this reason, love of another can only be love of oneself. And so the obvious and immediate question: *"Of what in the other are we loving?"*

PLATO: "Explain therefore, when one falls 'out of love', and in the extraction of the equation between the two, moves into greater self-realisation and worth – when the very walking away from, empowers the individual. How does one explain this?"

Mr P: When two people fall in love, they are falling into discovery of themselves – of the parts of themselves they either enjoy expressing and 'enlivening' or wish to unearth within themselves. They literally *bounce* their atoms off of the other, and all manner of equations and links are fired up into existence. These new energy formations create new pathways and greater diversity, and the one fuels the other: the *enjoyment* fuels the growth, and the growth fuels the enjoyment.

Some equations are intended for a 'reason' and some for an 'effect'. What I mean by this, is that some connections are *purposeful* in one's subconscious – and it is always the subconscious that 'calls' these connections in – to enable a 'preordained' experience of growth and evolvement to occur; an *agreement* if you wish.

The other are intended, usually by the conscious mind, for the *effect* they bring. Whether comfort, to satisfy desires, to enable wealth or conscious growth. When the effect wears off, the desire for the connection wanes, and the person 'moves on'. It is in these circumstances one observes the greater self-realisation and self-worth, as you refer to it.

The 'intense' relationships man experiences, are the ones which combine both reason *and* effect. And these are the ones which 'pull' man, either together or apart, and often to a flow of both at intervening times. These are the connections which turn into *relationships* as the acknowledgement between the parties of the spoken and unspoken intricacies 'bond' the equation into a continuum of time and space.

It is these connections which confuse man, for to enter for effect but find reason can overwhelm as the subconscious becomes conscious in one's awareness. *"How did this happen?"*

is uttered as man is pulled towards what is unknown yet familiar; of a level which touches the divine yet is oh so tangible. To leave these equations, when the initial effect has been realised, the 'job done' so to speak, wreaks havoc on man's understanding of 'what-is', for confusion abounds.

PLATO: "Would man not enter for reason and subsequently realise effect too?"

Mr P: No. This is not a 'viable' equation, for 'reason' is of the external. The edge of reason is the reflection of the inner in the outer. As we have discussed, man sits on the border of the edge of reason (the outer) and the edge of belief (the inner). To *enter* a connection for reasons of reason is to *know* what the equation is about – there is a purpose to it, it is 'business:' the work of the soul.

In these connections of purpose, the effects are *anticipated* and therefore 'managed' by man from the outset. The boundaries are clear and defined; if not always exercised. Man *knows* at a deep level his role in the equation, and this is 'played out' and experienced to great effect. There is immense value and enjoyment in realising a connection of reason. Many 'marriages' and 'partnerships' provide this stability and grounded environment, and indeed, this is the role of parenting.

But it is the connections of effect which 'spark' man, for these create an intense sense of *aliveness* and vibrational 'electricity' – both within and without. A *coming together* for mutual effect of both parties can seem so profound that man believes there is 'reason' to it, but this is not so. It is what it is, which is intense fulfilment and enjoyment in the moment, for personal effect, through the effectiveness of the combination, but it is no more than this. Because man may experience so little of this, he can mistake it for 'reason', for *something more*.

PLATO: "Tell me dear fellow, where does creationism 'feature' in this?"

Mr P: A timely reminder to bring the discussion back to our purpose: of awareness *creating*. And this is what connections of 'effect' are: awareness creating. Connections of reason are awareness fulfilling. And connections of both are profound creators of all-that-is.

THURS 27TH NOV 2014, LONDON AT 8.30AM, SESSION 71

PLATO: "So why does man not just seek the connections of both reason and effect, be they so fulfilling in capacity?"

Mr P: Man does, but it has been an evolvement over the millennia. As two became four, became sixteen, became thirty-two, the 'possibilities' of encounters of effect grew accordingly. Man's interest became 'sparked.' Literally. Man needed connections of reason to survive, but he enjoyed connection of effect too. And this can be the pull when they present simultaneously. For the safety of the tribe, man is encouraged to choose reason. And there is much sense in this, and much permanence by way of preservation of what has gone before. But it is an energy of stability, of honour, not of creativity. And underneath all that man sees and lives, is a desire for creativity.

PLATO: "I would suggest that peace is more of a base desire? Is it not peace one seeks in and at the end of one's days?"

Mr P: Peace only comes dear Plato, when the creativity is done, be that creating a family, an empire, or harmony within. But man's unique perspective, through the eyes of the soul, is to create his fortune and to spend it *in* his destiny. Matters not the currency, for energy is energy.

PLATO: "There are few I suggest who would understand a young person for instance, 'snatched from life', having achieved his or her 'creativity'. When evidence proves there is so much more at all times to create – which man *can* create – how to qualify that 'the job is done?'"

Mr P: And this is where the unfathomable allows not just its presence but also its mastery. What I suggest by this is, man is in charge of his 'time', whether consciously aware or not. But as time is again a perception of one's experience, man is both 'in charge' *and* at the mercy of his perception. Many a soul enters the physical element of his or her time-line with the intention and desire to 'get the job done', to continue with the grander time-line, and to evolve in ways man cannot observe from where he stands. But whatever the experience of intention – however brief – the full spectrum of emotions will present. For to experience another human is a gift.

So it may seem harsh to those who mourn a loved one, but it is always perfect, and always *true* for the soul who has departed the physical. The 'creativity' is not always *seen*, for to depart the physical is also creationism in itself. Man views it as a loss, but perhaps he would do well to consider and trust the unfathomable both within him or herself and within 'the experience'.

It is one's perception of a need for a *justified experience of time* which creates distress. The belief held by mankind of an 'eighty years of living' serves to destroy '*life*'. Many a man elongates his activity, spontaneity and creativity to 'fill' his years. Oh how shameful a waste!

PLATO: "Indeed one does not *need* many a year to create ones' fortune if the desire exists, and is allowed to flourish. But man finds it not easy to alter his timepiece to that of spontaneity, and creativity for creativity's sake. It requires, I feel, an attitude of enquiry into what the day can bring as opposed to how one fills the day?"

Mr P: It is exactly so, that the exchange within the day is partaken between man and the unfathomable, and that the creativity occurs in response to the enquiring mind. Man sees what he wishes to see, and his days become as full as he allows the creativity to spark and rise within him and within the exchange at the border of reason and belief.

PLATO: "Tell me, where does the unfathomable reside at this place of reason and belief?"

Mr P: It resides in the energy of all-that-is. *It* is within everything. It is energy, as we all are. The beauty of the physical is that the contrast of what man 'reasons', by way of form, *accentuates* the experience: in the direction of either -1 or +1. The *purpose* of man's experience in the physical is to live the very desires of the unfathomable within.

These desires will not be of 'war,' or 'love', or association, but of the wish and desire to evolve. And the unfathomable always, always supports this, for it is a joint, linked desire held by every man, woman and child on planet Earth. It is the unanimous agreement all have, but all exercise in their different and unique way. It is the challenge of living *with* others, whilst living one's unique life which is not the purpose but the experience all partake in. The purpose is evolvement, and once this is understood, the journey becomes so much softer and gentler…and loving.

PLATO: "Loving, you say?"

Mr P: Yes. For once man *knows* his journey of evolvement, once he has connected with it in both reason and belief, he is able to *know* love – not as an exchange with and between others, but as a state of love. When one *knows* love, it is not 'seeked' but felt, and all is fused with its softness and benevolence.

PLATO: "So you suggest therefore that man, in seeking love, is seeking connection with his evolvement?"

Mr P: And not just his evolvement, but also his demise. For there is always balance in the equation.

Man's innate desire, I suggest, is to live his life *and* to live his death. For when he can confidently create either, to his or her unique time/space, he becomes master of all-that-is.

PLATO: "I understand the wonder of being able to create one's 'end of life' to suit one's destiny, but how does this interplay with being at the mercy of the collective energy of mankind's consciousness? How can personal will play out within the greater will of all-that-is?"

Mr P: Through desire dear Plato, through desire.

6

A DISCUSSION ON DESIRE, LOVE AND VIRTUE

Mr P: Desire, through the very desire *of* desire *creates*. How could one have creationism, the very existence of a planet and its inhabitants of all form if it was not *desired*? Yet what a struggle man has had with this most effective, rich and oftentimes destructive of energies!

Man believes he loves – or hates – but for the most part, he desires. And this is as it is…and should be, though mostly 'dis-couraged' by societal infrastructure. It is permissible to desire what 'fits in' with perceived comforts, or to desire what will lead humanity but it is not permissible through example or deigned consent to desire for desire's sake – to satisfy one's innate senses for no reason other than it feels good. And therefore man keeps his true desires to himself, shrouded in emotions yet unable to be expressed in an energy of pure self-realisation.

The desires I speak of are the ones which 'don't fit' or 'don't form part of the collectives' direction'. But in truth, if the collective allowed its true desires to surface, the direction would be oh so different!

As man desires, he judges and expresses it – or not – based on his combination of reason (of the external) and belief (of the internal). The 'reason' he or she observes in the external will affect the belief of whether it should be expressed. And this is why the external *affects* the internal.

The desire in itself, is neutral: whatever the desire. As it rises, it begins its colouration based on one's reason and beliefs and hence becomes 'judged' and energised into a direction of output, much like an electric motherboard. It will 'be there', within the energetic make-up of the unit, but indistinguishable in its form – unless released. But herein lies the conflict – for man's desires bequest his downfall, or so he is led to believe.

And this belief that mankind carries – of desires being 'wrongful' in nature – leads us to wonder at the greater picture. For perhaps, just perhaps, man has evolved to be able to trust his desires, to trust that he *knows* his own mind and being'ness and innate sense of Self? For if he trusts, he 'knows'.

PLATO: "Man's instinct is a desire, yet in its expression – in being so spontaneous – it has colouration as you describe it. Surely the instinct *requires* control in order to effect the desired outcome?"

Mr P: 'Instinct' is very different to desire. Very. My suggestion is of desire being an energy of creationism, of growth, absolutely pure in its form – a free-flowing tap of wellbeing and opportunity. Instinct by contrast, is a 'linked' and 'drawn-upon' automatic response of the Self: of the physical, the heart, soul, ego, the whole psyche of what exists within and without. Perhaps one would call this self-preservation, perhaps 'natural instinct,' perhaps desire – but when one is in 'response' one cannot be in desire – for desire is pure action.

PLATO: "Yet all response requires actions?"

Mr P: Indeed. However, all action which is in *response* to something is coloured by the emotions. Action which is a result of pure desire is neutral – until it links with reason and belief – and therefore becomes 'emotional' in nature. But when man allows the desire to remain pure and 'untarnished' it retains its power and dynamism.

PLATO: "Explain more of the contrast between desire and instinct if you will, for whilst your point of observation facilitates clarity, when man is navigating his day, it is without such distance of viewing."

Mr P: Distance of viewing notwithstanding, man is capable of viewing his actions within the context of *feeling* the energy of the moment, and in so doing is very informed of whether instinct or desire is at play. But before this differentiation can occur, the 'difference' must be felt.

PLATO: "And how best to feel this difference?"

Mr P: Through love. For in love resides instinct *and* desire.

TUES 2ND DEC 2014, LONDON AT 8.40AM, SESSION 73

PLATO: "Before we address love via instinct and desire, I have a question: for to know love is, we agree, subjective to the linked connections and emotions, and the 'direction' of the intention. A state of love would have no intention I suggest, other than experiencing more of love, more of what is being experienced. So is this experience of love – for no reason other than to experience the love – within the 'state of love,' an instinct or a desire?"

Mr P: The question of whether instinct or desire exists within the state of love is one that contributes to our discussion well, for the notion of a 'state of love' creates I suggest, in man both instinct and desire: the instinct towards the state of love, and once touched, the desire for more. But when one is experiencing that very state, there is neither desire nor instinct – there is just the sensation of pure love. And I would suggest that the closest man gets in achieving this, is peace and joy – different to the state of love, but very, very enjoyable and profound in its own way, and more of a 'vehicle' for the physical life. But it is virtue which man desires as the stepping stones to states of peace, freedom, joy and love. I believe and offer that virtue and love have become 'confused' and have brought all other aspects – such as freedom and compassion and self-care – into the confused mix. But the 'state of love,' what most would call divine love, is 'above' and outside the realms of desire and instinct.

Man's experience of the physical is I suggest, to experience and navigate desire and instinct. It seems a challenging yet potentially rewarding of journeys, no?

PLATO: "It strikes me that the challenge, of reaching the balance between the contrasts offered by man's world, is the very *intention* of man's journey, yet it is 'understood' that man's journey is to reach the 'state of love?'"

Mr P: Indeed. But I propose that the true 'direction' has been lost…for a direction considered through a sense of separation: of being 'apart'. The desire for connection – through love, desire, instinct – is grounded in a sense of separation. And this desire for connection draws man instinctively towards a state of love, yet pulls apart all that he has desired in the process to that point in time and space.

PLATO: "Yet is it not permissible to love without intention of the state of love? Would it not offer a *kinder* experience as man *lets go* of the instinct to be 'in a different state?'"

Mr P: There is much merit in this suggestion, yes. For two reasons – a duality within themselves – for when one releases the 'seeking', we find; and when one accepts, we find. But it takes great skill and courage to accept one's reality *as it is*, for this relies on '*being* love'. And in this place, desire and instinct are very different to when one is seeking. For it is the acceptance that one is perfect – and perfectly acceptable – as one *is*; and so the instinct changes focus, from self-improvement to the improvement of 'what-is'.

PLATO: "And desire?"

Mr P: Desire will always be present, but in a very different form for the colouration alters – becomes 'clearer' and purer – as the intention alters via the changing atoms and sub-conscious intricacies of the energetic fields, as connections fuelling seeking are 'dropped' in favour of connections giving and offering support to 'what-is'. For in the acceptance of the present being perfect, the energy flow is stronger and powerfully 'spreads' outside of the individual to the greater sphere of attraction. The 'desire' becomes to enjoy the present and to positively affect the dynamics of one's reality. It is peaceful yet enlivening. Instinct in these circumstances becomes to fulfil one's existence as it appears in one's now of time and space. It is very efficient and very rewarding. The state of love as a destination has been relinquished in favour of expression of instinct and desire, and the wonderful irony of this? That this becomes in itself expression 'of' the state of love – by the beauty of relinquishment of the seeking.

PLATO: "Yet man's instinct is towards betterment and self-realisation? Virtue, being the vehicle to self-acceptance creates the very growth and learning one needs knowledge of?"

Mr P: Yes…and no. It is a path to peace and harmony, yes. But it is not essential, no. For at any stage in his time-line man can 'let go' and accept the expression of virtue he or she is.

PLATO: "And so instinct and desire would indicate being of virtue more than 'love' perhaps?"

Mr P: Indeed, and worthy of our explorative discussion, for how can one not desire to desire?

WED 3RD DEC 2014, LONDON AT 11.30AM, SESSION 74

PLATO: "We speak of virtue, of love, of desire, of instinct, of peace, of joy. All worthy of expression, but wherein lies the 'thread' of a profoundly satisfying life? For you speak of desire, yet desire, being considered man's 'downfall' dost not warrant the accolade bestowed on love or virtue I feel?"

Mr P: My suggestion, is that desire, like love, has been mis-understood, and that crucially, it is *desire* which fuels man, keeps him 'going'. The thread you speak of, the underlying support of all existence, is desire: desire for peace; for food and nourishment so man can exist; for expression; for companion-ship and intimacy; for connection.

When man laments the very desire which fuels his life energy, conflict arises. Hence 'depression', illness and misfortune. For when man is unable to express his true desires, a 'blockage' appears. In this blockage, emotions form, fear forms. For an inability to express one's truth creates an energy of fear.

The doctrines espouse that desire is 'wrongful' and must be tamed, that one must honour the God, not of the soul, but of the church or 'religion,' that in one's dedication to 'a bible', salvation will be sought…and bestowed.

My suggestion is that man's desire *is* man's God, *is* the divine energies wishing to express themselves through each and every person. The creationism is a 'joint-effort' by all who walk and observe planet Earth. The 'accountability' is in what man created for not just *his* benefit, but also the benefit of all – for his physical brothers and sisters. The choice is for what man wishes to experience and contribute *now*, not for when he 'passes over'. For then it is too late. The power is in the now.

The *vision* man is 'missing' is the awareness that he holds his or her own bible of truths. Many wonderful scripts and tales have been offered and enjoyed over the years of time and space, but it is virtue – the act of reflecting *within* oneself – which plays out and creates expression of one's unique wisdom. Virtue *is* the expression of each man's unique 'Bible' or 'Koran'. For whilst man does not have all the answers he needs, he has the means to absorb and *attract* the knowledge which will guide and fuel him. Man's *answers* can only ever be a response within the moment, and as each action creates a reaction, his inner bible is updated and amended. It will always be this way, for awareness *creates* knowledge. When man feels worthy of this knowledge, of his or her belief in what he or she *knows*, virtue is expressed. But it is the *desire* to express virtue which creates the 'space' for growth and expansion. In honouring one's God within, one knows the God without, whatever one's chosen reflection of deity.

PLATO: "And so I hear your suggestion that one must *accept* and *welcome* desire in order to express one's inner divinity to one's God?"

Mr P: Indeed, for the alternative is to negate one's desire, forsaking one's inner wisdom, for the wisdom of the 'external'.

PLATO: "Yet man observes true wisdom in the external deity?"

Mr P: Undoubtedly – for he observes the reflection of himself. But when one's God is deemed without desire or instincts of the physically human, a conflict exists. For how can man 'compete' with such a differing set of tools at his disposal?

In believing that each man, woman and child *is* perfect within their sphere of virtue and potential, desire becomes a tool for good: for the movement and wellbeing of all.

PLATO: "And how does man differentiate between desires which serve wellbeing and those which don't? For it takes a virtuous man to honour the difference?"

Mr P: And therein lies the solution: virtue.

<u>THURS 4ᵀᴴ DEC 2014, LONDON AT 8.45AM, SESSION 75</u>

PLATO: "So tell me dear friend, your difference in reflecting on virtue as a desired object of humanity, and the virtuous man. Which comes first in expression and subjective observation?"

Mr P: The 'object' is not virtue for the sake of virtue, but virtue for the sake of man's goodwill and benevolence. It is in the understanding of what constitutes 'a good life' that man creates the laws of the land, with the intention of the ability for all to experience 'a good life'. The emphasis though dear Plato, has been on the 'good' and what constitutes good versus 'bad,' as opposed to 'life'. As with all things of a worthwhile nature, the answers lie within the contrast.

PLATO: "You talk of goodwill and benevolence?"

Mr P: Ah, the 'crunch-points' in the system. For man entangles in goodwill and the greater benevolence which is felt *within the air.*

Man chooses to forget the scientific dynamics of the planet he resides on. All is 'electrified' and all, when sparked, becomes magnified. When a feeling of goodwill for others and benevolence for and of, both oneself and others colours one's awareness, these sensations can override the *virtuous* response or action. For to be virtuous is not the same as to have goodwill or benevolence towards others.

PLATO: "Yet surely an aspect of goodwill towards one's fellow humans is a necessary requirement for a virtuous life?"

Mr P: No, I suggest not. Contentious I agree, but perhaps one could question it in the following context of a discrimination against a woman for slight of favours. A 'court of law' would question each party's intention and the occurrence of improper action. In finding 'agreement' with the lady, judgement is made against the man. But where lies the goodwill? For if no 'actual harm' came of the lady, if her refusals were met – if not perhaps in the most gracious of ways, but met nonetheless – is the goodwill in 'charging' the man or allowing his freedom? The courts, in their role as arbitrator, require a 'decision', yet the goodwill for all – for both the man and the woman – exist in intention, through a desire for *society* to experience the freedom to live 'a good life'.

So the courts of law exercise their virtue in deciding on the woman's 'good character' and whether the man is a 'danger' to the greater community or not. It is in upholding the goodwill for the greater community that the law makes a virtuous decision.

The same 'result' would ensue with an opposing judgement. For if the man had been found innocent of wrong-doing, yet the woman admonished for improper action towards him, the goodwill would play out in favour of a state of peace between both parties and 'removal' of the lady's ability to commit such wrong-doing at a future date. The goodwill is for the greater good of the community, not for either party, although the acquitted will benefit in benevolence.

In all cases, virtue is the decision-maker, *in favour of* goodwill for all. But it is not *a deciding factor* in the equation. And such with benevolence too, for in making a virtuous decision, one has to decide on the 'direction' of the action. One cannot be benevolent towards all parties when a choice is required.

PLATO: "Yet one can be benevolent towards oneself? Surely a necessary aspect of conscious decision-making?"

Mr P: Indeed, yet perhaps part of the 'air' one stands in? For to experience goodwill and benevolence for others, one must by default experience it for oneself too.

The *crunch* comes when man is guided by goodwill and benevolence – for both feel very enjoyable and pleasing – *instead* of virtue. For when man expresses virtue, a feeling of goodwill and benevolence ensue, but when man chooses goodwill and benevolence for a person above virtue, confusion and conflict ensues, as the direction 'back-fires'.

My suggestion is that man expresses virtue through the ability to differentiate and navigate the contrast. Most get caught within the contrast, drawn into a combination *with* a person or emotion, as opposed to flowing through what presents towards resolution of the experience. For instance, a desire to choose the virtuous response to an invitation or offer, can pull one in many directions of goodwill or benevolence. Often no response is given rather than a confident decision. Yet to exercise virtue towards one's host is to respond with dignity and honesty. This is just one example. So the expression of virtue has to come before virtue can be experienced or understood.

PLATO: "And how would you suggest man's ability to decide on the virtuous action or thought creates movement towards the greater purpose of 'a good life?'"

Mr P: Through the desire to create a better life. Not a good life, but a better life. The self-realisation of how one's life could be 'better' is what drives man. And this could be a betterment in a multitude of ways: perhaps more peace, less action, more security or stamina. Perhaps more love and connection. But through the desire for a better life, man makes virtuous decisions. It is only when he is stuck and troubled he chooses otherwise.

MON 8TH DEC 2014, LONDON AT 8.40AM, SESSION 76

PLATO: "'Betterment' is an interesting topic of discussion. For what constitutes 'better' in one person's eyes denies the other of this effect and affect – the contrast which is our each unique combination of wishes and desires. But the virtuous response will need to cut through not only others' ideas of betterment, but also one's own. If man is to act virtuously at all times, there will, by default, present at times a conflict between what is virtuous for oneself and what is the virtuous response."

Mr P: Ah, but not in the eyes of the observer, for only one 'response' can be given. And surely *truth* can only be a dualistic response? For there will always be the subject *and* the object, the decision *and* the action, the observer *and* the observed. So although one response can only be given, it is a 'split' dynamic within itself.

PLATO: "I sense the direction of your wisdom…"

Mr P: Yes, for all is an equation, but man would do well to spend more of his time and space on his inner equation of balance. For one of his unique abilities is the gift of subjective observation – of the ability to observe himself.

This very discussion is just that, is it not? I am conversing with myself and through the dialogue of observation and inquisitiveness I offer my own solutions yes, but also, one wishes and hopes, greater virtue in the awareness. In navigating my very own contrast, the option of a 'third way' arises, for although I may profess wisdom, the discussion itself allows greater knowledge and 'stability' of thought. We are always *increasing* in energetic flow of movement, whatever the vision.

PLATO: "Though not always achieving betterment?"

Mr P: No, always moving, yet the direction will be one of two: +1 or -1. And what presents as one person's +1, will be another's -1. And so the virtuous decision must rely on a different dynamic, a different 'set of rules'.

PLATO: "Say more…"

Mr P: The set of rules man, in the whole, lives and operates by is that of betterment of one's tribe. Even when a 'solo-expedition' is observed, it is to fuel a desire to 'return home' with the accomplishment to share amongst one's tribe – be that on a physical level, or on a soul level. But there is always, underneath all action, a desire and belief one *returns home*. So this creates a wonderful sense of adventure and gain – whether of peace, experience or love. It all enables *feelings* and 'tales to tell' and *share*. There is a communal sense of belonging, which even if not visible in one's reality, exists *below* the consciousness; in the sub-consciousness.

Some will refer to this as oneness, others as group consciousness, some as family ties and ancestral dynamics. But the rules are the same nonetheless. It is when one's fellow man 'breaks' these rules, by jeopardising the groups' chances of betterment that objective criticism arises within. To the outsider, the *virtuous* action is the one which allows *all* groups to experience betterment with no one given more lenience than another. The group virtue is to enable betterment for the whole group. So as man ponders *his* virtue against that of a group, he will either align with *his* group, his family tribe, or align his tribe to the greater group. In truth there is no 'wrong' answer, for all are attempting alignment and betterment in the direction of growth.

PLATO: "Yet for the man or tribe experiencing continual minus-one, such as extinction, surely the virtuous action is to prevent this?"

Mr P: Or perhaps not? Perhaps in 'allowing' its physical ex-tinction, greater growth is enabled on a soul level? For if the edge of reason is aligned with one's edge of belief, harmony and growth result. Is it not man's fear which prevents him *see-ing* this?

PLATO: "And so you profess *betterment* includes aspects of 'afterlife'?"

Mr P: Indeed. Yet this is always, always a personal choice and decision. But in exercising virtue towards another, this must always be taken into consideration. The alternative is to decide 'without all the facts', to include one's *right to life* in the equa-tion, but not one's *right to death*.

When one's edge of reason is aligned with one's edge of be-lief, if it is wished, transition to the 'next life' – to Source – will occur. This is also an act of betterment for the person who wishes this next step. Unconditionally so. Yet the edge of reason for all who 'remain' is affected forever. One's experience of virtue will adjust accordingly, as will one's wishes and desires for betterment.

So I offer that this set of rules creates both contrast and movement, yet an alternative set of rules is available too.

PLATO: "And this would be?"

Mr P: That of non-compromised desire, where the drive for betterment is relinquished in favour of experiencing the bet-ter in this very moment, in allowing the tribe to 'land' right here, right now; in enabling man's movement to be consciously manifested within the 'what-is'…and so the experience of being rules the desire for doing. It is a complete 'about-turn' of what is most often experienced in this time and space.

PLATO: "And so man would choose both the more peaceful and more enjoyable option. Yet is this the most virtuous?"

Mr P: If one observes from the intention of wellness, self-realisation and provision of harmonious expression and care, then yes.

WED 10TH DEC 2014, LONDON AT 10.15AM, SESSION 77

Mr P: Perhaps it would be wise to recap on what desire means before entrenching in a discussion of such worth? For 'desire' means many things to many people: a desire *for*, a desire *to*; a desire *of*; a desire *in* – the object creates a differing subjective interpretation.

PLATO: "Yet if the sensation is within, then it matters not what the object is?"

Mr P: I suggest otherwise. For all emotion 'draws' on *something* – a recollection of a past experience which colours one's view of a future one too. A feeling of desire is in response to something – it is always reactionary, whether to satisfy hunger, thirst, sexual instinct, fear or abandonment.

The suggestion I offer, is that this reactionary instinct or movement can be lacking virtue when it is exercised without awareness, without consciousness. Consciousness brings with it a clear state of action, so even when one desires, the response will be a considered, observed action which is endorsed within itself.

By this I mean the person exercising the action would be pleased with the action, even if there were no preceding reason. An example would be someone returning from work exhausted and consoling herself with a large dose of sugar-coated delicacies. If she would have enjoyed the delicacies as much without the desire for consolation or the feeling of exhaustion, it would be a conscious choice. If the consumption is in response to a feeling state, and only because of that, then this would be unconscious and lacking virtue. So we have a feeling of desire, but two – of many – different examples of 'reason'.

In addition, we have the belief the action or choice (which is also an action) supports. An inner belief the sugary delicacies will enable wellness is very different to an inner belief the consumption is 'bad'. And therefore we have a clearly virtuous observation by the consumer. Yet to others, it matters not which belief is felt, for the aspect of virtue is purely intrinsic. There is no 'wrong', and there is no 'right'; for no harm has come to anyone else in the process.

But often man casts judgement on others, and decides for them if a 'good' choice has been made. And in the absence of the acceptance of this opinion, will *enforce* feelings of low worth or virtue. Yet virtue can only be intrinsic. So as man attempts to express his innate inner virtue, through the trial and error of life, he begins to fear and clam-up his true desires in favour of approval by others, namely the tribe.

PLATO: "And yet there can be much value in the 'advice' and guidance of others?"

Mr P: Yes, but only when it is an offering, not an objection. For man must honour his inner guidance above all others, including above the divine. For how else can he exercise *his life?*

PLATO: "And hence the conflict of desire versus virtue. For desire is always intrinsic, yet man perceives virtue as extrinsic – although it is not. Virtue will always remain an intrinsic choice. And so I understand your suggestion that desire and virtue are inextricably 'linked'.

Mr P: Indeed. And so we will explore this 'connection' further.

THURS 11TH DEC 2014, LONDON AT 11.45AM, SESSION 78

PLATO: "Tell me, if you will, the benefit man experiences in leading a virtuous life? For if 'life' is about living the contrast, it would seem that one cannot *be* virtuous, but walk between virtuous and non-virtuous paths?"

Mr P: It is a fair assumption, but one that feeds to the harm of judgement of 'right' or 'wrong'. For what is virtuous to one, is not to another – purely by the circumstances each person finds himself or herself in.

It is not so much that man 'falls off' his path of virtue, but that he leaps into experiences of growth. For in all 'non-virtuous' actions or responses, there is always learning and growth. When there is no self-judgement, and no cast of failure, the virtuous course of subsequent action more than 'compensates' for any feeling of 'wrong-doing'. Man is always 'self-correcting' – indeed the ego is very good at supporting this inner dynamic; one of its powerful assets. But man always walks but one path and so the contrast which appears is not to pull awareness into different directions, but to highlight the options so the awareness of what is *preferable* is cast forth – perhaps not accepted, but always offered by the conscious mind in some form.

And so, it could be said that man is always leading a virtuous life, but with varying degrees of awareness.

PLATO: "And the awareness you speak of, is different to 'intelligence?'"

Mr P: Yes. For many 'intelligent' people do not honour their desires, but place their intelligence above all else. For society rewards well those with displays of mental agility. And so, such intelligence can be seen as virtuous. Yet it is not the *intelligence* which is virtuous but the action and choices which led to the absorption and expression of such matter. Man excels at what he practices, especially when the heart and soul are allowed to intervene. But untold 'intelligence' is of no worth if it is not put to use. And to put it to use, one must desire. For the risks are high when we speak one's truth.

PLATO: "High, you say?"

Mr P: Yes, high. For to walk along one's path by oneself, without one's tribe is always a risk. It requires great awareness to hold one's nerve and to trust the beckoning unknown. And this awareness is moment-to-moment awareness – so that the virtuous response or action can be made. The risk I speak of is that of 'regretting' one's direction, for once one takes this path, there is no 'return'. For the practice of a virtuous life becomes one's highest desire, above all else. And so, as all feeds into one's path to support this self-expression, the risk of tumbling becomes at once inconsequential *and* man's overriding concern. It is the flip side of the coin, for there is always contrast...

PLATO: "Yet why, if man is leading a life of virtue and ease, would this fear reveal itself? For surely the desire will encourage the forward movement?"

Mr P: Indeed, yet the further man walks his path, it is with the awareness he is walking further and further from his past. As he is beckoned forth, he leaves behind. And this challenges not the soul, but the heart.

PLATO: "The place of all desire."

Mr P: Yes, the place of all desire.

<u>FRI 12TH DEC 2014, LONDON AT 8.35AM, SESSION 79</u>

PLATO: "A question which arises most naturally, is what of those whose desire is to harm others, to create desolation? For in such circumstances, no manner of subsequent virtuous action can balance the loss one might feel at say, taking one's life, or losing a loved one at the expense of another's actions. For surely in such circumstances, a strong desire of the heart must create such strong action, and whilst it may be a desire for one person, how can this be deemed virtuous?"

Mr P: This is an area which is somewhat difficult to explain, for each person will have examples of such occurrences which fuel strong emotion. And it is the emotion which is the reaction, not the underlying state of love or understanding of what has occurred or the reasons why, for there is always growth for all.

Each man, woman and child is on a unique journey: to self-realisation, via the route of virtue. Love in this instance, we will leave for discussion at a later time. But virtue, we will use as the means to create growing self-expression for the purposes of this discussion.

Desire creates the identification of the stepping stones of the route. Suppressed desire, withheld route. Desire, in conjunction with virtuous choices of action creates a dynamic journey of wonder.

Now when man is suppressed to the point of great inner discomfort he will 'lash out' at others as a means to create balance.

It is a very uncomfortable and disharmonious energy to be in. He no longer *sees* or is aware of the 'what-is' and hence his view becomes jaded and egotistical in nature. And in this environment, if a coolant is not applied, the heat creates 'disaster'. For the 'perpetrator', whilst he or she is in a place of non-virtuous reality, the act itself may be the effect which creates an inner release and balance. One can never truly know another's 'what-is', and when one is tormented so, one's edge of reason and edge of belief encompass no further than the torment itself. It is an unfortunate place to be and yet the only panacea is often to *create* the disaster to dissolve the pain being felt in the moment.

The contrast is the hurt, pain and loss felt by others as a result of the action or 'disaster'. But again, there is always reason – by the very nature of it affecting one's edge of reason.

It must be understood that a soul never leaves the physical timeline until the perfect moment in time and space. It is not for those 'left behind' to question the *appropriateness* of the timing of others – just of oneself. When it is *known and felt* that all is perfect, loss is not felt – it is not possible. The challenge is in managing and expressing the emotions which accompany change of one's 'what-is' and the safety and comfort of the known.

PLATO: "And the 'perfection' you speak of, I recognise as the divine aspect of virtue."

Mr P: Yes, when this is felt and known, one understands that everyone desires a virtuous existence, for man knows what eases torment and conflict; under all conscious action, the soul whispers *truth*.

PLATO: "And yet not all man hears."

Mr P: In this physical timeline, perhaps not. But man cannot withhold his own self-expression and desires to love, create and heal for the sake of others. *Because* of others' torment, he must walk through his own discomfort for to pause for longer than a blink of an eye is to succumb to the inevitability of regret of virtue not lived. For one lives one's desire and one's virtue.

PLATO: "And how best does man live his desires and virtue?"

Mr P: By creating a world like no other – a world which pleases enormously his or her edge of reason, and supports and cradles his, or her, edge of belief. For when one's beliefs become known and expressed in one's reality, pure peace, harmony and joy is felt and shared.

PLATO: "And this can only be a desired thing…"

MON 15TH DEC 2014, LONDON AT 9.55AM, SESSION 80

Mr P: Let us turn our attention back to the subject of betterment. For to seek betterment is not, I feel, the same as to create one's ideal world. It is always the energy and the intention 'behind' something which creates the outcome. And man can have many reasons for 'betterment' which are not part of an *ideal* vision.

Take, for instance, someone caring for an elderly relative. Whilst on one hand he or she may wish to *better* the life of the relative, on the other, the 'ideal' life is perhaps deemed as 'un-available' due to responsibility and compassion for one's relative. There could, in potentiality, exist a split in the person: of *"I can begin living my ideal life when so-and-so passes on."* Whilst the relative is alive, one's edge of reason offers the obstruction, supported by the belief…which currently knows *"life is not ideal right now."*

In reverse, it may happen with one's child who is about to leave home for further studies. One's edge of reason may offer that the happiness now felt – of the ideal situation of one's child being at home – will come to an end shortly, and that the 'ideal' situation will end. One's belief may offer that happiness will diminish, and fears rise for the wellbeing and safety of the child.

So we have just two examples of what a person may be feeling in a day – and there will of course be many more pulling at the psyche. And within all these exchanges, man must differentiate and strive for virtue. We can appreciate how worthwhile and useful virtue is to guide a person within a multitude of directions, no?

PLATO: "Indeed, yes, for I cannot imagine an existence without the pull of virtue. And yet does virtue support betterment of others or an ideal life for oneself? It seems to me that virtue involves both?"

Mr P: Yes…and no. The examples I have offered, by their nature of being 'generational' create a strong contrast we can observe. And indeed most people's examples are so. But they very clearly encompass emotions of the person, in relation *to* the elderly relative and *to* the departing child. Both 'exist' in one's *edge of reason*; in the external. So therefore, any expression of virtue cannot directly create an 'ideal life' for either, for both the elderly relative and the departing child will have their own beliefs on what constitutes an ideal life for them. But an intention of betterment for the individuals can indeed be held; and as long as there is no imposing of demands, no infringement of what *their* ideal life may be, then one could consider this holding of betterment *for* a person an act of virtue.

But with oneself – with the intrinsic – virtue is subjective, is it not? For the *virtuous* response to a child who steals may be to inform the victim of the theft, to reprimand the child. Is the virtue of oneself, or in relation and for the benefit of the victim, or the child? The decision 'to inform' – in whatever context, whether to impart knowledge, wisdom or good intention, or not – is an intrinsic act in response to one's belief on what would be *better*; for in the case of a stolen item, the 'ideal' is no longer possible.

So we observe in this example virtue being used *for oneself* so that we can feel comfortable with our movement towards betterment for all parties. And yet this can also be viewed as directional and encroaching our beliefs into someone else's reality. And hence the dilemma. For man is drawn towards helping others as a means of an 'ideal life'.

In the act of saying *"this is how I chose to live my ideal life"*, one has to stand within one's beliefs; wholly. And yet the beliefs, by the nature of continual fluctuation and growth on no less than an atomic level, are continually in flux and adapting to the environment. So is the virtue an expression *of* one's ideal life, or is it the means to create an ideal life?

PLATO: "One would assume, by way of observation of the common causes of happiness that virtue is as a *result* of a good life, yet as we have already addressed, it is the expression of man's authenticity which is virtuous."

Mr P: And it is this which I wish to pursue: the idea that virtue *is* happiness. For if we equate happiness to +1, and unhappiness to -1, then the decisions one makes will always create a greater sense of happiness: for oneself.

Using the example of the stolen item, although extrinsically it may not make someone happy to disclose of one's child, intrinsically, if it is the 'better' thing to do, it will create an effect of +1 within. For the child, this may be felt as -1 or +1, but either way, the child's reaction will compensate and adjust his or her inner equation.

So perhaps the question is, does one need a requirement for betterment for others in order to be happy? And if so, does one's ideal life *rely* on this need or is it compromised by the very reality one observes in the external as the needs of others draw one away from the needs of oneself?

TUES 16TH DEC 2014, LONDON AT 10.35AM, SESSION 81

PLATO: "We could take an example, of a young child, growing into a young adult, from a background of financial poverty and hardship – and perhaps encompassing emotional challenges too. The 'good life' may not be apparent visually and yet expressions of virtue may abound. The *assumption* would be in this case, of a young person who has a desire and wish for 'betterment' of himself and his community. And yet it strikes me that an acceptance of one's social standing is required in order for the humbleness virtuous acts need for an avenue of expression."

Mr P: Humbleness is a term of acknowledgement of one's entity, is it not? A thoroughly misunderstood word carried through centuries as a means of deprecation of the Self – and a word which creates the very *withholding* of creationism, I fear. Humbleness – to be humble – is not, as perceived, a sense of graciousness towards one's fellow human beings, but a sense of the grace which flows through all beings – human or not. It is an acknowledgement of one's place – one's rightful place, by the very nature of time and space – within the grace of 'what-is'. And therefore, yes, 'humbleness' if it is understood in this form is indeed a *requirement* of virtue. For to 'express' virtue, one must be *present* and *engaged* with the time and space which provides the *scene* for the show. For is not one's physical time-line a mere play of expressed energy?

PLATO: "And this *grace of 'what-is'* as you describe it, will encompass others as much as oneself. And therefore 'others' cannot be ignored within a wish for virtue."

Mr P: No, for 'others' exist within one's edge of reason – unconditionally. But one's edge of belief can only encompass the self – and there we have the conflict of man. It is not, I suggest, a conflict between man and the divine – for the divine is in all, *is all*. It is not a conflict between man and other men. It is a conflict *within*, between our 'reasoning' of man and our belief of one's divinity.

PLATO: "And for the man who has no belief in divinity?"

Mr P: I would suggest that there is no such man to walk the planet, who does not have a belief in divinity. For although divinity may mean very different things to many different people, a desire to *breathe*, to *experience* and to *create* is by nature consensus of participation within an energy of *something*. No single man can control or dictate his reality and therefore an acknowledgement of one's wish *for* something is an acknowledgement of forces greater than oneself which are *contributing* to the 'what-is'. It is not 'other men' who withhold one's ideal life but man's retribution between his edge of reason and edge of belief. And so mankind continues…

PLATO: "And virtue, as an expression of the divine, allows the retribution to soften, for 'movement' forward to betterment, and *therefore* an ideal life."

Mr P: And so, we always begin with the soul of man. For when man can feel his soul, he *knows* virtue, and he *knows* his truth. There is no conflict, just the discomfort as the energies held for so long begin to dissolve and fade, to allow a lightness to rise and transmute into joy. For joy is virtue in motion.

7

A DISCUSSION ON SELF-REALISATION

MON 22ND DEC 2014, LONDON AT 15.00PM, SESSION 82

Mr P: It is with great flourish we move to this part of the works. For *ambition* for an outcome creates great flow and diversity. And the desired outcome, aside from awareness, is a change of focus. For the focus creates the impact. And so, let's focus dear Plato, on not virtue, but the wondrous experience of self-realisation!

Perhaps my exuberance for this of topics underlines my belief, in its qualitative demonstrations of wonder, yes, but also resonance and fulfilment. It is when one is self-realising that synchronicities and sparks of Randomness abound. It can be tangibly measured if closely observed.

PLATO: "And yet, one does not always know when we are self-realising as opposed to 'creating'. For they are very different I would suggest. Self-realisation *originates* in the soul, does it not? Creationism is as a *result of* sparks and visions, but nonetheless powerful and intrinsically satisfying."

Mr P: Yes. I would agree that the difference, is one of origination yes, and also *expectation*.

When man desires and therefore creates, he or she creates both what is desired – and also what is not desired, if that is the focus. If we remind ourselves of the equation: Vision > the positive/negative alignment > the neutral acquisition > the attracting forces, when one is in 'negative' output and input through an *uncomfortable* frequency, one will attract exactly that. It is law. And often, the more one does not want it, or desire it, the more it comes, as the volume – or electromagnetic output – is increased.

So man *expects* different to what he is answering in response to 'cause and effect'. And when man is aligned in the 'pluses' he gets *more* than he expects. And so man is always responding, through a consideration of 'more' or 'less'. A tiresome yo-yoing.

By contrast, with self-realisation, the inner call is from a place of neutrality. In resting in the comfortable place between the minuses and the pluses, man finds his inner equality and balance. This is a most powerful place to be, for in this place of neutral alignment, wonder abounds. We could equate it to the eye of man's needle aligning with the soul.

When man remains aligned in his or her neutral 'zone', the soul is heard and received, and if given the space and tools to trade with, will seek realisation.

The tools I speak of are patience, virtue and energy.

PLATO: "Yet all is energy?"

Mr P: All is energy, yes, but beyond energy is the vision. The vision *drives* the direction of the energy. And so we have harmonious energy and dis-harmonious energy. When man is aligned, he automatically 'calls-in' attracting energy and if he holds his vision, his focus, and his intention, the flow of sparks carries one on a journey fit for kings.

PLATO: "And yet *expectation* will trip even a king…"

Mr P: Ah, but it is not expectation which conceals trickery, but expectation which tricks the conscience. The concealment in expectation is the inauthentic desire. When man is in neutral alignment, he can be nothing other than authentic in energy, and so there will never be expectation, but a good dose of healthy ambition and focus.

You see dear Plato, man does not often trust enough to apply effort, consistent focus, and energy to something without the lure of an expected outcome. The mind creates 'reasons' to substantiate 'belief' of cause and effect: *"If I do this, I will get that."* And yet when man is in neutral alignment, he just 'does' what feels good and virtuous and fun to do. He just does without reason or belief – for he *knows* and *en-joys*. The self-realisation is of himself and not of extrinsic energy turned into 'product'. *He* is the product.

TUES 23RD DEC 2014, LONDON AT 12.05PM, SESSION 83

PLATO: "I am not sure that the difference between expectation and ambition can be understood in a 'rational' way by the mind. For ambition is felt in one's bones, not in the flesh of man."

Mr P: And if only man understood the impact of such faith: to trust one's bones, one's depth. The flesh of the mind and the wounds of hurt so often cascade into prominence. But the bones – the givers of the very essence of wellbeing and the structure man *stands for* – are the illuminators of wellness. When one loves his or her bones, wellness pervades all action. Self-love is the greatest healer of a broken bone.

It is for this reason man endures the toll of the dentist: the visible bones of man. Ambition, a desire to learn and experience, and a faith in oneself enable the strongest of teeth. And yet man considers not this aspect of desire. For to seek virility and stamina is to enable 'progression', but woefully, not ambition.

PLATO: "I understand not your deference to man's desire for progression and creativity, yet your disdain for the same? Surely stamina and virility are the very components of an actively alert consciousness?"

Mr P: I distract myself perhaps with too much by way of 'measure'. But it seems to me that the methods man uses to measure his virility and stamina both create more requirement (for no reason other than to exude 'success') and less self-realisation.

Ambition – and I talk of the deep innate desire to be one's absolute best, for no reason other than it feels the most wholesome way to be – surely has to be of unequal importance in one's ability to be authentic. Yet ambition is not applauded; most likely refuted to aspects of conceit'ness and extravagance. And yet when observed in physical endeavour it is praised in others: the woman who can sail single handedly the deepest oceans of the world; the man who can climb the most challenging of mountains; the child who can survive the longest of days beneath rubble – these expressions of physical ambition, one recognises.

And yet, what of ambition of the soul, the heart and of the breath? The stamina and courage needed to ambitiously speak one's truth – be that to a single person, or an arena of faces – so often overlooked and discouraged; in oneself and others. *"Come with me, for I know the way."* And man follows. The ambition to find one's own way, in just the smallest of acts or movements, worthy of praise and reverence. *"What is your ambition"?* is a question not many can answer, dear friend.

PLATO: "And I sense a difference between 'an ambition' and 'being ambitious.' Is that so, in your eyes?"

Mr P: Perhaps not a difference, but a measure of belief. To express an ambition, is to believe in one's ability – one is aligned to the vision. 'Being ambitious' by contrast, is a perception of oneself or others through a lens, and in this awareness, the alignment is loosened. A question has been raised, and failure is now an option, a possible outcome. Expectation has entered the equation; and a sense of judgement, of observation. When one is aligned however, there is no observation, just the act of expressing in the moment one's connection with the vision. The commitment is palpable. This 'state of ambition' *is* self-realisation.

<u>WED 24ᵀᴴ DEC 2014, LONDON AT 17.00PM, SESSION 84</u>

PLATO: "Self-realisation, whilst powerful, can be challenging and demanding of one's courage. To know when to move forward and when to question is an art in itself. Would you agree?"

Mr P: I would so.

PLATO: "And the questions raised, at the junction of self-realisation and the 'logic' of the ego of man-in-the-physical, pertinent perhaps to not just one's destination – or ambition – but also to one's past. When man 'rests in the present' – within neutrality – he is in danger of stagnation and confusion I fear. So how best to *drive forwards* whilst containing one's presence?"

Mr P: A good observation my dear Plato of the confusion of desire. All desire.

It is oftentimes the ego which drives man, but the soul can too. And it is a question of which is in the driving seat of the vehicle. But…it is important to know *both* are required for forward movement: an interchangeable team of driver and navigator.

Man refutes the goodwill of ego. Ego has evolved with a 'bad' reputation. Now whilst there are many occurrences of unhealthy and unhelpful ego dominance, its gifts and strengths are usually overlooked. For it takes ego to climb a mountain, sail the seas or create a business. It cannot be done without; indeed 'life' cannot be *done* without the contribution of one's ego.

So at the junction of self-realisation of the soul or logic of the ego, a 'discussion' must take place. And the question is: who needs to take the wheel now, in order for us to move to our destination?

When the answer appears, if it is virtuous in nature, and aligned to one's vision, there will be no conflict – the one will move aside for the other, for it is the vision which carries the power. Maintenance of the vision is the required solution for the posed problem.

PLATO: "And how does one 'facilitate' such a discussion? For it is intrinsic in nature."

Mr P: By way of allowing the vision to be held, without 'need' for its execution. By this I mean...if one wishes to go to Timbuktu, one must set the course for Timbuktu – no point in heading for Alaska. And so the decision is: what do we need to do now to set off for Timbuktu? It may be that the soul 'takes charge' and *carries* the energy and nudges the vehicle forward, step-by-step. Or it may be for the ego to rise and display its strength and resolve, for the benefit of all aboard. And yet, in allowing the flexible agility of all passengers to contribute to the journey, no strain is felt. It is a fluid mergence of abilities and commitment. It is a state of allowing – by all parts of oneself – the forward movement of the vehicle. In holding the vision, the journey takes care of itself.

It is when the ego feels challenged or under the spotlight that 'detours' are made. Perhaps a swerve into a layby, a 'wrong-turn' or collision; and no passenger can be heard, no decision made. At such time, the soul must provide and resurrect the good fare.

Conversely, the soul can mislead when the journey loses direction. A happy soul can forget its role as it enjoys the view. And the self-realisation is relinquished in favour of temptation of the divine. For whilst 'a good soul' is a happy soul, a happy soul needs realisation to continue its evolvement.

A journey requires much by way of, not planning, but consideration. If one keeps in awareness the considerations of the moment – of what is needed by all parts of oneself for the benefit of the journey – a wonderful journey it will be. At times it may be challenging, at times scenic, at times perilous, or perhaps uplifting, but whatever the 'weather conditions', it is the conditions of the passenger which dictates the pleasure. And so this is the discussion to be had with oneself. Where are we heading? Where do we want to go? And how are we feeling? When all parts of oneself contribute to the considerations, all parts of oneself are 'communicating' in harmony, and decisions at the junctions of life become decisions *for* life.

FRI 26TH DEC 2014, LONDON AT 18.15PM, SESSION 85

PLATO: "Righteous belief in one's abilities though, a consideration for growth of the soul *and* the ego. And yet the balance between harmonious wellbeing and driven stamina for expansion and movement can be a fine line, visible in its extremities in society in general. Evolution of the cities and the sub-culture of new generations *creates* life but it beckons the life out of people too. And to this end result we observe oscillation between *wanting* things to be better and wanting things to be calmer."

Mr P: It is at this point re-addressing the flow of energy is pertinent. At the beginning of these works I briefly mentioned energy companies: the external reflection of man's inner energy. For where one collects energy, one distributes it in accordance with societal demands. And society demand, demands, demands.

Now whilst realisation of society does indeed require 'energy', it is the energy man 'takes' which hinders his ability to give. Yet it is in the *giving* man self-realises. So already we have a basic conflict.

Rarely does man decide on his location of homestead by the means of what he can give: does not search for a home in a location where he can 'better' the environment, create a more desirable place for *others* to live. More commonly man will seek a neighbourhood which will better his image of what he has, and which will elevate his image within his reflection. And so he 'takes' energy, and expels energy paralleling his inner source with his chosen external. He is operating within energy deficit, and so, conflict creates cascading effects on the younger generations who now live within a society of 'keeping pace'.

PLATO: "And yet self-realisation requires a vision; and a desire for betterment is powerful in its ability to create the very movement a growing, expanding society needs?"

Mr P: But betterment, being purely intrinsic in value is but a perception unless all members of the society feel the grasp within. For when the seed of growth is laid, the energy waters its flourish. In this instance, when all members are connected intrinsically to the betterment of society, the energy rises from within effortlessly and dynamically.

When man gravitates towards an environment (whether a neighbourhood, a corporation or a cause of any kind) with a desire or instinct to 'take', he sucks energy *from* the source or well, and redistributes it by way of 'keeping pace'. Society suffers from this kind of energy depletion.

Alternatively, when man approaches an environment or situation with *"What can I bring to the table, how can I make it better?"* he *brings* energy and fuels others. The flow creates the breeding ground the seeds of realisation of self and society thrive on.

And so, whilst the planet's energy sources are plundered and spent, mankind will feel its effects. The quicker the energy 'runs out,' the quicker man will wake up to his self-destruction and the reality of his actions. All is in the flow of energy.

PLATO: "And the alternative to this direction of waste of potential?"

Mr P: Appreciation of one's abilities and the power of giving. In the giving of oneself, man finds himself. It is not the seeking of betterment, but the giving of betterment which creates the energetic realisation of a global impact worthy of the deepest pools of oil and the vastest plains of soil. When man *gives* energy, he *creates* energy: a formula decreed by one man or a nation of men. It is the direction of the flow which affords the results.

PLATO: "And so the answer provides the solution, yet the solution requires the action."

Mr P: And perhaps the action requires not just the vision, but the *willingness* to partake, to stand by one's conviction, and to stand in sincerity.

SAT 27TH DEC 2014, LONDON AT 9.55AM, SESSION 86

PLATO: "And so, it is not without vanquor that man creates a better environment, but through the battle to be a better person perhaps that betterment is exuded. And yet man often resists betterment in favour of the known. Betterment is subjective, and hence disparity between citizens – or indeed deep parts of oneself too – creates a battle, not for evolvement, but for continuation of 'what-is'. How does an individual, or a society, understand true betterment?"

Mr P: The solution is not in the answer for society, but in the answer of each contributor to the society. When man responds from the soul, or from a virtuous place within, the answer will always allow for others too.

Each man, woman and child is contributing to society – whether they 'see' this or not. But when man's energy is of a 'taking' kind, there is instant conflict within. When man is grounded, considerate, truthful to his individual needs, and able to care for his family, he will always wish to 'give' outwards. The same applies to a child, whose energy flows outwards with abundance. And yet it is a journey to one's truth; and so we experience frustrations and obstacles along the way: the contrast which enables the very evolvement of the emotions needed to create desire. And yet, for man to see his truth, he must only look inwards, to what *feels* right.

The loudest advocate for change in society will be the one with the most to give – and the most to accept within. For those who know their truth and understand their role in society, their purpose, are already creating betterment. For the only improvement of note, is the improvement to the quality of one's existence – not the quantity of such.

PLATO: "And quality creates beauty I suggest."

Mr P: Again subjective and so we have inclusion of all of society. Yes, how wonderful when one *feels* the beauty of life. To strive, as a society, to each *feel beauty*, in whichever way pleases each soul would be a society worthy of its name.

FRI 2ND JAN 2015, LONDON AT 17.10PM, SESSION 87

PLATO: "And yet, the aspect of beauty I find so intriguing, is that in honouring one's perception of beauty, we automatically extend the honour outwards. The recipient can only but receive one's acknowledgement of beauty: even if it is unspoken, the energy and disposition towards the enquiry of beauty creates a feeling of thankful grace. As I honour my perception of beauty of this flower I observe, the flower receives the beauty. The 'image' is both subjective and objective in its expression: 'the flower is an object of beauty'. And so, there is little by way of *barrier* between the within and the without; the 'description' is both *mine* and the flowers."

With beauty, one is always *willing* to accept, but with deceit and ugliness, one is not so ready to acknowledge nor accept. And so, 'beauty' must in itself be of a different quality, of a different *dimension* to other states of observation and 'feeling.'"

Mr P: And it must be said, that although love cannot be 'judged' with the purity of beauty, joy can. But the difference between beauty and joy is that an object cannot 'hold' joy in its perception. Joy is purely intrinsic – it is a feeling state. Beauty is both a judgement, and a trigger for a deeper sense of *something*.

Society strives for beauty, but does little to recognise inner beauty; for to *feel* creates a contrast. When one has felt beauty, one also feels its absence; and this becomes uncomfortable. The boundaries between beauty which is imperceptible yet tangible and beauty which is overt yet, shall we say, shallow, are *loose* and therefore susceptible to not contrast but omission from the qualifying criteria for a 'better' society. Let me explain…

When a decision is made to seek improvement to one's immediate environment something is triggered within. A vision is created and focus is applied to *making it happen*. In wishing 'betterment' a *link* with what constitutes one's definition of beauty is triggered. To one, a new wall may create beauty, to another open wide space may reflect the vision. Neither is wrong and neither is right. But the difference is between beauty which is *visible* and beauty which is *felt*. For it is not, as commonly supposed, that outer beauty creates the inner state. It is indeed the reverse – in all occasions.

PLATO: "And yet if beauty is *held* in the object or person, then it by definition holds that title; if only by the observer. For if I call a pink rose beautiful, it will undoubtedly forever remain beautiful to me."

Mr P: It is true that if something is judged in an instance 'beautiful' it is likely to remain so in one's perception; yet as times change, so do one's perceptions of what constitutes a feeling of contentment or beauty. And so tomorrow, a red rose may be more beautiful.

The psyche is quick to label: to detect or defer. And in the detection, the person or object is put through a 'qualifying process' as its worth is 'scored' for relevance. It is a process all souls do, whether consciously or not.

The higher the *score,* the more relevant to one's experience. Again, most judge it the reverse. And this explains how a lack of self-worth creates a recognition of differing 'standards' to when one is in a position of higher self-love and compassion. It is when one experiences an increase in self-love that one *allows* the recognition of beauty into one's reality. This in turn creates a feeling state of beauty and wonder, and so the pattern flows. As one *feels* more beauty, one allows more beauty and society benefits.

Because beauty is intrinsic, and mirrored in the external, it can only be subjective: what is beautiful to you may not be beautiful to me; and what I cannot see in its beauty today, I may observe tomorrow. But what I do suggest, is that the inner trigger to what constitutes beauty in itself, is, as you say, of a higher order and 'separate' in its definition to any observation we can make. And this, my dear Plato, creates does it not, a sense of wonder?

SAT 3ᴿᴰ JAN 2015, LONDON AT 12.40PM, SESSION 88

PLATO: "Ah…the sense of wonder! The question and the exclamation of life. Which is 'greater' in capacity and definition? For beauty and wonder seem both interchangeable and yet uniquely individual. As with joy, wonder is felt intrinsically, yet we wonder *at* something or someone, and so it is also subjective in its observation of the object. It has, it would seem, the same resonance as beauty – and yet it raises questions. For beauty *is* beautiful. Wonder begs the question of how, why and for what divine purpose can such an occurrence happen, whether desirable or not? And yet the *sense of wonder* which pervades all existence is often 'over-looked' in its simplicity; the unrecognised seed of all fruit."

Mr P: It strikes as a great shame, does it not?

PLATO: "More than a shame, it strikes me with sadness. For it is the magic of life which creates the 'wonder' in itself – it is the life force which creates the questions *and* the answers. The unknown, driving one forward, giving the very reassurance in its stability of creating the exclamation of not just wonder but knowingness. In my wonder at the view of beauty I *know* beauty and yet I also know, reassuringly, I will never know how the beauty came to be. For what I cannot create, I cannot take away – and that is where the reassurance lies."

Mr P: This being, I would suggest, the very essence of creationism.

It raises the question, does it not, of why man feels compelled to create more stability in the external when he is surrounded by it in this moment. For one can observe beauty at any time should one wish: even darkness is *beautiful*. And yet this is not enough…man seeks more.

Creationism varies in origin, and in delivery. To *create* beauty one must be connected within, to *something* which gives birth to the seed. I suggest that man, through a desire to *connect* is addicted to the seed, to 'touching base' within. And so, it would deem that man is not seeking 'more' but seeking connection with his or her innate state of wonder. A view, Plato, that affords discussion, no?

PLATO: "Yes. And the discussion, perhaps not of *why* man wishes this link, but '*because of what?*' For the 'what', the *end result* or destination is what calls us forth."

THURS 8ᵀᴴ JAN 2015, LONDON AT 10.00AM, SESSION 89

Mr P: The *sense of wonder* we talk of, is perhaps a little 'deeper' than the wonder at how something can occur on the surface of it. By this I mean, one can wonder at how the blade of grass grows so strong – a *surface* questioning – or we can wonder at how grass came into existence: the order of the protrusion and the countenance of its offering.

Perhaps such observation of thought is unnecessary on a practical level, for to *stop and wonder* at all existence would create a rather full day! But the sense of this wonder can be retained in perpetuity if one chooses. And this not only affords great striving for mankind, but also great depth of peace. For to know that *things are taken care of* is…peaceful in the extreme.

PLATO: "To *strive* is perhaps at odds with the gentleness of inquisitive wonder? As all is 'taken care of', *striving* therefore must be born of fear? Perhaps the disparity therein belies a truth of man, that he values fear above all other?"

Mr P: It is true that fear has a hold on man – but not in the manner most commonly thought. Fear is, I sense, man's resistance to the sense of wonder. It is rooted in a wish to excel and to

206

align with one's inner source of wellness and *aliveness*. And yet it has 'bad press,' is renounced as an evil fuelling destruction. But Plato, I question man's relationship with fear.

All is of the scale: +1 or -1. One feels better, or one feels 'worse'. It is perceived that fear makes one feel worse – but not so. Fear, I suggest, presents a mirror – it makes the person decide which direction to move in, in order to feel *better*. The 'problem' is that man does not honour the movement; conditional behaviour 'gets in the way'. It is not fear itself which prevents movement, but the behaviour of expected attached outcomes. Fear in itself is a useful and highly 'designed' method of movement. Indeed, to be 'rooted to the spot' may be exactly the required stance in order to *feel better*. It is one of man's great tools, a natural instinct.

An 'instinct' is always towards +1. Always. And this is where the confusion lies. For mankind is perceived to have an instinct to self-destruct, to 'destroy' the world through actions rooted in fear and lack; through selfishness. And yet man is striving, he is – if we observe man non-judgementally – *trying to make his world a better place*. We may not like what he does in this action but we must respect his instinct.

The desires we instinctively have are the expressions of our sense of wonder – of wanting to understand more. An addict who instinctively reaches for cocaine in order to feel better is not moving out of fear, but moving towards what he or she perceives will make them feel better. The presence of the mirror of fear will have created the decided movement. The movement is 'pure' in itself. But when the direction or movement presents itself and the action is *not* taken, when the sense of wonder is not honoured, and when the 'opposite' or habitually known behaviours are chosen instead, then one experiences -1. When cocaine is chosen *despite* knowledge that +1 is 'over there', then it becomes a journey into -1.

PLATO: "And the minus one is, as you say, resistance to the sense of wonder."

Mr P: Yes. Fear is a wonderful barometer of movement, but not a destination in itself. One who feels fear is moving through life, is encountering new and renewed occurrences which require decision making: a signpost at a fork in the road. Sometimes we make a choice and find ourselves back at the signpost of fear. We choose again. And perhaps again. And when we one day make the *other* choice, we continue on our path…until we meet another signpost. And so it goes.

Now fear is just one of the guiding emotions and high-lighters of our soul's desires. Joy may be a decision maker, or excitement or, indeed, wonder. But none of the signposts in themselves *are* the path. And this is the misnomer with fear.

Resistance to moving towards one's true authenticity despite society's pulls, is what keeps one hanging around the signpost or mirror of fear. There is no 'forward' motion, merely a circling of the area one is in. But to accept the fear, and to recognise one of two paths, to -1 or +1, is to use a blessed tool for one's advantage.

Mankind is quick to disregard those who 'choose fear instead of the light'. How judgemental and belligerent of a most natural of human conditions: the inability to accept one's potential. To recognise someone trapped at the junction of fear and to 'walk away' without offering direction is to *journey alone*. For those who know themselves, know that all encounter the fear which belies the path to wonder, and that in recognising this journeying, one never walks alone.

FRI 9TH JAN 2015, LONDON AT 17.20PM, SESSION 90

PLATO: "And why, one supposes, is it so tempestuous to accept one's potential when surely the 'relief' is in doing so?"

Mr P: It is both understandable…and not; depending on the point of viewing.

Self-realisation of one's abilities to not only express oneself, but also love oneself, create movement in different 'directions' to of old. The movement both invigorates and 'disturbs' the status quo. There are infused energies and signposts of fear denoting new paths previously untrodden. The movement both 'electrifies' the equations and sub-structure of one's reality *and* makes one breathless and struck by what is being asked by way of forward movement.

For some, this 'behaviour' will entice and excite and all will become flowing with belief and enjoyment. For others, it will frighten and render devoid of energy – the transmission towards the object of desire will become fraught with insecurities as the energies are 'given away' and not harnessed to fruition.

PLATO: "And the characteristics to determine outcome?"

Mr P: Purely dependent upon the space/time variables. And this is why not all movement is 'equal'. For some, movement in a chosen direction will be +1, for others, -1. The *determining* factor: the relationship between one's reason and effect: "*Why am I doing this?*" It is a question so often unacknowledged, yet so, so powerful in comprehension; the solution in the answer.

Accepting one's potential is a very different affair if taken too soon, or too late. Perfect symmetry of time and space allows the effortless acceptance. There are those moments dear Plato, are there not, when everything just 'falls into place?' But man pushes himself, tries to make things happen *now*, in order to justify his potential, to create self-worth. But this is in fact the antithesis of worth; it is undesired outcome. For the desire will always be for flow and ease. It is man's rightful 'position'.

When one is in flow and ease, time and space moves around you. Like a revolving shelf from which one picks one's fruit of choice. "*Shall I have this, or shall I have that?*" The question provides not the answer but the very requirement for flow: choice. For there is always choice.

When man moves within a desire for self-worth, he seeks, yet finds a long road taking him further from himself. Yet when he rests, acknowledges his time/space placement and *observes*, he sees choice of reason or choice of effect. The self-worth is not in *what* he chooses, but the very choice. The contrast of the *alternatives* – all powerful within themselves – creates the worth of the Self. And this gives a taste of freedom, and powerfully, a taste of ambition. For the choice creates instant movement towards a better-feeling place.

PLATO: "This 'better-feeling place' is not, I am supposing, the same as *betterment*?"

Mr P: No, for one – the former – is intrinsic, and the latter, extrinsic in nature. *Betterment* involves one's ability to 'create'. A 'better feeling place' involves one's ability to feel with authenticity one's emotions and one's placement. And this is the key to a smooth ride to accepting one's potential. For when it 'feels good', the ease and flow enable the joy. And when there's joy, man needs not self-worth but the avenue to express this joy, for it is a wonderful thing…

MON 12ᵀᴴ JAN 2015, LONDON AT 9.00AM, SESSION 91

PLATO: "Tell me dear fellow, the meaning, for you in your time/space placement, of love in relation to self-worth. For as man seeks betterment through a *better feeling*, he seeks love, suggesting 'love' is the aim of desire?"

Mr P: Ambition is of course a love of *something*, so there is always an aim, yes. But in truth the equation of choice is a simple one: is the ambition intrinsic or extrinsic in fulfilment?

PLATO: "But surely all desire is intrinsic?"

Mr P: In the 'launch' of the desire, yes. Although it will always contain the 'colouration' of one's external as the contrast too. But where one wishes the effect to *land* is another matter.

Some desires and ambitions (for they differ somewhat) are intended to fall into the laps of others – for their intended benefit, or for their intended conscious or subconscious attachment. The aim is to create 'links' and *involvement* between two parties. *"If I do this, she will then <u>have</u> to…"* or *"If I allow him to do this act of help, I will need to…"* The 'result' is an extrinsic 'landing' of the action, affecting both parties' time/space placements.

On the other hand, some ambitions and desires are purely intrinsic – in launch and landing. They are self-motivated self-realisations.

Now both have feelings of desire and ambition; the intrinsic and extrinsic both need a *launch* but only the fully intrinsic in nature has self-worth and self-love at its core.

All ambitions relating to extrinsic offerings have within them a desire for the love of others. And so we have the *connection* which fuels humanity. And yet the kind and gentle soul who 'helps others' and feeds others before he feeds himself is a part of this connection in just the same way.

PLATO: "This raises questions in relation to virtue, but please continue."

Mr P: 'Desiring' the love of others is *seen* as 'un-desirable'; as vanity and insecurity. And yet I offer that this is a most basic of instincts, it is what man and woman was 'put on the planet' to do. And yet self-love must at all times be protected for without the love of the Self, one cannot love another. It's an impossibility of nature.

The 'problem' is not of needing the love of others, but of not having the love of oneself. It is the awareness of this lack within, and desire for others, which creates the inner turmoil and 'hell'. But when inner love, self-love, is attained it becomes the most natural 'reaction' to express love towards others, with the acknowledgement that 'love' is what is desired. For to be in a 'state of love', in its purity and non-attached freedom, is to be open to giving and open to receiving love in equal measures. It is the acknowledgement of the desire which creates the delivery of one's wishes.

And so the ambition becomes intrinsic; reflected in the external, but fully intrinsic. Man wishes to love, in order to receive love – but this is the crucial difference, Plato, the 'nugget' which eludes man: it matters not where the love comes from, for it is the 'love' one wishes, not the person. The person is the conduit for the energy of love. It flows…

WED 14TH JAN 2015, LONDON AT 8.50AM, SESSION 92

PLATO: "Changing one's focus to *loving oneself* above all else is not an easy thing to achieve when society considers such 'behaviour' as *un*virtuous. And for how long, how many millennia have men and women been struggling with this dichotomy of being? For the solution – when one feels self-love – surely a requisite for a wealth of knowledge to be passed to the generations which follow?"

Mr P: It would seem my dear friend that there are some things man is reluctant to share, for above all else he is a creature of vulnerability and assumption. The dichotomy – expressed as *either* love of self or love of others – is in whether he displays his vulnerability or assumes 'no-one cares'. This worth – to himself – the decision maker on whether to share or not.

Self-worth has to be realised (and this is the 'objective' of *reason* and being *reasoning creatures* I suggest) before the combination of self-love and love of others can be 'integrated'. Without self-worth, there is not the 'container' to hold the contents; it is all of a reductionist nature...

Cellular activity happens because of the power passing through the atmosphere of the physical body. In wishing to 'partake' in the exchange, cells are formed. It is in the cellular components that the *activity* happens, and it is within the exchange of forces that the merging of energies creates the birth and death of what is needed at each moment of time. The 'container' which holds the positive protons and negative electrons also holds the *potential* for further activity. Without the cellular aspect of nature, nature would not exist. Likewise, without the vessel of man, mankind would not exist.

The profound nature of man is not in the obvious components which a science book offers, but in the fundamental question of *"What creates a cell?"* What drives the birth of the smallest of containers which holds the potential of all-that-is? For the smallest cell in the smallest corner of one's consciousness has the potential of altering one's reality to such a degree that one begins to question not only the nature of one's existence but whether we have a place in it at all. And yet, no single cell can exist without another. An embryo needs the cell of the male and the cell of the female. A diseased cell needs the healthy cell to contrast against, the dying cell needs the birthing cell to create the space for transmutation. An idea needs the parts to enable the outcome. Life is a canvas, and yet it is the picture we cannot see.

Self-worth is the container which creates man's 'base' for the exchange of energies and life force. Love comes after – an ingredient added to the pot. But it is in the *exchange* of love that man finds meaning and in the expression of joy that pleasure abounds.

FRI 16TH JAN 2015, LONDON AT 9.30AM, SESSION 93

PLATO: "Consistency of movement creates a dynamism which aids connection – the more frequent and more congruent the action, the deeper the connection is forged. And yet with love, it seems not always the case. For not all 'temperatures' allow for action to be both consistent and *regular*. Often the action is launched and yet never arrives at its intended destination."

Mr P: Ah, but it always does land, Plato. For it is the intention which corresponds not with the desire, but a deeper wish. One can have a desire for expression or communication with someone or something, but a deeper intention may be 'running the show'. And it is always the intention which is in line with the soul which carries the greater force.

If I wish to communicate with you, but my soul's wish is that I not, 'obstacles' will appear in my reality. These obstacles are never the manifestation of *the other*, but of oneself. When a connection has been formed, the manifestations will always benefit both parties – for what affects one, affects the other. It is those who 'ride with the forces' who experience the most fruitful and charming journey.

So if I wish to express my love towards an individual, but my soul understands the impact such a conversation may have – for 'better' or 'worse', although there are no such states, but let's say for +1 or -1 which do exist as quantum movements – then the conversation will not 'happen'. It may be through the *other* being unavailable, not 'present' to hear or willing to acknowledge, or it may be the passing incident which pulls me from my task. And yet all of these possibilities are manifestations of my soul's intention. They are expressions of my soul energy.

The 'interaction' between the heart and soul is of great interest, no?

PLATO: "Indeed. And yet the heart feels more *comfortable* as a place of discovery and growth."

Mr P: Why yes. And this is because it is a 'visible' and beating part of man's ecology. It is the in-and-out route of desire. But the soul *carries* the heart, is the container which supports the addition and purification of love. For love can be a messy affair, can it not?

PLATO: "And yet its purity, as you describe it, is not questioned for love is accepted as *love*. Yet throughout this book of words you decipher a difference in meaning and component of love?"

Mr P: *Meaning* perhaps not, but component, I fear yes. And I use the word 'fear' as an acronym for analysis. Fear has been misunderstood by humanity and so its worth as a form of analysis overlooked. It is the **F**eeling **E**nergy of **A**ctive **R**esponse which in turn enables the forward movement – around and past the obstacles of resistance. Man sees fear as the boulder to be pushed through. How misleading!

My growing observations of the components of love are striking in me discord of what constitutes 'love'. Yes, I would agree there is a *base* energy of pure love but its name is often taken in vain and combined with expressions of fear and so the feeling energy of the active response no longer has its purity for within are the elements which constitute one's response – the cause from the effect of standing at the boulder.

PLATO: "And so love is launched from a place, or including energy of, a place of 'stuckness.'"

Mr P: Yes, a case of *"I'm over here, and I want to be there"* and so I will launch this form of expression so you 'come to me'. And all the time trapped behind the boulder interpreting the feeling energy as a wish for and from another. When in fact the pure essence of love is to open, share and move *towards*. And so 'love', I suggest, has components of inactivity which renders it 'messy' and uncomfortable. For when one is called into action in the name of love there is a purposefulness, a congruence and a lightness, is there not? This is the purity I speak of.

PLATO: "And yet man also seeks stillness and peace."

Mr P: My suggestion, dear friend, is that stillness can only be achieved *within* movement. For in allowing oneself to be carried upon the forces, one requires nothing but balance and alignment, for one's intention 'does the work'. It is when one is stuck and 'intending movement' discord is felt, and it is when one attains inner peace that one realises the movement happens not despite one's stillness, but because of it.

8

MR P REFLECTS: OBSERVING HISTORY AND THE MASTERY OF VISION

Mr P: We come to a different section of these works now, one in which the observation is not of the *functionability* of love, but of reflection of when love 'worked'. The times and moments in history when it can be said that not virtue, not pleasure, not the 'right action' but something else, all pervading and infused with a sense of all-that-is, permeated the atmosphere.

Observing history is useful. It is not a direction to *go in*, for all is of forward motion, but to stand in one's awareness with the gift of hindsight affords observation from the 'top of the mountain' so to speak. And although one must never wish to have 'done things differently', for that is the gravest and most soul destroying of energies, to take learnings is the work of mastery. But to integrate the learnings requires the letting go of such, so that the energies remain pure; otherwise discord strikes and the inner battle ensues. For within one's awareness are all the components needed for such action of spirit. The trick: to let go and let be. And this is man's challenge.

To observe history, one has to let it go from one's present; to allow it to become components of one's past. For a country as an individual. It is the reluctance to accept oneself and 'what-is' which prohibits such energetic release. When a nation accepts their part in the battles of war, they accept their ability and desire to move forward. The 'war' becomes a released aspect of what-now-is. And so all becomes possible. The healing and integration of the learnings creates a new status quo of energy and absolution.

Unless one accepts the responsibility for action and non-action of past, one cannot accept one's potential, for the past is the component of the present. Without the desire to explore one's potential, there is no desire to accept one's past. And within these two energy fields, is man...today.

A warring nation needs equal desire for growth, and desire for acceptance and recognition of one's history, in order to live in this moment in peace and prosperity. It is the nation which carries a sense of victimisation and aggrieved behaviour of expression which remains stuck and entrenched in *no-man's land* as it seeks neither forward growth nor responsibility for its part of the equation of what-was, but a helping hand towards safety within another's power. And this is not helpful, nor is it love.

The moments which created the greatest impact on mankind were, without exception, those of a solitary figure expressing an energy of acceptance and, not humility, but innate power of gentleness. And it is this quality of powerful gentleness which distinguishes love from need. For when there is no *need* to love, no attachments to be maintained, and no reason within one's external creating one's decisive actions, one can stand in one's true power. The safety comes from knowing one's place, not within the greater picture and canvas of life, but within one's own time-line. And so the expression of energy becomes infused with a gentleness of character, soul and heart as one's conflict exists not in actuality but in perpetuity. For in observing one's history, the learnings are integrated into all that becomes. It is in accepting oneself in completeness that all is released, and then, the gentleness and powerfulness that is one's innate character becomes the most natural of expressions. One becomes available for oneself, one's future and others. We become connected to love.

TUES 20ᵀᴴ JAN 2015, LONDON AT 11.15AM, SESSION 95

Mr P: Without the connection to love, life's twists and turns become rather all-consuming. The need to 'put things right' is played out in one's external as opposed to being in the state of love – *without need.*

It is very easy to observe the individual who resides in love, for there is a peacefulness about them; a calmness. And yet *something* grabs our attention – they have a spirit and fire in them which 'contradicts' in some ways, makes us enquire to ourselves, makes us take note. We sense their energetic output and find ourselves 'in a different zone' as we leave them. We take with us a sense of *something more*.

Time operates at a different frequency for residence in love. Because it has 'depth', of quantum formula, 'time' is *greater* in mass. It is why a child will most usually notice fuller and longer days to an aging elder. For his or her days are spent residing in love. Whilst for an elder, it is not so much love which arises but a contentment; a peacefulness. A child moves towards love – for it guarantees connection, it is subconscious – but for many elders, the move is towards peace with love as the 'standby'.

When an individual is operating through searching, through the need to achieve, time is 'skipped over'. The destination 'holds' the prize. Moments are not felt and self-love is compromised in favour of self-realisation of the ego. When this energetic striving is relinquished, a beautiful tumble into the present occurs, and oh what depth!

The moments which have provided the anchoring and swivel points for humanity have been the moments where man has operated from this tumble and depth. When it happens to such a degree that many 'take note' and connect to the *something else* being expressed, powerful change and awakening occurs. The collective exchanges of energy within the state of love literally 'lifts' humanity and so it is able to observe its past as history and feel the depth of space available for its innate self-realisation – of expression of love.

The scriptures refer to unconditional love as the destination of man's journey. Perhaps, I would suggest, it is not

unconditional love, but expressed love which creates the 'results' man seeks? It is one thing to reside in *unconditional* love
but another to express such energy. It is the individuals who
resided and *expressed* who have led humanity. The search for
one's meaning of unconditional has, I fear, distracted man
from the ability to *be* love. And with all equations of matter,
one cannot be what one is not expressing.

When one ponders one's history and personal reflections,
the question is not *"What could I have done?"* but *"What can
I give to this moment? What makes me who and what I am, and
what fuels my desire to live?"* I suggest that *this* is love, and this
is something every man and woman can express. And more-
over, it is the unique qualities and personal histories of each of
the planet's beings which 'creates' the unconditional diversity of
love. The wonder of man is that he *is* the unconditional nature
of love.

WED 21ST JAN 2015, LONDON AT 8.45AM, SESSION 96

Mr P: 'Rightful action' is a funny aspect of mankind's movement towards self-realisation. Pray, for what benefit? To *show
others their error*, or to create change in one's external?

The more others 'do as we ask', the more disconnected we
become from ourselves. It's as simple as that – underpinned by
science, and the 'cause' of the lack of love in society.

We can use the physical body as an example. When a
limb or muscle is isolated in attention, the 'infrastructure' of
the body compensates, and then rebels by disconnecting and

absorbing the tension. What happens in the body happens in the greater and wider reality of the external. And yet man overlooks this parable of the Self. Indeed he often treats his physical body as needing to prove 'rightful action': *to step up to the mark.*

When one expresses inclusion and understanding of all parts of one's physical body, the reflection occurs in the external – it is a law of nature: as within, so without. And yet with matters of mental capacity, this *softness* and desire for self-understanding is so quickly relinquished in place of the 'daily battle'. Softness and gentleness, adopted as a luxury as opposed to a comfortable state of being.

When one does tip into the state of love as a base state, excursions into rightful action and tension become stark in their nature of aggression and discord. The highlighted awareness is of unwanted energy and misplacement of focus. The sudden nature of such tension begs the question of: *"Where did that come from?"*

The answer is always: from within. What matters is not why the energetic output is needed, or what is being expressed in the exchange, but what lies underneath the tension. For all tension is holding lack of movement. As the desire to move grows, so will the tension. And as movement occurs, tension will release. It is the observation of what is driving the desire to move which offers the answers man seeks. These answers will never be found in one's external, and yet the whole paints the picture: one's physical being, the 'display' of one's complete Self.

Beneath all tension lies the softness of love. And within all love is a gentle powerfulness. It is connection to this most wondrous of energies which offers the healing and innate energies of divine expansion and peace. With this connection, 'rightful action' becomes no longer a desired response, nor a required outcome. For to love is to accept all parts of oneself and all parts of others, whatever the movement. The impact of softness is the strength of having acceptance of one's Self and therefore the need to exercise restraint is diffused into the ether. For to love oneself is to know oneself and to know oneself is to know that what shall be *will* be and that is our part in the play of life.

THURS 22ND JAN 2015, LONDON AT 9.00AM, SESSION 97

Mr P: Love. *To know one is to love one.* And yet the elusiveness leaves us wondering…for can we ever know anyone? And so if we can never know another, for what, love?

Randomness creates movements and action, via thought, in the spark. It is in the spark two souls collide and ignite. The encounter will always be *even* and balanced in nature, and yet, if one can never truly know the other, what are we seeing in our external? What is being reflected back to our edge of reason?

It is well understood that in falling in love with another, one falls in love with oneself, and yet I sense more: that in falling in love with another, one falls out of love with an aspect of relinquished Self. And that *this* is the enticement. Not what we gain, but what we release. In the distraction of the encounter, we do not notice what we no longer notice.

Man has evolved to a time of great distraction – indeed it is challenging to remain present and aware with such visual and mental stimulation – but it does not afford the release that falling in love does. It has become for many a case of accumulation and hence the distraction becomes the object. It is, I would suggest, the resulting tendency to overstimulated appetites… and there is much on offer to stimulate one's appetites, no?

But falling in love creates a vacuum that a substance cannot. Yes, cocaine or alcohol or exercise, or disconnection of any type will create a reprieve, but not a vacuum. And so, with such distractions as one would call 'addictive', the emotions and senses are heightened yet numbed (for there is always a contrasting balance) and energy is *accumulated*.

The vacuum created by two people 'connecting' and igniting is one of 'repelled forces'. As the encounter occurs, a shift happens within each party's subconscious energetic make-up. In seeing oneself reflected in the other, an inner link occurs – as if a piece of one's inner puzzle is found and carefully put in place. This *satisfying* of one's 'being' creates a comfort and sense of belonging – of *completeness* – and so the space is created. The energies of 'seeking', satisfied and 'bounced back' to self. It is in this connection with 'an-other' that one falls in love. This I suggest, may never be found in a bottle, an increased pay-cheque or in any appetite other than love.

Self-worth and self-love create the foundation for being able to fall in love with purity and awareness – yet without the ignition of a spark with another; a vacuum is not created. It is, I suggest, *the vacuum* one 'falls in' to. And so we understand that we reside in love.

Falling in to love is the 'pull' of life. It is wondrous, awakening, enlivening and awe-striking in its complexity and innate simplicity. And yet man will 'reserve' himself to conditional moments of allowing. Falling in to love can happen at any moment, to any degree, if one is open to it and its possibilities. Falling in to mutual love with a friend, a companion, a neighbour are all possibilities of expansion and awareness and yet it happens so rarely – for it requires both parties to acknowledge the exchange, the spark. But when it does, the effects contrast so beautifully within one's reason. And this is the divine nature of the exchange, for such connections are made on the borders of belief and reason, in the neutral territory which honours the space: the vacuum.

It is always within the 'space' that the vibrancy and *heartbeat* of life resides. It is *within* love that love is found. And it is within one's own love that we reach and extend to love another. And so, perhaps we can never truly know another, but we can know the love that another knows, and to know love is to know…love, for this is the breath and heart-beat of life.

FRI 23ʳᵈ JAN 2015, LONDON AT 8.45AM, SESSION 98

Mr P: A mother's love is different, for the vacuum is created not by the encounter with one's child, but as a result of an encounter with another. And for this, the reflection is both intrinsic and extrinsic. Her child is 'of' her yet also not 'hers'. She knows the creation before her is for the benefit of others, that her part in the birth of life has been facilitated by another…and yet no-one will know her child as she does.

The energetic link between a mother and her children is one which supports all of existence. For the very understanding that life be created for the benefit of others, with the complicit involvement of others, yet with a love so deep it can move the mountains and stars in their placements between heaven and earth is the understanding mankind operates within.

Rather than involve another in her reasoning to bear children she will involve her femininity and her prowess as a giver of life, and it is in honour of this medal of worth a child is born. A woman, in bearing her child, is honouring the female race before the reasoning for such child within her encounter. Her belief, her inner belief, is of a deep commitment to her sexuality and placement within society. She is a partaker of her commitment.

And yet, what of those who chose not to bear, who relinquish the honour to her sisters? Ah, and as such, where the partaking in her femininity?

A woman's 'role' in life, I would suggest, is not to wonder at her role as mother, but to embrace her role as giver of love. For all *acts of creation* give rise to the birth of imagination and energy. 'Femininity' is the movement and expression of an energy intrinsic to planet Earth. It resides in everything and is *sparked* by male energy – in whatever its form of Randomness.

The belief that one must *bear children* in order to experience and delve into the feminine is interesting, yet I propose 'unnecessary'.

The forces of nature will always ensure consistent and balanced continuation of the sexes and 'life'. As such it is a divine task. It is not mankind's role to shoulder the burden of ensuring continuation of life, but instead to enjoy the blessing of life. In the *effort* given to ensuring one's placement and continued ancestral 'obligations', one's placement and reasoning for why such *bringing to life* is desirable become overlooked.

When man lets go of the *need* to reproduce he will discover why such desire was sparked in the first instance. For the wish to 'live' bears little resemblance to how many choose to exercise this gift. And men, as the 'complement' to a woman's sexuality have such wondrous opportunity of discovery!

To be a man within a world of female energy is to be the receiver of both a blueprint for expansion and a comfort of the womb. For a woman is unconditional in her acceptance of her man, as she is with her sisters and her children. Yet she will not suffer a fool, and this perhaps is where humanity has reached. For in taking her for a fool, she will turn away – it is a natural response, one of survival. Her solace? To express her femininity via her children; to continue 'by herself'.

It is when male and female energies – in whatever form they may present – work 'together' and honour each other in mutual desire for growth, fluctuance and wonder, that peace is attained. But peace in itself is not enough, for one is capable of so much more! What benefit peace without joyful expression, without a journey of discovery, and without the simple complexities of the entanglement of love and passion combined?

MON 26TH JAN 2015, LONDON AT 8.45AM, SESSION 99

Mr P: It is the combination of love *and* passion which enables a different aspect to one's vision, for through the eyes of the soul one observes the soul of another. And it is passion which both creates soul energy and is the recipient of the reflection.

Now to 'link' passion and the soul, indeed passion *for* another no less, may seem at odds with one's *impression* of the soul. *"The heart is the birthplace of passion"* you may think. But I propose not. The heart is the heartbeat of life, it is the 'balance' of flow, the thermostat through which input and output exchange. It is always moving and always responding and driving forth. It is 'busy' in itself and whilst capable of immense growth, expansion and capacity for flow of love, it is not the source of passion.

Passion arises out of stillness. Each person's passion is unique to them, unique to the soul where their being'ness resides. Passion is ignited by *life* and one's encounters – or absence of them – and yet it is never reactionary, never 'in response', always *pure* in intention. It is the soul expressing itself in the physical world of planet Earth.

And the passion aroused between two people? Of the same; individual to each and yet in combination the 'explosion' creates a magnitude in quantum calculation. For the combined offering at encounter is supported by the mathematical substructure of exchanges. In the all-powerful moment when two people's passion comes together, it is 'more' than just the sum of the parts. For both stand in their truth and the souls speak.

The passion I speak of is, as I mention, of the soul. The doctrines reside in agreement to defence of one's stillness, to turn *from* passion, to instigate energies of reason and *otherworldliness*, to reside in the sense of 'Godliness' of humility and disallowance of the pleasures of the physical. And yet, I propose, such creates in one a suppression of the soul. For man must find his own way to inner stillness, and whilst for one, peace is in the reverence of 'what-is', for another the path leads through exploration of oneself in a manner not undertaken by all.

A passion of any type is, I suggest, the soul expressing its direction and its need for clarity; a breaking of the chains of others. It casts not stones, nor kills in the name of truth, yet it will always display its colouration in one's energies and virtues.

To deny one this most basic of 'human rights' is to 'kill' another. Nature provides that there will always be a complement to one's journey; there will always be another to assist on the path. It is not therefore the role of the peaceful to 'dictate' the methods of peace but to support seekers of peace on their individual paths, to *encourage* the expression of passion and to assist all in 'understanding' the messages of the soul. For letting go *into* one's passion is perhaps the hardest encounter man will have. It is the avoidance of this truth which enables and fuels man's disparage of what he uptakes not. The denial is the doorway through which answers lie and passion, I suggest, one's natural energy and friend. In the exploration of one's passion, lies the exploration of one's soul.

TUES 27TH JAN 2015, LONDON AT 10.00AM, SESSION 100

Mr P: To watch those embroiled in the energies of passion is to observe magic unfolding. The haste to absorb disallows the intention, yet creates the effect. Both the edge of reason and effect stimulated into action. The particles, atmospherically resonating in frequency, *attract* correspondingly high vibrations and so, the observation is creating ever deepening energies. As one observes a passionate 'exchange' one can only feel of the same – even if it is then, latterly, 'suppressed'. A raised frequency will always raise the frequencies of others.

And so, when the atmosphere becomes 'charged' with intention, the *result* will indeed occur. The question is, what is the intention behind and fuelling the passion? For if the soul speaks, it has a voice. The message of the soul will fuel the passion, and the passion gives voice to the soul. The greater the passion, the greater the message to be heard.

A passion 'for' something, such as art, poetry, human kindness, is of importance, yet not as powerful as the passion sparked simultaneously between two souls. A passion *for* something, once found, will be life-long; it never goes away. But a passion created by two people – purely for the sake and benefit of the passion itself – will dumbfound all senses. It will carry on streams of gold and harness one's virtues in abundance. It will rock reality and shape one's future. And yet, in itself it is what, other than energy?

It is when one enters the embrace of passion with the inquisitiveness that tells of its provenance that the wonder exudes. For when one knows it is not the other, but the contrast and combination of the two which pours forth the charged energies, one resides in the freedom of the moment. For as with all things – all things of reason and wonder – the solution lies in the question. The inquisitiveness of the passion supplies the energy of the soul. And this, is a beautiful sight to uphold. Just beautiful.

WED 28TH JAN 2015, LONDON AT 10.00AM, SESSION 101

Mr P: Randomness results in connection. It is the means to enable the links, movement and exchanges. It 'glues' the world together, *is* the form which manifests as matter. And it is driven by desire and passion. In truth, no more need be said for this is *it*.

And yet, men and women 'interact' in this world in large part oblivious and de-sensitised to its wonder. For when one *steps into* the energies of desire and passion, a world unbeknownst opens before. Its depth and beauty, mere peripheries to what is contained within. And this is man's gift, his and her 'omen' of love.

Falling in to love requires great courage. For the ego is in jeopardy and the soul 'gaining ground'. Now I speak not of the illusion of falling in love 'with' another, or 'lust' and exchanges of the superfluous kind. No. I refer in this dialogue to the awakening of love within, triggered by, but not dependent upon another. The love that exudes and provides, attracts and emphasizes. The love that surrounds and yet…eludes. *This* is awakening, and this is the essence of life. The rest…mere formalities perhaps?

Love of such intrinsic nature can be awakened indirectly and without warning, but when it involves the passion of another, it involves the forces which provide for life. It *is* life.

There is not a person on planet Earth who has not, or will not experience such emotion of the soul. It may involve another, it may not. But it will always, however brief, awaken within. The degree to which we allow such emergence will vary, and for this, the divine provides. For what one cannot experience in another, one can experience within all-that-is. For all-that-is, is love.

THURS 29TH JAN 2015, LONDON AT 13.30PM, SESSION 102

Mr P: Now I am very much aware that my 'tune' on the subject of love has altered over these works – and yet it remains a mystery to me. And that is how I would wish it. For to always wonder, to always become entranced at the magnificence of what arises and appears in one's reality is just how we would want it, no?

And yet we search. We search for more, for understanding, when in truth we have the answers. For 'the answers' can only be what we experience right now. To be *satisfied* with what we have whilst open to 'more'. And with this outlook, one can never be without, can we?

Falling in to love with the moment – finding the love in the moment – is a skill, yes, but also a natural instinct *underneath* the cloud and clutter of the mind; one's reality clouded by uncertainty as opposed to the fertile ground of being'ness.

And so, I question not what *is* love, but why man continues to search for it in others when it is always to be found within? To reflect the *reason* of love is skilful. To attach to the provider of reason…not. And this 'entering the exchange' with reason is perhaps the opening question I have not asked: *"Why does man wish to love?"*

Historical hindsight offers clues. Plenty, and yet regretfully no answers. The likelihood of a war being fought 'for love', whilst promising in its offering, does not satisfy the cruelty and despair one will inflict in such circumstances. We cannot say that we killed for love, can we?

We could consider honour…the love of one's heritage and evolvement; the wish to defend this. But if the honour is for one's past, one's inheritance, can we call this love? It seems not.

Which suggests that perhaps provision be the driving force for expressions of love: to provide for one's 'loved ones' by taking or defending property and possession. But in such circumstances, can we truly say that to deny another for the benefit of one's own and oneself is born of love?

And so, history teaches us little. Yes, we have observed great acts and displays of love, and have all experienced the everyday gift of being the beneficiary of an act born of love, and yet...and yet it seems we cannot learn from such experience. Man still needs to create contrast, to 'shake things up', to play the role of the defender *and* the aggressor. And this is what fascinates me.

There are words, very wise words, to say that this is all perfect, that what works for one, need not work for another, that what I enjoy, you do not need to, for you enjoy your own pleasures. And this is accepted and understood. Yet, I ask, "Why the need to distil one's power of love to 'fit in' to a world which allows not one way but many ways? Why create '*reasons*' for being, when one can just be?"

The act of reasoning has not solved man's problems. For not all men reason the same meaning. And so, the *reason* for reason necessitates inquiry, no? For if my reason only works for my benefit, dare I offer my reason to another? Dare I share?

FRI 30TH JAN 2015, LONDON AT 11.45AM, SESSION 103

Mr P: To share one's reason is to share one's vulnerabilities if the reason differs from those of others. When our meaning aligns with the meaning of those closest and most impactfully present in one's life, we experience comfort and resonance. But times come, when what resonates within is in conflict with the reasoning of those whose attention we value, and so we have a choice: to adopt a silence, or to express our reason and risk abandonment and exile.

I refer to the latter as a risk, for in truth our expression will, if authentic, most probably inspire. And yet we dare not share, through fear.

With fear as the feeling emotion of the active response, expressing one's truth must therefore be of an emotional nature – not of the soul. A thought-process has entered the mix. For passion, by contrast, overrides fear – is not held back. The soul, in expressing its emotion is heard. But with reason, there exists no passion. It is of a wholly different energy. It *lacks* the spark of creativity, does it not?

I suggest that whilst passion can feel no fear, reason is ruled by fear. Not merely the fear of what will happen if I express my reason, but more paralysing: *"What will happen if I don't express my reason?" "Will I 'exist' and hold my place in society?" "Will I, without my reasoning and meaning, ever 'have' a place in society?"* And so, man is ruled by reason and as such, by fear.

To love is to operate 'outside' of the confines of reason. And yet society is of a reason-making infrastructure. The laws, the dioceses, the roads of communication and elevation: all founded upon reason.

So for man to *operate* and flourish in society, he finds his reason, and searches for his love. But what of the man who discovers his innate love, his joy in living and purpose of expression? For he is surely in possession of his worth and his abundance? Where do we honour *this* man?

The search for inner peace is often viewed as a 'stumbling across' process: 'by *default*, man finds his purpose and his contentment.' But perhaps this is not so, perhaps it was always there…hidden in the undergrowth.

The creativity of man, of *creationism* in itself, would therefore suggest one's answers are found in the creativity of expression: the man who 'finds his purpose' has found his soul. And so, where does reason contribute to this discovery? For one must operate and choose *against all reason* in order to walk such a path. Never will one find an example otherwise.

If creativity creates an effect, meaning enables a reason. As such: if a painter creates a painting, the painting creates the painter. But does one need to *be* a painter in order to paint? At what point does the suggestion of one 'being a painter' kill the very creativity which created the painting? And if one 'paints', is it for effect or for reason? And where in such expression is found love?

MON 2ND FEB 2015, LONDON AT 12.20PM, SESSION 104

Mr P: The conundrum of reason and effect is the same as day and night, the embryo or the mother, the stillness amongst the movement. And this is just it: amongst.

It is not as it would appear: one 'or' the other; that one leads 'into' another – but that each exists *within* the other. The day rests in the night as the night rests in the day. They exist *at the same time*. As such with effect and reason: the reason exists within the effect, and the effect within the reason.

The suggestion that man is a meaning-making persona is true…in that reason must be 'present' in order for man to *ground* and *exist*, but equally (and no more than of equal share) he must experience effect for the reason to have shape…form. The 'effect' can only be of an energy without form, for the inspiration which allowed the creativity is what created the painting. The inspiration the formless; the finished canvas, the form.

And yet, before the painting has landed on the canvas, it 'exists', does it not? The idea and the parts: colours, textures, hues, strokes – all 'present' before the *coming together* on the blank screed.

The 'inspiration' and the unformed parts of the creation *require* the form to come forth into existence. Without the canvas, 'it' cannot exist – and this is the duality of creationism. The maker maketh the storm.

The disparity between reason and effect is the 'hole' man finds himself in. And yet it exists not. It is perhaps at dawn and dusk when man appreciates both the night and the day but he enters the world of 'split' existence if he *believes* one is present before another. In daylight hours, man resides in the darkness of night and in the midnight hues, daylight also shines.

The *alignment* of one's light *and* dark is what creates the 'wholeness' man seeks. He does not have to choose, to prefer, to have distaste for day, or preference for night. He just has to accept the totality of existence – which is that the very contrast he creates, creates *him*, and yet exists not. And this is both the question, and the answer.

TUES 3ᴿᴰ FEB 2015, LONDON AT 11.40AM, SESSION 105

Mr P: Wondering *how* we might create more peace, more acceptance of our darkness and our light is, dare I say it… pointless. The question of 'how' is neither philosophical nor helpful. It merely creates more division.

The question one should ask: *"Why does this bother me so?"* And therein lies the answer: that 'I' am bothered. 'It' involves no-one else and therefore requires no-one else. 'I' can be bothered to rest and observe, or *bothered* to take action, but either way, 'I' am solving my own problem – creating, if I wish, my own peace.

The question posed of *"Why* does this bother me so?" also involves a further probing – of not just my edge of reason and why in my external reality I am concerned, but crucially, of my edge of belief: my *inner* reality. And in doing so, I *bring together* my light and dark – my contrast. I become *available* – to myself, or to others. I have choice.

Now one may read these words and observe: *"That's all very well, but what about the wars man rages, the destruction to our planet, the evil 'out there?"* And I would answer: *"Why does this bother me so?"* And within one's answer, all is told. But it is another thing, another reality, to *take action* and to offer +1's into the world. It is a man or woman who has aligned his or her edge of reason and edge of belief who 'takes action'. *All* other observation, if triggered by disharmony, is a lack of alignment of oneself.

Many are in wonderful alignment, with a deep compassion for man's suffering, and yet within their alignment they seek no need to 'change' what is happening, or to offer disdain. For such an energy would enhance the despair, create no solution, and destroy their alignment. And yet they affect the whole. For in holding the vision of peace and sitting within love, they in fact are the most powerful proponents of peace: world peace.

Holding a vision, whilst residing in the neutral territory of alignment within the +1's and -1's, between reason and belief, is the most powerful, most healing of states. It *is* the state of love…and joy…and ease. And yet man does not, on the whole, trust this 'place'.

In resorting to the dialogue of *"What can we do? Why does this happen? They should know better!"* one resides in -1. There is no actual attempt to raise the vibration and reduce suffering, just a greater distance created between 'them and us', when indeed that division exist only *within.*

In order to 'heal the planet' (and indeed there is no such requirement although greater compassion towards one's planet would serve all) man must reside in love. And to reside in love requires man to ask the question: *"Why does this bother me so?"* and when he realises it does not in fact 'bother' him, he has found some peace. Long may he share it.

WED 4TH FEB 2015, LONDON AT 8.50AM, SESSION 106

Mr P: Timelessness is a source of ease. Those moments when we drop into just being – when there is no *thought* in itself, when we have become one with the thought.

It is commonly considered that for man to 'quieten the mind' and lose the distractions he must *empty* the mind. This is not so. What is to occur, is a *melting into* one's thought, becoming one with and within one's mental process and flow. It is a stillness which enables this. And in truth, when the mental aspect of Self stills, one 'fills' – the reverse of what is considered. In stillness, a completion is attained as the alignment between the bodies occurs. It is this place of neutrality – of emptiness and timelessness – which enables the integration of one's reason and belief. It is the border of chaos and flow, and it is filled with not just love, but wonder.

At the borders of reason and belief, an effect is felt. Indeed, an effect is always felt, whatever one's 'circumstances', but the effect I talk of here is one of transcendence. The peacefulness and wonder create both the desire for movement, and the contentment with 'what-is'. One ponders the greatest of questions, but understands no movement is 'required'; and in that very understanding, movement has occurred. In being one with one's thoughts, the thought *moves*. It is a 'live' process of being: *"Am I thinking this, or is the thought carrying me?"* But this is just an awareness, for as I say, there is no 'thought' when one *is* the thought. It is an alignment of supreme quality which carries a resonance of cut crystal in the glow of a multitude of stars.

Man searches for these moments of transcendence, for he knows them well. It is in such moments when he connects with his soul and knows all his questions and all his answers. The 'emptiness' is full to the brim and so no *need* exists. All is perfect, and all is understood to be as it is. The creation has created, and in such creation, man has his answer.

The ability to merge with one's thoughts involves a single process: that of letting go. For it is the counterbalance of creationism. It is the out-breath so a new breath can occur. It is the Achilles heel of man, for the greed is not in wanting more, but in not being able to let go of what one has. And this is what causes war and famine and suffering. Man is not searching for love within war, but refusing to let go. Yet in the letting go, he will transcend his pain and enable the balance to be sought within. For the seeking is of the transcendence of one's emotions to that of a balanced emotional being: one that can create *and* let loose. This is flow, and this is man's journey. And the path? The edge of reason and belief; in the neutrality and the distance between what one *sees* and what one *believes*. For when the two meet in splendour, the integration has begun.

THURS 5TH FEB 2015, LONDON AT 8.50AM, SESSION 107

Mr P: Reasoning as to what constitutes credible effect is perhaps where man 'loses' himself. For in the act of reasoning, 'advice' and contingents of others are brought into the mix. And so a purity of awareness is lost as one's sensation is diluted to include the beliefs of others too. And yet man must reason if he is to make decisions and choose movement in life.

When man chooses to reason not for choice, but to *judge* the value of something, is when the dilution occurs. For in one's worth belongs one's belief. The very act of 'judging', of rating and discerning, affects one's sense of worth. For our edge of reason reflects one's edge of belief. In *lowering* expectation of others, of society, of the 'infrastructure' of humanity, one lowers one's internal worth. Yes, of course the ego will rear to provide ever more fuel to the cause, but independent to such 'small talk', a deeper, more systemic lowering of one's inner value has occurred. Imperceptible, yet tangible to one's soul – and reflected in one's cellular make-up. For how could a self-beating not affect one's inner circulatory and bruising? It is not just the ego which bruises easily, is it?

And so the balance between walking through reason and belief? In allowing the true effect of one's energies to be re-alised and felt. It would surprise if man knew how little he allows himself to feel and to experience his or her true emotions. You are like walking parcels – so tightly constrained and withheld!

It is the fear of losing control which creates such stiffness and restraint – and all because man resists letting go. In the accumulation of energies a compound effect is created, and to hold such accumulation in place, forces and 'strapping' are required. Man literally binds himself together. Yet *underneath* such bonds lies one's answers, one's freedom.

Letting go is not to be feared or approached within com-promise. It is within trust that movement occurs in such direc-tion, for to allow release – a loosening of one's bonds – one must trust that all is well. With trust the bonds untie them-selves, but to experience trust, one must endorse the effect.

Trust does not involve reason, but it relies on belief. And the counterbalance to this belief is the *effect* that is felt when one is in a state of trust. This effect cannot be judged, reasoned nor retaliated with. It is just…trust.

The first step in allowing the release of the bonds which tie, is to allow oneself to *feel*. Nothing more. Just to feel the effects of what presents. This is letting go. And it is that simple.

When man permits himself to fully feel the effect of himself he will find himself. And this is the journey we undertake together, for when one lets go, we all let go: "A*s above, so below.*"

FRI 6TH FEB 2015, LONDON AT 11.30AM, SESSION 108

Mr P: *Letting go* is not for the faint-hearted and yet it requires a 'loosening' of the heart, a softening. It is often in such moments, when man experiences a situation or exchange which *pulls at one's heart-strings*, that one releases and relinquishes control: we *give in*. And this is what I mean by a softening; in the pause, we let go and allow what is, to *be* – and breathe.

In permitting a child an allowance of note – a 'relaxing' of one's admonishment perhaps, or a smile within an argument – the softening is not of the child, the situation, nor the energy, but 'within' oneself. As a result, of course all of these change in effect, for the links *react* – but it is always from within.

An example, of a row with one's partner – my, how the distance and restraint can be held! And yet it is always in the softening of the heart that reconciliation is made.

And so how can it be, if the heart is but a thermometer of pulsing energies, of inwards and outward flow, that its *density* affects one's environment so? And for this, the answer lies in the letting go.

Energies are 'stored' in the heart – indeed within the whole physical body. But particularly within the heart. Each breath in, an absorption; each breath out, a letting go, a release. Man's last breath will always be a release. And yet such release is feared, avoided.

It is the fear of death which creates the accumulation of energies in the heart. And so, each out breath is a little letting go of life, of oneself. In moments of panic and fear, man involuntarily 'stops breathing', he *holds on*, and this is why he resists forward movement. The flow of energy: trapped within the heart.

But what if man understood there *is* no 'death', no *end* in sight. One just has to observe one's planet, the universe, the generations that both passed before and present before to know that 'life' continues. The 'hold' man feels within, and within his heart, is the *hold* he has on life: to remain stuck here in *this* life. And yet each moment is just a signpost, a choice.

As man learns to let go, wonderful things occur: a softening; space to allow in 'new' life; a release of pressure; an untying of the bonds which bind. In this creative space of *living*, man heals. For it is not 'God' who takes, or disease or disaster which inflicts, but man himself who slowly takes his last breath; for in restricting himself, he restricts his life.

Now I talk here not of *length* of life – for there is no such thing in 'real' terms – but *quality* of life. For how can we count the days spent 'in decline' as life? It is many a man or woman who has lived a plenitude of 'years' but very few days, and it is the measure of how willing we are to let go and experience our emotions which denotes how 'long' a person lives. Many a child has lived a longer, deeper life than a grandparent, and in such example one finds the solution of not wellness, but greatness. For the greater the life, the greater the wellbeing.

MON 9TH FEB 2015, LONDON AT 8.30AM, SESSION 109

Mr P: Today's tomorrow is what catches man out. Literally. For the desire to 'know' what tomorrow brings trips him up. And in *deciding* how he wishes it to be, he keeps himself both small and unavailable. It is he who opens and offers himself to *whatever presents* who is available for others. In one's desire to 'know', the truth is not permitted into play. For truth exists 'outside' of one's ability to see. One 'sees' or one 'knows'. Neither possible simultaneously. Ironic for a philosopher, no?

It is the 'desire to know' versus *knowing* which differentiates truth from narrowness. One 'sees' a future, the other, oneself, but one does not *know* at such times. For seeing incorporates potential and possibility. Knowing is the now, the snapshot of one's truth; as it is in that moment. It can be neither right, nor wrong. It is non-judgemental, it is 'what-is'.

247

But desiring to know is neither knowing, nor seeing. Its origination is in insecurity and doubt. A need to feel more comfortable than one currently does. The 'now', in its instability, a request to feel more security, more stability. And yet, how can one feel more stable than right here, right now?

The desire to know is what prevents men and women to let go. The further one wishes to see into the future, the more one hangs on to one's past. It is the counterbalance. But as one begins to appreciate *this* day, this moment, and crucially, not need to know about tomorrow, the easier and more effortless it is to let go.

Your society does little to encourage letting go. Quite the reverse! In planning one's 'retirement', one's 'old age', one's decline, the accumulation enhances the fear. It may not be the physical accumulation one experiences, but the emotional, energetic one: the fear, the strangulation of potential and possibility. As one's vision declines, so does one's spontaneous responses and creationism. *Life declines.*

There is much confusion between having vision or intention and a desire to know and have. It is those who master the former who 'succeed' in life. And by succeed I refer to the original meaning of 'gaining energy and outcome', not of 'accumulating objects'.

'Success' is attained as a result of vision and intention. And how to execute without a need to know? The answer: in letting go of the need to attain. For when one is connected within, to one's energy and the execution and flow of energy, success is known: for it is direct expression of one's potential in its purest form. In being in the now, with no expectation, one *is* one's pure potential. There is no doubt, for one knows one is at one's best. It is, shall we say, win/win.

The knowledge that one is truly present, available and executing energy to one's potential creates enormous freedom, and by default, involuntary creativity and letting go. The flow is so fluid, so clean and unencumbered that manifestation of one's intention creates greater vision and greater intention. Without trying, life moves swiftly – but with a connection to 'what-is' which gives its very own stability and meaning. This meaning, this reflection of one's edge of belief within one's edge of reason, evidence of being beautifully in alignment with one's inner and outer realities, yes, but also with one's understanding of such reality. It is in understanding this understanding that truth shows the way and calls forth to greater success. This is not *decline*, it is not a need to know, nor is it fearsome in any way. The signpost eagerly awaited, as each moment presents not decisions, but choices. And this is a very different energy. Very.

TUES 10TH FEB 2015, LONDON AT 9.15AM, SESSION 110

Mr P: Randomness allows one to step back from life a little, to take a pause. At times this is needed: a recuperation of one's energetic being. We still 'operate' and respond to 'what-is', but in observing, in handing over one's power to Randomness, we can 'check-out' whilst still *being*. For in observing the random connections – from a distance, rather than being *in* them – one knows that all is good, taken care of. It is a form of presence which is overlooked and unappreciated in its offering. For we all need a pause from time to time.

The transference of one's power to the role of observer is a classic 'tactic' of man's ancestral heritage – a necessary skill of the hunter and gatherer. For hunting relies upon Randomness as much as it does patience. In observing the play unfold, one's position of authority and standing is dependent on yes, the interplay, but also one's ability to remain present, centred and alert. It is this silent alertness which enables a successful hunter to gather his wares – the flesh of an animal as much as the components of his fortune.

Man would do well to cultivate the skill of the hunter – often lacking in a world of electronic pulsing and instantaneous 'exchange'. Yes, electronic pulsing and instantaneous exchange: a modality of human being'ness of all generations; but as the world acclimatises to its overtly graceful entry into conscious manifestation of this 'pulsing' via computerisation and digitalisation of one's infrastructure, it is losing the art of the pause.

In the blink of an eye all can change. The hunter knows this, and awaits this. Today's man avoids this and fears this: change both welcome, yet unwanted.

It is in the space of the pause that change occurs, and so man avoids pausing. And yet all thought of value and diffidence, reliant on this space of inquisitiveness. In the inquisitiveness one discovers one's Self and one's answers. Welcoming change is what the hunter offers, and so he catches his prey and feeds his family. The same true now as then.

When man realises it is not the change which is fearsome, but the inability to change which creates the discord, he will open himself to the greatest learning and safety of self. In the accepting the pause, one allows the Randomness to interplay with one's reality, and so, the change creates not pleasure – although perhaps so – but a purpose to align one's activity with the activity of 'what-is'. In this connection, the realisation is of a stillness and deepness of being which permits the expression of one's gifts and uniqueness. The pause creates the awareness to allow the change. And yet the change drives all. For man desires not the known but the change, for it is a law of nature.

WED 11TH FEB 2015, LONDON AT 9.30AM, SESSION 111

Mr P: It is one's inability to change which creates the discord, yes, but it is also the inability to ponder one's placement which prohibits the vision.

In pondering, reflecting, philosophising, an awareness is gained. And in this awareness one's outlook changes, and hence one's vision…and so the change occurs. The formula attracts new energies and experiences in line with the new vision. Some men and women update their vision *as they go*, others in *stops and starts*; some frequently, some rarely. And all update at different space and time placements. Hence the variety and spice of life.

But this awareness is not always of *what we want*, but sometimes, oftentimes, of *what we don't want*. And in moving from what we *don't want*, we attract more of the same. And so how to philosophise without 'attracting' the unwanted?

The awareness *of* something does not create it if we don't include it in our vision, but immediately *let it go*. And this is a skill. For most attach an emotion and therefore 'link' themselves to the unwanted. Emotional agility – the precursor to emotional intimacy – the requirement for analytical thought. In the detachment of one's emotions one is able to contemplate the greater awareness and so greater choice is available to one's vision. In choosing *"I want this, but not that, but yes this"* without attachment, the vision is protected. It is all in the detachment of emotion – namely of personal emotion. And yet there is an intimacy of the greatest kind. For in the detachment of self, there is connection to the whole. For there is always a link.

It is a desire for connection which drives man and yet his emotions get in the way of this connection – and yet you are emotional beings? Indeed Spirit 'has' emotion too – of a different colouration but nevertheless present.

It is the ability to play with one's emotions – to create them and let them go – which enables connection. Pondering, ruminating, dreaming requires the skill of letting a thought, opinion or belief 'go': so that a new one can come in its place; can take centre stage for a while. Likewise, when man holds on to an emotion, be that love, fear, trepidation, excitement or any such temporary state, he becomes *stuck* and ineffective. He is not within the pause, but quite the opposite, within a cloud of pulsing energies. There is not room for *him* and so he absconds to the place where he can't be touched: into his cave.

Exiting the cave is no mean feat, for to face one's vulnerabilities without the protection of the sword is to believe in oneself. And to believe in oneself one has two drivers: nothing to lose, or everything to gain. Always one of the two.

THURS 12TH FEB 2015, LONDON AT 8.45AM, SESSION 112

Mr P: Strangely, few recognise these two avenues of movement, or drivers. It dates back to when time began, when man first trod the lands: one was exiled from the tribe, or one sought a new tribe. Movement always founded on one of the two energies. Physical union, likewise.

It is in the pauses 'between' these two energies that evolution occurs: the embryo 'held' in limbo; the walk between the tribal camps; the allowance of the moment.

Perhaps the reason man is not aware of these drivers? For he believes *he* is in control. And yet if one is moving in an energy of 'nothing to lose' this is not so, he is moving within the -1's. By contrast, movement *towards* something is of the +1's ...very different.

When we move 'towards' our vision, we are within wellness and within a natural, expansive flow. It is why man enjoys house-building and home-making so much. It is creative and expansive to the soul…and heart. But when we move 'from' somewhere the energy differs for our connection is not with what we want, but what we don't want. Man will never, I repeat never, extricate himself from where he doesn't want to be. It is only when he finds the pause and connects with his desire for what he *does* want that he will achieve betterment. Always. If this one lesson was understood, so much of history would be re-written; the desire for peace would enable the very peace that avoiding war disallows.

A 'visit' into what displeases is extremely worthwhile at times – but purely as a visit. The agility to observe and extract the necessary to accomplish one's vision, a skill. It is in recognising the pause for the vehicle of transition, that enables excellence of outcome: the pause, not a delay, but a part of the equation; the 'link' between the contrast of +1's and -1's within the equation, the pause *creates* the time/space attraction.

The *degree* to which man exercises his energies of -1 and +1 varies depending upon the 'topic' being reasoned. It is quite possible for stagnation to display itself by way of a chosen energy within one's edge of reason and the contrasting within one's edge of belief. The +1, negated by the -1, and so, paralysis. This is not a pause, but a conflict – a lack of flow and movement. For there is always movement within a pause: there is always growth of the embryo; the steps walked; the awareness created.

When within a conflict, man tends to blame either his edge of reason (the external) or his edge of belief (the internal). One creates discord without, the other within. The 'war' played out in the physical: as for a country, as the one man or woman.

But when man arrives at the pause, and chooses the object or passion of his or her desire, he is 'lifted' forward. Movement becomes effortless and wonderful in nature, for he has reconciled his conflict in the -1's and so the +1's can carry him forward. It is the way of the universe. It is law.

FRI 13TH FEB 2015, LONDON AT 11.00AM, SESSION 113

Mr P: Perhaps to understand one's border between the edge of reason and edge of belief we need some clarity on *why* it is of importance.

The *reason* we entertain this balance between the external and internal is because all cellular activity is based on this state of coalescence. Without the inner, the external cannot be, and vice versa. The contrast creates the distinction. And it is in the distinction the 'fusing' occurs – the point of transition. As a cell 'attracts' it also dispels. A healthy cell, in attracting an unhealthy (although there is no such state – it is all energetic movement) electron or component, dispels a corresponding 'unhealthy' component. The 'activity' occurs at the borders of the cell, not as commonly thought *within* it. The change then proceeds to impact the inner and outer as the multiplication and division of the action creates such movement.

So if the cell 'changes' at the borders, what creates the change? The answer: awareness. The cells have an 'awareness' of their energetic base properties. It is when the awareness of this energetic stabilising force *kicks in*, the change occurs. It is not the energetic force itself which creates the change – although it can create 'discomfort' for the cells via tension and a sluggishness of movement (and all cascading effects thereafter) – but the *awareness* of this energetic base stability, or more to the point, instability, which triggers the change. One only has to call to mind an occurrence in one's life where the *knowledge* of the trauma or incident or news created the emotional reaction in the person – whether of the mind, heart, soul or body. It is always the awareness…

And so, the physical body reacts accordingly. When one is told of a diagnosis for instance, *that* is when the 'illness' *takes hold* – or dispels, depending upon one's outlook and edge of belief. If one believes *life will be better* then the energetic base force will reflect this distinction which has been created, and cellular activity will react accordingly.

But this importance of awareness is relevant not just to the physical wellbeing of man but also to his emotional and mental wellbeing. For awareness, whilst requiring the mind, is not of the mind. And hence one's ability to sense and 'know'. Man's cells, affected before he even consciously knows it!

The sharing of this 'information' bears two benefits: clarity on *why* events happen in one's body and environment (the internal and external on a greater scale) and an understanding, for those who wish to explore their 'placement' in life, of why *things don't happen when we want them to*. And for this latter element, the edge of reason is creating discord with the edge of belief; the two are not aligned. But…and here is the understanding needed…it is when they do align that the cellular changes occur. And sometimes, it is just not the right time for this change to happen. Sometimes, the energetic base force is creating a different outcome, one more suitable and beneficial for the person. Sometimes…is always. The awareness is, that *sometimes* is right now.

WED 18TH FEB 2015, LONDON AT 11.50AM, SESSION 114

Mr P: So if we can 'change' our bodies and our outlook via thought, why can we not manifest our desires as we wish them?

The answer to this refraction involves our placement with space/time, or more accurately time/space.

The *thought* 'goes out' into the universe, into the ether. It is dispatched into space as a thought, and whilst 'only' a thought, it is already *matter*. Matter interacts with energy (other matter) in differing ways, depending upon the constituents of the properties. It *reflects off, absorbs, distorts* or *encompasses*. Always one of the four, or a combination of.

Each time a thought is dispatched, it creates more interactions with energy. Eventually, until it is *broken down* by a change in belief, it becomes 'held' by the mind. It will have differing points of attraction and diffusing vibration depending on one's circumstances, but it will be *there* nonetheless.

We now have a thought held in 'space', not by its own forces, but by the forces of the attached energies. And it is these energies which reflect components of 'time'. The attachment of the *other end* of the energetic link – whether they involve people, situations or matter created from mass – affect the 'time' of the thought. It is, once again, an example of being at the edge of reason and the edge of belief. If we 'think' something will happen *as a result of* something else (even in our subconscious or unconscious levels) then this is what we will witness in our reality.

Let me give an example: if Delilah believes she will finish this book in ten months' time, all energies, matter and mass related to the production of this book will adjust in her time-reality to slot into place with this vision. If something alters her edge of reason or edge of belief contrary to this, 'time' will adjust for her. The *book* – the 'space' – has not *moved* at all; it remains 'held' in her thought and vision. But whilst she believes we will complete on the 15th December 2015, she *will* complete on 15th December 2015 – even though the mass to produce the 'matter' of the book is not *hers*.

By 'calling it in' she affects the outcome. And yet she plays a part in this outcome too. Belief creates reason, creates belief, and so it goes…

SUN 22ND FEB 2015, AIRBOUND TO LAS VEGAS SESSION 115

Mr P: To 'own' one's thought is a powerful example of how a person can change his or her outcome. And perhaps this is the 'crux' of why dissatisfaction reigns.

Holding a vision requires 'owning' the thought. To drop, change, alter, relinquish creates disparaged momentum. The equation of force (V> +1/-1> neutral acquisition> attracting forces) *relies* on the vision. Yet man changes his vision; doubts it; disbelieves it. And so the resulting momentum. When we understand the consequences, we understand our part in the play.

Oftentimes adaptation to one's vision is wholly appropriate, and this is desirable, part of the creationism of evolution. But this differs from one who: *wishes, disbelieves…wishes, disbelieves…wishes, disbelieves…* Much more effective, to hold a 'lower' vision, maintain it, realise it, and then choose a fresh one. Such behaviour affords an effortlessness, an ease and streaming of focus.

The requirement of a vision however, will always necessitate 'fine-tuning.' And this differs from doubt. With fine-tuning, the vision is quadrupled in velocity at each stroke of the artist's brush – and this is what is occurring: a work of art; a personal masterpiece. Each stroke, an *addition* to the canvas. Not a *"Shall I paint, or shall I not paint?"* What one might call a grave and distinguishing difference in the mastery of one's life. And it is…that simple.

Those that effect change, *effect change*. It is not the 'size' of the change, but the change itself which enables the feeling of movement and being *on purpose*. Little is understood of such processes as man seeks outcome and not the *feeling* of change, of movement. The power lies not in the system, but in the current of flow: the part being greater than the sum of such outcome. It is the ability to *take part* which affords the pleasure.

When mankind understands – and more effectively, *feels* this dichotomy of intelligence – he will realise that there is no 'wrong' in the world; that reality provides for an ability to feel. It is the vision which creates the path, and yet the journey provides the answer. Human nature, as such, provides. The soul of man, the star one follows.

MON 23RD FEB 2015, LAS VEGAS AT 5.30AM, SESSION 116

Mr P: Once the mastery of vision is understood, things become a lot smoother…and more interesting. And by 'things' I mean exactly that, that the *objects* of one's desire 'arrive' more smoothly – be they matters of mass, consequences, ideas or people. All arrive via connections, but in line with the vision.

Now you might say: *"But I didn't desire this illness, the event, this frustration which has appeared in my life today"*, and the answer I propose, is that yes, you did – your soul did. Spirit works in line with the soul – it encompasses the whole, including the physical, mental and emotional – but *concentrates*, or perhaps a better word…takes *instruction* from, the soul.

Man emits many signals – consciously, subconsciously and unconsciously. We all experience conflict at times between our conscious expression and subconscious thought – even in Spirit. But the most powerful signal is that of the unconscious: the 'group' emission. It could be considered the sea we all float on. Man sails his own boat – the conscious – but relies on the subconscious to know his direction. It is when the conscious and subconscious align, he reaches his destination.

But a third way is to align the conscious (the effort or energy) with the subconscious (the vision and desires), and the unconscious (the expression of 'what-is'). When this occurs, mastery occurs. It is akin to sailing *with* the seas, not atop or against; it is being present in the moment, with the moment; and it is what you might call being with "the Father, the Son and the Holy Spirit". The suggestion: that *man* is the Spirit – the vision amongst the seas.

There are always benefits to all events, whatever their nature. When viewed within one's edge of belief and edge of reason this may not always be 'visible'. But as moments pass, as events unfold and one's edge of reason reflects new beliefs, the learnings will present. One only has to look to historical events to see such evidence.

Supporting one's movement requires a connection to the soul – to trusting the unconscious nature of the occurrence. When alignment with the soul occurs, all doubt falls away – indeed one's reason and beliefs fall away too, for there is a *knowing*, a surrender to not 'something else', but the *alignment* – of which man is part. It is his or her 'inclusion with' the divine forces – as an expression of, and creator towards – that satisfies man's soul. The surrender is not to another, but to oneself. This is flow, and this affords *peace*.

TUES 24TH FEB 2015, SEDONA AT 9.30AM, SESSION 117

Mr P: In *succumbing* to the energies of flow, the 'force' of the current creates a 'slipstream'. A kind of fine-tuning, but with gained momentum as the equational links 'come together'. The attraction becomes more pertinent to the destination as the refinement of *effort* (the balance between +1's / -1's) enables, through less resistance, greater attachment to one's desires. Things 'come alight', are sparked, and therefore create new connections in turn. It is a veritable feast of delivery.

Since the *destination is oneself*, the feelings of connection abound – namely, a feeling of being 'on purpose', in the right place at the right time, and at-one with all-that-is.

Every man, woman and child experiences this at times, but when experienced in perpetual motion there is an 'excess' available for sharing. The benefit, not just for oneself, but also for others…for their flow too.

'Flow' is a somewhat difficult expression to describe – one knows it when one knows it…but it has 'qualities' we can observe. It is not an energy in itself, but the transmutation of *other* energies. It 'facilitates' life, enables things to run smoothly; the 'things' containing the matter, but the flow enabling their expression and connections. Man is the facilitator of mass. He may believe he creates and he destroys, but in truth, he 'facilitates'. The creationism is his expression of himself – all-that-he-is in that moment – and just as man cannot *not* express, he cannot therefore destroy. He can *make room* for something else, but all is always 'a creation'.

Flow enables creation which 'suits' the soul. The more the soul expresses, the more flow occurs. And yet man finds it a challenge to hear his soul – to allow its divine expression, does he not?

Strangely, this disturbance does not 'harm' man's ability to flow – just the effect and outcome of flow. Man can *choose* to flow at any time – it need not be learnt, but *allowed*. And this allowance is purely the act of hearing the soul.

If man can connect to *this* voice within, to allow its speech, no matter what 'it' says, he will automatically experience such wondrous energy. It is all in the allowance of oneself – a state of full capacity within one's energies: transcendence of the mundane to a grasp of the divine. Of what wonders to behold!

WED 25TH FEB 2015, SEDONA AT 14.20PM, SESSION 118

Mr P: Randomness relies on one's ability to manage one's energies. Flow is an allowance of energies, but one needs to manage oneself energetically in order for the flow to happen. It is not a handle on the energies or desires themselves, but on oneself *so that* the energies can express themselves within, without and through a person. If man could learn this one distinction: that at all times we manage ourselves – and this includes an 'obligation' to express what arises when it is 'called forth' from the soul – then he will save himself much discomfort and anguish. He can never manage someone or something else – purely his own response to 'what-is' within his own reality. And this is the misnomer of creationism: that 'we' do not create, we allow the manifestation to unfold of what we envision. And this unfolding can take many sizes, shapes and forms. All to excite!

Perhaps we would do well to ponder for a moment on the frequencies of man's request of desires. They come in many forms and permutations, but mostly from a frequency of need…of *reliance* on them for one's happiness. This is not the way of realising one's destiny, but more a way of ensuring the discomfort which keeps what man wishes at bay – behind the line of touch.

It is when the line of touch dissolves that one can touch one's desires. And as a metaphysical explanation, we could call this the degree of rotation of the time around space: the object of one's desires – the space – remains, but the connection with 'time' dissolves to enable the distribution of the energies via the 'link' of time and space. They become one, so to speak.

The line of touch is created by not thought, but by the absence of thought – and by this I refer not to a thought of the mind, but the thought of the soul. This happens on a different frequency and is 'orchestrated' by forces acquiescing to the soul's journey through not time and space, but through the energetic achievement of the soul's journey. The calling, from the place of energetic magnitude known as a 'feeling'. And so we come full circle: the *feeling* man is hesitant to allow, in itself allows the soul to be heard. And the frequency of such a voice is that which creates the greatest resonance. It creates the sound of the soul through the avenue of the body. The flow, the sound of the soul; the body, the mechanism – the instrument which plays the tune. A well maintained instrument will always permit the notes to flow. It is a gift...not of one or the other, but of the combination of the two. The management, needed to infiltrate the strings; the tune, needing a 'house'. That home is of the soul.

THURS 26TH FEB 2015, AIRBOUND TO LA, SESSION 119

Mr P: When it is remembered that we do not play our tune to the music, but the music to the tune, we can understand how we get in our own way. When we 'complicate' our days by trying to play Bach when we wish to play a sonata, we dissolve our ability to flow – and are mismanaging our energies. These affect the physical body too. If one deeply wishes to rest, but 'continues on', then what little energy is available is not distributed according to the soul – but according to 'reason'. *"If I do this I will feel better"* as opposed to *"I feel like doing this. Period"*. The lack of conflict: translated from the mental, through the emotional, by the energetic, to the physical. In a sweep of links and exchanges, man affects all elements of his status.

The underlying consensus of the body is either: a natural flow and ease – and expansion – or conflict, constraint and denial. Each choice made by man, a choice in which avenue he wishes to take. And interestingly, all his wishes, hinged on the choice.

He may think that he needs to 'do' in order to 'have' but this is not so. He *can* do, but what he will get will be off-set by what he loses in the process: it is law of nature at work.

By contrast, when he chooses in accordance with his energy flow (and he will always have enough energy for what he truly desires) he gains on all levels – for it is of equal law that the desire is acknowledged through the links of attraction. It is when man focuses on his vision, of what he truly wishes, that he is able to focus his energy accordingly. And when the soul is called in, the effect is compounded by the benefit of congruence. In the light of the reason and the belief: all is well.

9

REFLECTIONS ON TIME AND SPACE, THE MEASURE OF MAN AND A NEW STRAND OF SCIENCE

Mr P: *"Once upon a time…"* as the saying goes. Hmmm… and so much truth in four short words. Have you ever pondered the deeper significance of a story placed in a time gone past? For how can 'time' be of the past when all that exists is the moment so presenting as *now*?

Space and time are the 'basis' of life – in as much as all events are quantified by the turn of the clock – but if time passes and is acknowledged as 'lost' or 'gone' what does this say for space? Einstein's Theory of Relativity touches on the causal links between the two, but it does not go far enough to explain – in understandable terms – the significance of the combination.

Life, death, birth, decay, enlightenment, despair…the harrowing passages of time for many, 'accepted' as the process. But the process of *what*? Is it just a passage of time, or is it a claim on space? And to know the link purports to a knowledge of what involves the combination of space *and* time – and how many dare observe this wonder within?

Many…most, separate time and space in their reality. They attempt to live life according to the watch on their wrist, judging their success by the creation of space. As their attempts slide away from their ownership of Self, they experience a disconnection.

It might be suggested a reversal: of living life according to the space we inhabit, judging the use of time as a benchmark for a *fait-accompli*. But this too as a method of displaying energies creates incongruence and limited feelings of expansion.

Time and space, I offer, are not merely linked, but one. There *is* no separation between the two. One does not travel through the two, but *is* the two. Man *is* time and he *is* space. He just understands himself as being not 'of' the world but 'upon' the world – and this is the misnomer.

There is no *"Once upon a time"* but there is *"Now, within this time"* – even as a 'past'. Indeed there is no past, nor future…nor present.

Pertaining to live in the 'now' is a *step* in the direction of aligning one's space and time, but it does not truly encompass the truth of one's existence – for there still remains a separation: of the 'now' or the 'not-now'. Existence is greater than the now; it is 'all-that-is' and it encompasses all of time and all of space. No story that happened 'before' exists other than in the current awareness of its existence, and yet it 'existed' before. It is *its* existence which man dips in and out of, not the story dipping in and out of man's existence. Both exist, in all time and all space. Both *are* time and both *are* space.

The daily practice of such awareness enables a fuelling of mergence with Source…of the existential understanding and connection with one's existence. It is in the dropping *into* the combination of space and time that one understands one's placement within, not upon, the reality known as planet Earth. When man understands he exists *in* time and space; is an expression of his experience of time and space, of Source; then both time and space become invisible in daily living. The 'now' opens up to enable the complete experience of what is available within. For the within holds an infinite degree of Source available through infinite ways of being. Such is man's unique expression of himself or herself.

<u>TUES 10TH MAR 2015, LONDON AT 9.00AM, SESSION 121</u>

Mr P: The causal links of space and time – or time and space – can be explained through an analogy of the forest.

A forest – any forest – *is* space and time combined, for it cannot exist without either component: the 'space' for the growth to occur and the 'time' for the growth to occur. The growth occurs *because* of both, not despite both. And yet neither requisite for the potential held within the growth. It is the 'growth' one observes but it is the potential which enables and fuels the outcome.

A forest floor contains the seeds of growth but without the elements of the infrastructure of the planet *as a whole* it cannot germinate into existence. Is it time or is it space? It is neither and yet it is both. And such with man.

Time and space are an *effect*, never the *cause*. They are the result of the potential and the effect of the germination of an expression of the whole. A small sapling shoot relies upon and exists because of the abundance of the environment, and the environment produces growth because of its causal traits.

Likewise, man creates his space and his time as an effect of his or her potential. Neither can exist without the other and both rely on man exercising his duty to create an effect via the cause he or she *is*. As man expresses, both time *and* space 'open-up' before – as the forest came into potential, the space and time arose to enable this interaction with nature: the laws of nature.

The 'natural world' one observes is an unfettered expression of time/space. It is the application of the laws of nature in motion. Nature creates itself and 'rules' itself without any *need* from man. And yet man needs nature to exist. A thought well-worth pondering, no?

Common sense tells us that without the intrusion of man, the planet's natural world would flourish and blossom. Whilst there is truth in this, as a component of the same laws of nature man lives in, there is an 'exchange' between man and nature which nature relies on to exist. Any exchange is always dual in purpose and potential.

The 'natural world' exists in purpose as both teacher *and* student. It teaches man and 'it' also learns from man. Time and space, for the natural world, affected by its interaction with man. When nature no longer provides, man 'removes' it, replaces it with man-made space and time. And yet the replacement, subject to the same rules of nature – also expressions of, and acts of, time and space. A building: needing the same elements of space and the same elements of time to germinate, adapt, grow and evolve. But it is only with the inclusion of human *life* that the building 'comes to life'. As with all…

The natural world – whether a forest, an island, a vegetation – exists in potential 'for itself' and 'for others'. It *is* time and space, *is* the effect of the potential, and in itself *creates* potential. Space and time – the very potential for life, and also the effect *of* life.

When man lives his existence not within the descriptive of the restraints of space and time but as an expression of potential without the *need* for space and time, is when he discovers both. For he drops into his 'reason' for expression supported by his belief in its abundance. The question of *"Who created the forest?"* answered by his observation and enjoyment of it. For without the belief that the forest 'exists', the existence pertains to potential only.

FRI 13TH MAR 2015, LONDON AT 9.00AM, SESSION 122

Mr P: Randomly, the extension of one's belief in a world, or reality, 'outside' of time and space creates a discord which fuels the need for both time *and* space. Man, on the whole, feels separate from time and separate to space. In part there is some observational truth in this, for the physical body creates a boundary of sorts – both spatially, and as it grows and declines – but in actuality, there is not. For how can man be separate from the ocean which created him? A cake mixture, for instance, becomes a singular cake, divided by slice, or a plateful of individual smaller cakes. But the mixture is the mixture: it is all cake.

The belief that we have to capture time, and space, is one rooted in not creationism, but idealism – and this is not truth.

The difference between creationism and idealism is one of outcome. The outcome itself may be the same, but creationism relies on the experience of the creating – the journey, so to speak – whereas idealism pertains exclusively to the outcome; there is no perceived benefit in the journey, just the net result. It is this drive towards a 'net result' which creates a society – and inner feeling – of reductionism: that life is running away; disappearing; dwindling…

Idealism *reduces* one's time and space as life narrows, creationism *increases* time and space as life expands. The question of 'living in the now', invalid and unattainable, unless one changes one's outlook from idealistic to creative – for the sake of now.

To drop the tendency for an idealistic outlook challenges the psyche of man, for he has to let go of the desire for outcome in totality and pick up the strands of desire for right now…*and allow himself to do so*. This is man's greatest challenge. It means not requiring an 'extension' of time or space, but accepting and dropping fully into *this* time, and space. The acceptance of the 'reality' one is in: both the giver of time/space and the destroyer of idealism. It is in accepting 'what-is' that one moves *within* time and space, as opposed to 'skirting over it'.

To accept oneself and all-that-is in *this* moment requires a letting go of all past attachments and recalibrations desired by the ego, *and* a letting go of all future outcomes. It is no mean feat, this has to be acknowledged, and yet it is the simplest of acts and forays.

The foray into the present, via the portal of this – and each – moment of time, opens one to a world of untold possibilities and dimensions of awareness and understanding. The 'altered state' man seeks, always within. The gift of the acceptance of each moment is that it encompasses, effortlessly and 'by default', all-that-is: all of one's past and all of one's future. The present moment *is* 'all', yet can only be accessed by relinquishing 'all'.

It is the space/time awareness which enables the transition to letting go of the need to capture the *uncapturable*. Why would one wish to 'capture' a moment when one can enjoy the freedom of a moment? The vision man must hold, is of the desire to feel good and to express his or her truth towards enabling others to feel better. The vision, not of obtaining capture or an 'ideal' formula of being, but of bettering one's enjoyment of the now. The vision is not a destination, but a reflection of the potential within one's being-ness for greater being-ness. When the vision is recalibrated from one of idealism to one of creation, worlds shift and time and space open before one.

MON 16ᵀᴴ MAR 2015, LONDON AT 9.00AM, SESSION 123

Mr P: Transition from a life of meaning rooted in the exterior – the edge of reason – to one lightly holding the wonderfully unattainable within one's belief – one's interior – bequests the involvement of the divine. For to *believe* and rest easily within the unattainable, to recognise that what makes us wonder is the very essence of what we live within, and lives within us, *is* divinity.

Man searches for knowledge and understanding. He makes, makes, makes: to create more of what he knows, so he can know more. But there is little wonder in all this; little of the unknown. It is the pursuit of understanding our relationship with the unknown which offers the greatest learning, and it is the acceptance of the unknown which gives the ease and sense of absolute belonging man seeks. And yet how can this be?

Space/time is an accepted form of measure, and yet man is trusting in an unattainable and incomprehensible method of measuring. The mind, at the end of one's life in the physical, will not be able to 'compute' its data in either time or space; it will measure it purely within the elements of reason and belief: *"Did I have a good life? What created my good life? What beliefs did not serve me?"* These are the questions we ask ourselves as we seek not understanding, but learning to take forward, into the next portion of our master life.

In striving for our *ideal* life, man often misses the point *of* life. The man or woman who regularly asks themselves these questions – not as a means of getting somewhere, but purely to learn for learning's sake and to create not understanding but wonder at what is and what may be in possibility – has the greatest potential for a transition of ease and flow.

When one adopts the *absence* of space or time as a basis for one's viewpoint and resonance of one's lifestyle and life choices, opportunities abound. For without the self-imposed restraint of the twenty-four hour timepiece on one's wrist, without the control of the influence of *what* one has created within the constraints of time and space, we can observe our levels of influence over and to ourselves.

Everything life offers is a tool. This includes: the use of time, a method of 'making arrangements'; and the use of space, 'the place arrangements are held'. When we can observe the details of life as a series of arrangements, it is the arrangements and our interaction with them which creates the meaning. Man's use of the tool of time – the 24-hour clock – and the tool of spatial awareness, not the destination or a measure within themselves, but perpetrators of a point of viewing.

Viewing one's life-time with wonder and appreciation of the unattainable and unknown relies on not needing to know time or space. It is within such a point of viewing that a deep sense of freedom is tasted and felt. For without the constraints of past, a 'difference' is felt. It is this difference, this altered state, that man seeks; for within this unknowable of spaces a timelessness is experienced which provides a connection surpassing the physical, and enabling the expansion of both the soul and the heart: the communion of the physical and the spiritual.

TUES 17TH MAR 2015, LONDON AT 8.40AM, SESSION 124

Mr P: *"Tonight we dine at 8pm"* – is this a ritual or a necessity? Is the movement towards food, or away from hunger? Are we filling the space, the time, or is the food calling forth our attention? At what point is the awareness of our actions, as opposed to the automation of life's ritualistic nature?

There is peace, safety and harmony in the easy system of not routine, but rituals. But routine can enter the movement if permitted, and this perhaps is what causes the 'tip' into space/time complacency. Once the emphasis has changed from desiring to eat, to presenting at 8pm for food *"because this is what happens"*, then the tipping point has created a lack of awareness as the power of the action is handed over to the space/time dimension of '8pm'.

Conscious awareness of one's thoughts and actions defies the encroachment of routine, and I would suggest that without routine life can never be 'dull' or unchallenging. For to remain consciously aware requires the challenge of upholding the awareness, and this in itself surprises those who believe an 'easy' life goes without awareness.

Rituals by contrast 'play' with space/time, for the awareness remains of *why* they are proposed and partaken. In holding a ritual of taking seat for dinner, the appreciation is held of the movement and gift of the moment – neither the food nor the space and 'arrangement' of the dinner are taken for granted. Rituals are our conscious awareness of what space and time is offering – and as such the power and intensity of the moment is acknowledged.

Now this may sound rather convoluted and abstract an offering of what man does on a daily basis, but this very aspect of the 'routineness' of one's life is what can create temptation to *ignore* and disregard the 'necessary'. Yet it is the lack of acknowledgement of the reason *for* the 'necessary' that dulls man's experience of life and nature. In dulling the senses within the everyday movement, life dulls in the without of one's experiences. The *necessity* is for an exchange of energy, and of awareness of, and partaking within, the moment. The consumption of food 'enables' man to live, and to express himself. This appreciation of such a necessity lost to the demands of a day where an 8pm routine is 'met or not met'. Time has overtaken *life* in the pull for one's attention and aim, and as such 'life' becomes a routine, a series of moments which are *"achieved, or not", "met or not met".* The demand tips onto the person or structures – bodies of people – to complete a series of tasks and routines. The easy, pleasurable partaking of rituals, lost to time and space demands.

When one tips out of space/time, the moments have the awareness of a level of being which, whilst oftentimes challenging to maintain in a society running to a different clock, delivers what the moment promises. Movement is neither 'to' or 'from', but enjoyment of 'what-is'. Within this place of lightly holding the experience, an appreciation of *why* we are doing so provides a contrast to the wonder of one's greater sense of being.

The provision of space/time absence is available from either direction: from the energy of *letting go* or from the energy of appreciation, for both encompass an acceptance. When man accepts himself, he also accepts his life and all it offers and promises. And for this, time/space is not a requirement but an available tool. It is the art of using one's tools which defines the master from the student. But all learning, all processes, require the handle of the lesson *and* the handle of the tools to enable the integration of the teaching. As such with the awareness of one's motivation for life: is it a routine, a 'dead-line' to meet, or a series of beautiful rituals, rich in experience and learning? It does not take a philosopher to answer, does it?

WED 18TH MAR 2015, LONDON AT 9.00AM, SESSION 125

Mr P: *"Streetwise and knowing."* Perhaps 'useful' characteristics and talents? Or perhaps degrees of routine and complacency? For how can we *know*? We *think* we know but there is little to truly know in the movements we take other than the automaton of our environment. *The train comes at 8.15am, the bus at 9.15am, the bell to commence the session, the break for lunch.* When the 'pointers' of one's day are of the automaton nature, both space and time 'narrows'.

But *'streetwise'*...this differs. There is a complacency, yes, but also an alertness. The complacency...of acceptance of the status quo and of the nature of one's surroundings – a 'knowingness' clouding one's openness for a change of energy, but there is also displayed an air of possibility as to one's interactions within the field, the field being that of 'life'.

Space and time provides an arena, a field, a playground to have fun in. But consistently 'dismal' interactions are observed of society: an assumed knowingness; a disregard for appreciation; assumption that today will be the same as yesterday, and tomorrow too; lacklustre participation in 'effecting' any impact onto one's society; an expectation that 'danger' and harm will ensue; a closed and hurried speed of movement; a dis-allowance of life-force through people, and into the environment.

The compounded effect creates not only routine and attachment to time, but an awareness of *decline* and *time-running-out*. One's observation: of loss and dis-ease, for oneself and also for one's society. The lack of ease...a reflection within and without.

When one steps out of time and space, this ease is regained – for it is always there, always present in potential and possibility, an offering of the soul. In not needing the routine and restriction of the automaton of oneself and life, a space opens for *appreciation* of life. One does not need to be streetwise or knowing when one is 'at ease' and in harmony with oneself. A child, not yet accustomed to the fears of adults, needs neither to enjoy his or her day. Yet adults do not trust that the learning of life and of one's interactions with life are sufficient for a child of ease to grow into an adult of ease. Preferable it seems, is the desire to create dis-ease for children, to show them 'real life'. What a shame!

SAT 21ST MAR 2015, LONDON AT 10.05PM, SESSION 126

Mr P: 'Today's date' serves a purpose. It is a 'log' of time in space and a means to 'mark' an event within time; for reference, so to speak. But other than that, the logging of time serves no purpose of use. It is a means to measure, but man uses this measuring stick against himself. Admonishment of what he has not done as opposed to grateful reflection of what *has* occurred and resulted from his actions and non-actions.

A date of birth, and a date of death are the only units – or dimensions – of measure worth their salt. For within these lines of space and time a man or woman's worth can be measured – not against the time but *because* of the time. Did he or she lead a good life? An enjoyable and purposeful life, spreading love and joy? A life another would be happy living? Did this person cause learning and comfort to flow from their very being? To inspire and receive in gratitude? To provoke thought and discussions? Reflection and diversity?

'Time' does not measure these qualities of living. *"He reached a good age, made it to 90"* – never more farcical such words uttered! Where is the soul of the man captured in a life dragged out to 90 without degrees of being which can be reflected for growth? For if we cannot capture learning and inspiration, if the living cannot epitomize the 'dead', how can we call that a life worth living?

Each man has ownership of his life, but we each have opinions and reflections of the lives of others. In the Spirit world as much as in the physical world. Not as judgement, and forsaking questioning; however, reflection causes observation. Man's edge of reason, a reflection and therefore an observation of 'what-is'. And if man cannot be inspired by those who pass before, how can he know how to inspire others?

The lack of reflection for growth in those that pass is two-fold. As the dying decline, their ability to use their skills and qualities decline too. And as such, their ability to enjoy their days becomes compromised as all effort is placed on 'holding on in'. But perhaps more 'destructive' and disheartening: something also dies in the living. In an attempt to reconcile one's observation of decline, and in order to satisfy a desire to live, a compromise is made: in reasoning our own place in the space and time of decline, we run the risk – the veritable risk – of judging our performance against what we have *not* achieved. And in a world of untold, never-ending possibilities, this is not a comfortable observation.

The benefit of moving to a continual observation of what one *has* done, felt, experienced, achieved, fundamentally alters one's outlook. It is those that appreciate the beauty and energies of reality – whatever that reality is – who experience a profound peace and harmony. In appreciating 'what-is', desire for new experiences takes on a systemic reasoning. The 'belief' is no longer in question and so the mind can rest.

When the mind stops *comparing* it becomes free to accept the moment. There *is* no decline, for one does not need to be elsewhere – either achieving a future state, or reconciling one's past mistakes or 'missed opportunities'. In not comparing, one also stops comparing time itself, and so the moment grows in depth and potential. In not trying to make this time special, before it 'runs out', time itself offers itself to be enjoyed. For it is only when one *accepts* time that one can enjoy time.

Many of man's reasons for wishing things to be different from generations before is because of a wish to prove betterment in order to heal past hurts and traumas. By proving himself or herself, man believes he will *feel better*. But in truth, he creates a need to *stop*. For the more he *tries* to make himself feel better, the further he moves from feeling better – and the closer he feels to 'decline'. When he stops is when the healing can occur, and the true enjoyment of being in and of this world be experienced.

SUN 22ND MAR 2015, LONDON AT 11.00AM, SESSION 127

Mr P: It is the person who is inspired by previous generations who understands his or her role in life. For 'purpose' cannot exist without a basis on which to apply the wisdom.

All movement and creationism 'relies' on the learning of what went before – it is an *integration* of 'what works' with the imagination, and collective enthusiasm and energies of the present. Change cannot happen without enthusiasm – otherwise it is labelled as 'disaster' or 'challenge', is it not?

Likewise, change cannot happen from a place of non-acceptance of 'what-is'; of the now, of the ground man stands upon. When one denies one's past or ancestors, one is attempting to stand on alternative ground. And when one does not *appreciate* or incorporate the learnings and inspiration from the past, one cannot learn from one's future. The further 'back' one travels, the further forward one is propelled – it is a law of nature.

It is the point of viewing which creates the outcome. This one protocol underpins all phenomena. But it is only in standing within one's acceptance that truth can be viewed. This is the journey of enlightenment. But many men, in searching for truth, cast their glance to the past whilst desiring the future. And so, they feel the 'passage' of time, not time itself. For time itself contains no measure. In requiring no measure, no comparison, the possibility of the very change one desires presents itself. But the vision, the point of viewing is always of ahead. One does not walk a path backwards. In not needing to prove oneself, one can enjoy oneself.

The measure of man, of a life well lived, is whether he or she was able to inspire and elevate others to greater understanding of themselves. For no action of influence is created *for* someone, but *by* someone. In inspiring and elevating others, the growth and expansion man seeks is enabled in an effortless and beautiful way. The continuation of symbolic measures of contentment are enabled through the very chain of exchanged ideas and thought-form. In inspiring the formless, man creates the form. And within the form, is found all of the formless which led to the creation. All of one's past, held and captured in this instant. As such, the depth of man holds the key for man.

MON 23ᴿᴰ MAR 2015, LONDON AT 12.30PM, SESSION 128

Mr P: Symbolic movement through time and space creates little ripples…but great waves. It is the process of continual movement in the direction of one's desires and vision which enables one movement to lead into another, into another. But the effect of seamless flow creates an enormous wave in outcome – an outcome one does not see until in the experience of the resonance. Like an earth's tremor which builds below the surface of the ocean, the impact to hit the shores and reverberate in effect.

The movement of time and space, in the instance of a tsunami, is measured by voltage and vibration. The electromagnetic frequency is both powerful and immeasurable in quantifiable outcome – until the impact is felt. And such it is with man.

Man's frustration is in holding a vision of an outcome, without connecting to the daily and momentary movement 'below the surface'. For it is in the measurement of the flow of the current that a satisfaction is felt. A tsunami feeds off its own power, its roll effortless and compounded by the elements but requiring neither to execute its impact.

The planet experiences many 'tsunamis' which diffuse into 'nothingness'. It is only the movements which create impact which go noticed. A calm day strikes no chord, and a diffused energy stream creates no outcome in itself. And yet it completes a function: that of combined effort. For it takes innumerable components for an outcome.

The appreciation of the unnoticed movements and contributions of nature's way and man's involvement allows for appreciation of our individual role within the collective symbolism of 'life'. To calculate all the movements which contribute to any moment in time would give immeasurable degrees of calculation. And yet this is taken for granted as most consider purely what they have *not done* or not considered of worthy an outcome. Nature does not ponder on what it has not produced; on what has not evolved. And yet man seeks to do so – *to go back in time*.

Tsunamis cannot be recalled, earthquakes not rebuilt. But buildings *can* be rebuilt, fields re-planted, water re-directed. When called to the practicalities of life, man excels in creating security and growth. What he can build with his hands, he can observe in matter-form. But what quantifies as completion of time and space, what cannot be measured confuses him. And so, in the quest for betterment, for a fuller, greater life, man must look forwards and within. In using what he has at his disposal – namely the energy of all that has contributed to this moment – he is able to move with an effortlessness and an ease. The outcome – for the pleasure and benefit of others – provides not the means, but the vision to enable a new collective, a new time in space where all converges to provide what is needed, and desired. The faculties are the gift: the provision of what is needed for each man, woman and child to express the greatest version of themselves.

WED 25ᵀᴴ MAR 2015, LONDON AT 12.15PM, SESSION 129

Mr P: Today's nature is not the same as nature of past. It may have the same 'qualities' but it differs in that it is an evolved combination of causes and effects, and so its *receptivity* differs today compared to 2000 years ago.

The interaction between man and nature is reflected *within* time and space, yet not dependent upon it. Man observes, today, elements of destruction of the planet, and depletion of its resources – and this is the reflection of mankind, of man himself. Within this 'time and space' is also the opportunity for opposing energies – of rejuvenation and replenishment. It is not time which allows the unfolding, but intention which changes, and creates the outcome – the possibility of something different and a life well lived – the same for a planet as for man.

As man heals himself, he heals his planet. As with all change, it must come from within – originate from its source. And one does not heal from looking back, by trying to do things *"as we used to do them"*, but by using our learning from the past to create solutions and ideas for the future.

A solution to a problem is a desire to gain balance: to create safe ground, and an air of openness and potential – the components of perfect harmony. The 'problem', as much part of the balance, of the equation, as the solution. This is how movement occurs, how growth is enabled.

Man's planet is his territory and man's body is his ground of experimentation. Depletion, rape and rage as uncomfortable for a person as a planet. And yet without such 'explorations' can one know the panacea to one's conscience? Although we can think we don't *wish* to experience such 'atrocities', can we experience our true range of emotions and possibilities without them?

In accepting what does not resonate within, acceptance of what does becomes visible…and possible for inclusion. But whilst man remains fixated at removal of the unwanted, he cannot see the contrast. The exacerbation of forces of destruction, compounded by the very resistance to the alternative.

It is those that focus not on the *un*-wanted but the desired who create the greatest impact within themselves and their environment. The 'action' – of focused intention, and inclusion of all aspects of expression – is greatest when held lightly and with disregard for opinion. For the regard of those held by the forces of others cannot contravene the nature of those held within and by themselves.

TUES 31ST MAR 2015, ROME AT 10.30AM, SESSION 130

Mr P: Space and time as a combination contravenes understanding and yet without knowing the intricacies of how equational divergence mirrors constant fluctuation, it is possible to gain a 'sense' of the rules and measures of relativity.

Digital life is measured on this understanding, and quantum life – by way of observation of theoretical studies – supports a 'move-on' from *standard time-space mechanics*. But what if the combination – the 'pairing', to extrapolate a bigger picture – were not of time and space but of the *theory* of time/space in combination with, not the theory of quantum observation, but the understanding of quantum 'results?' Let me explain.

Man mostly observes time and space as the 'background' to life, and quantum theory as the mechanics of life. Whilst this is a broad example, it is nevertheless prevalent. The planet's scientists seek understanding of the great questions of humanity, to gain the key to *how things work*. In 'chunking down' it is possible to observe the parts of the puzzle but not the puzzle itself. And so man observes either the part or the whole but not the 'links' – the invisible strains of 'scientific' value which *bring together* the whole. The law of the parts being greater than the sum of its part, in itself and of the whole, creates a compounding effect of invisible 'matter'.

Observation of one's historical ancestry is a perfect example of this law. One can observe the centuries and whilst standing as an 'outcome' of all centuries that have passed before one can also not know the sum of each century: as each generation led to another, the 'sum' is passed on to create a greater sum in effect and outcome. Man is the greatest, and most complex and diverse, example of creationism to exist.

Man operates not in a background of time/space but is in fact the essence of the time/space combination. The measure of outcome – the quantum exchange within the dynamics of matter – is not the 'answer' but the *other-half* of time/space effect. The cause creates the effect as the quantum measure creates the time/space.

It is in 'chunking up' that the understanding of the laws which enable creationism can be observed...and hence the limitations of 'science'. To understand the unknown, reference and observation of past, yes, but the outlook has to be of an openness to the unknown, to creating a masterpiece of unknown outcome. As with human instinct and wisdom, so with 'science'. It is in creating a strain of science to support the observation of the 'unknown' outcome which will provide the understanding of what the 'combination' of time/space and quantum measure enables, which will offer the answer man seeks. It is in creating 'nothing' that the visibility proffers the sum of its parts. And this is both a challenge to man – and the healing he seeks.

THURS 9TH APR 2015, LONDON AT 14.30PM, SESSION 131

Mr P: 'Creating nothing' is an out-standing skill – for it requires utmost seamlessness and stillness. For humans, it requires tapping into inner being'ness whilst remaining open and wholly creative – imagination and 'permission' wise. Scientifically, it requires nerves of steel and trust. It requires 'going against the grain' and trusting one's instinct to hold back and observe.

The *requirement* aspect is one of movement within the 'space' of stillness. How is this possible you may ask? Well, all movement is 'held' within 'stillness'. It is just not visible to most people who walk the planet. A few understand and comprehend this phenomena, and some 'see' it.

Stillness is avoided by many – until one day they collapse in exhaustion. Cultivating stillness requires a willingness to pause and temper one's emotions and feelings…so that the sensations may arise. *Sensations* permit the movement. Humans are indeed sensory mammals, are they not?

Numbing one's sense occurs in the presence of too much movement, and not enough movement does the same. It is a fine line; the border between reason and effect, in a different form. Yet the principle still applies.

When we observe a *frenzied* external reality, we have two choices: to comply or to distract. Stillness, inner stillness, will distract and 'neutralize' the pace. Likewise, when we observe a calm exterior, we have the same choice of compliance or distraction: we can join in stillness or combine with increased inner pace to 'shift' the energies.

Whichever the decision – whether to counterbalance or join – there comes a moment, a 'linking' of the energies, when the borders 'meet' and movement – a sort of *friction* – occurs. It is in this delicate and exquisite capture of space/time and quantum results that the transformative space is created. This neutral space – an emptiness if you will – holds all potentiality. It is man's choice as to how to 'fill' it.

This 'place of potentiality', which is held within the awareness of all quantum and material atomic matter is the birthplace of creationism *in a sensory capacity*. Feelings and emotions lead one to the sensory *choice*. This occurs in all movements – hence the ability to alter the course of one's life in the blink of an eye.

But it is the *inner* sensory base state which affects the outcome – not the outcome which affects the state. This is a fundamental learning to understand – and one that 'goes against the grain'. *"If this happens, I will feel better", "If we achieve this outcome, we will find meaning", "If we delay so-and-so, we will avoid feeling this"* and yet we all know this fallacy. And yet man pursues…

The cultivation of the desired sensory state is the most fundamental act of man. For it affects all outcome by tingeing with the hue of the sensory state. Feeling happy? Then happiness prevails; feeling sad, then sadness prevails.

Our 'state' affects our feelings which affects our emotional colouration of the moment. *Trying* to feel something different will not change the base state. 'Wanting' to feel something different *will*.

People who find manoeuvring between states challenging are overly dependent on outcome; all attention is placed in the external, at the expense of flourishing stillness. By contrast, people who cultivate a resonant stillness – in particular in the face of adversity – have control of their sensory movement. And in being able to 'move' and adapt their senses, they elicit a trust of humanity's offerings.

Consistent awareness of one's inner state enables an awareness of what is desired. Acceptance of both the prevailing sensory state *and* the desired state enables the change of outcome. It is as effortless as a walk in the sunshine on a balmy day.

As all 'space' contains movement, all atomic matter – whether human thought or material aspects – are *moving* towards the next moment. Cultivating awareness of the desired state – a uniquely human ability – is what enables and creates man's power. In choosing how to 'fill' the space, man chooses his life and experiences. It really is that simple.

For scientific analysis, the method is the same...until someone challenges this instinct and 'withholds' a desired outcome. It is in such moments that flashes of inspiration transcend the limitations of mankind's thoughts. 'Divine inspiration'...no more than movement within stillness!

It is man's emotions which prevent the ease of flow. All emotions – whether 'high' or 'low' – 'mask' the ability to experience this deep *inner* stillness and movement. And yet the *reality* of emotions cannot be ignored.

Emotional response occurs in two forms: as a 'release' or as an 'acquisition', or to explain it differently, as a *letting go* or as an *accumulation* of energy. The desired effect is *always* a letting go, for it is the exhale of life. To create, one must let go. To breathe in, one must breathe out.

Emotional acquisition burdens the emotional body of man. This can be seen in the heaviness and stiffness of the physical state of man and in the heaviness and burden of his or her visible lifestyle and choices. In accumulating external references, man accumulates inner deposits of emotional energies.

Emotional release enables the opposing effects as it lightens and 'broadens' ones aspects. It facilitates healing and rejuvenation. And it enables creationism. In the clearing of the unwanted, the wanted can present. But oh, the task now present: *"What to choose?"* What will man choose to allow into this neutral space? And will he allow it?

Magnetic attraction is a pervading force of the universe. Not *the* pervading force but consistently impactful nonetheless. It *brings together* atomic resolution. And it tears apart inconsistent elements or strains of signature atomic decay: to enable the emptiness for the evolving *new*-ness. Emotions 'hold' magnetic charge. Feelings, somewhat less so, and states even less. It is the emotion with the greatest magnetic charge which will be attracted into the space – *unless* it is denied permission. And the sole way to deny the permission is to choose an alternative base state.

The clearing of unwanted emotions is powerful as an act of healing. It also, through links of exchange, reduces the charge of 'surrounding' emotions. But it is the attention to the base state which creates the powerful outcome.

Man, through technological advances has focused primarily on outcome – as a panacea to the 'hurt' of humanity. But it is *holding the space* within stillness where the visibility of movement – including all its attracting forces – will present itself. No truer word has been said.

WED 22ND APR 2015, LONDON AT 9.50AM, SESSION 132

Mr P: Today's answers to tomorrow's problems cannot be forecast through a desire to 'solve' the problem. Rather, in forging a desire or ambition *beyond* the problem, and beyond the solution, can the panacea be discovered, and applied.

A desire to provide water, for instance, to a rural community with no infrastructure, requires planning a thought for the building of not just a pipeline, but outlets, reservoirs, drainage, sewerage, access points and riverlets. In factoring the impact of such development, consideration is given to the impact *today* and also, more importantly it would seem, the impact 'tomorrow'. As a future growth inclination, the *potential* of the future impact creates a firm base for additional growth in the here and now. Before it is even built, the *intention* to build a water supply will fuel development and growth of other structures. Before the first spade has entered the ground, ideas for schools, roads, homes will abound.

This example, of what has commonly occurred since man has walked the planet, assumes one fundamental point of interest: that of the developing psyche. It is man's intrinsic inclination to develop – both internally and externally. And this is a law of nature.

The balance between *solving a problem for today* and *building answers for tomorrow* lies within man himself. He is the purveyor of the 'instance of time'…the keyboard player of the tune to which he dances to. He may *live* in the today, but it is in operating in the tomorrow that the developing psyche has the most strength and capacity.

How is this a desirable state you may ask? How can an outlook requiring a pull *from* this present moment create inner peace and acceptance? What of the wisdom of old and the lessons of the quietened mind and deep contemplation for *this* moment?

All of these conducts apply to the developing psyche of man – are worthwhile and valuable in themselves – but presuppose a wish to 'still' the speed at which man operates. It is the *speed* – man's passing of time and space – which is the inhibitor of the developing psyche.

In resting in stillness, man *brings back* to centre his developing psyche. He creates a container – a safe space – for its measure and assessment. He can, when centred and focused on his inner being, observe and relate to what his psyche wishes to say and wishes to 'produce' as a *next movement*. As he listens to his developing psyche within, he intuitively knows and feels comfortable with his evolvement.

This practice will give light on man's *problem solving for today*, but for his or her *building answers for tomorrow* a different awareness is needed.

The passage of time is man's greatest battle. And as a result, his energies are centred not within himself but against himself. Man *is* space and time and in pressing against himself, he creates discord and splits. Within these splits energies and emotions surface and lie. The battle, now against aspects of himself which require little more than a cleansing of, yet trap him like glue to an aspect not desired by him, but created by him.

Solutions gained through the discovery of thought outside the aspects of time satisfy all problems. When thought is devoid of limitation it enters 'a different realm' – for it satisfies the unrestrained soul and aspects of the psyche which operate on the knowledge that all is equal, irrespective of time and space.

But to enter thought without limitation, one must relinquish the 'passage of time', the need for outcome at a certain point or in a certain way, and most crucially, in a desired manner. For the expression and development of thought itself creates an ever-changing backdrop of life. *This* is the passage of time and space: the ever-changing development of thought. As the purveyor of thought, man rests at the very centre of this unfolding reality.

In adopting limitless thought, there *is* no problem, nothing to be solved. Of course there is contrast – an unfolding reality – of which man interplays, but the objective vision is of a greater connection to the passage of life: of oneself.

THURS 23ᴿᴰ APR 2015, LONDON AT 9.20AM, SESSION 133

Mr P: The passage of time, when observed yet not with attachment, enables one to *have a benchmark* for the passage of life, but, when used 'as' life, all objects of worth become 'worthless'. Let me explain…

As purveyors of space and time, man has the ability to 'create' what he wishes, and crucially, to *enjoy* it. It is the 'it' he is enjoying, as an inner experience of what he creates in his or her reality. A beautiful walk at sundown on a summer's day creates a feeling of tranquillity within. But it is 'it', the *aspect* of 'the walk' – the formless aspect of the experience – which creates the impact and sense of wellbeing. The walk – 'it' – is not space and time, but an expression of it.

When man takes the same walk, but is walking against the clock, he is interacting with *the clock*, not the walk. The clock – the passage of time – has become the form, and the experience of the formless aspect of the experience has been overlooked, ignored. For this reason, those who 'worry' about time miss out on the very offering before them – and created by their soul.

Now, man's interaction with reality, what he sees as 'life', is not *life* itself, but his interaction with the passage of time: of what he is losing and is passing him by. When this awareness is gained and in those moments where he operates in *life* and not 'time', he is living in the formless – in a world where the meaning of one's actions and behaviours enable a greater resonance and *fruitfulness* to the day. 'Doing nothing' – the most enriching of experiences; as with doing what needs to be done – equally enriching. For when one resides in the formless, form becomes *fun* and the enabler of greater benevolence and creativity. When we reside in the formless, we become available for others, for now we are free of the restrains of the ego. The ego becomes our friend: the creator of the expression of what man is.

FRI 24TH APR 2015, LONDON AT 8.30AM, SESSION 134

Mr P: "Today's experience creates tomorrow's outcome." Hmmm. Whilst there is some truth in such a claim, there is also great misunderstanding. Yes, what is created today (whether judged 'good' or 'bad') will combine with the energies of force to impact tomorrow's combination and colouring, but the aspect of the formless is always free of constraint. We may have a 'commitment' to uphold, but our approach – our distilled formless approach – decides the experience and hence the outcome. A commitment approached with vigour, inquisitiveness and presence will result in a very different outcome than one approached with regret, resentment and reproach. The *act of doing the commitment* is the form when it controls man's experience. In transferring his power, control and aggression to the commitment, whatever it is, he creates the form itself: outside of him.

By contrast, when he decides the colouration of the approach, when he maintains all power within, and all attachments *with himself,* his experience is of the formless. He is in flow. And he is free.

The reality of the formless confounds man to such an extent he can doubt his sanity. For it is as 'real' as the ground he walks upon, yet as elusive as a grain of sand on a windy day. The trick: to call the sand to oneself.

Man's power is as elusive as a single grain of sand...and as essential to the planet. Man *is* but a grain and *is* all of the grain. The stars, the moon, each wave upon the ocean: all reflections of man's power. When he connects to this realisation, that he *is* the very essence of life – the formless shown in the form of the planet he resides upon – he catches a glimpse of the elusiveness he knows he belongs to.

Man's journeying through space and time is an expression of his power. Power has two directions, no more. It can be given away, in service of the Self, or it can be called, harnessed, cultivated, in service of the formless of others. All action is one of two flows of energy: the harness of form or the giver of formless. As such, it is law, and it is the ebb and tide of humanity.

———

Mr P: The purpose of these words and discussions has been to create not just awareness of offering views and outlooks, but for some, it is intended, greater connection with the formless within.

Everything touched upon in these pages can be scaled to greater or lesser capacity. The principles within these pages apply to scientists seeking answer to universal dimensions as much as to the man, woman or child seeking perhaps not answers but harmonious peace. They are intended as metaphors for interaction with life and as such, are quantum theories of the emotional, spiritual and 'combined' aspects of man and nature. The *passage of time* offers hindsight, but the moment offers clarity of being, and as such, man is in the most exquisite, and most *appropriate*, of realities.

The next section of this book will offer ideas and translate some of the thoughts and offerings into suggested practices for orientation of the soul within man's psyche. It will focus on combining man's power with his greater inner knowledge. And it will pertain to not just the aspects of man's reality, but also his connection to the greater reality of his place within his own time and space. For man, as the purveyor of his loves, his passions and his experiences *is* the capacity he seeks.

PRATICES OFFERED BY MR P.

Seeking Full Capacity. Practices for the Orientation of the Soul Within the Psyche

Steps towards an inner quietening: in hearing the silence, stillness offers.

MON 1ST JUNE 2015, LONDON AT 15.20PM, SESSION 135

PRACTICE 1

These practices are intended for incorporation into daily life; as a pleasure, never a chore. They are all of an awareness creating nature – recognition of that intention alone will give results of note. But whatever the awareness, know it is growth and creationism in itself; for thought *is* creativity.

New thought – as opposed to repetitive cycles of judgement and admonishment – is rare and most lovely when it presents. Books, films, stories offer narrative and lifestyle viewpoints, yes, but it is the self-generated *new* thought which tantalises and sparks the soul and inspiration of man.

It is cultivation of *these* thoughts that the exercises in this section of the works will address. Each practice: either a quietening of the perpetual cycles, or a deepening of the silence to allow the new-thought to emerge. The intention: the inspiration of man.

Proclamation towards new-thought will not be offered – for man is justly and amply equipped to profess his knowledge and opinions. Attention to this effect by a source other than of his choosing would not respect the nature of these works. And rightly so. For no man can suggest the thinking of another. And this, dear reader, is practice number 1.

<u>TUES 2ND JUNE 2015, LONDON AT 8.40AM, SESSION 136</u>

PRACTICE 2

Practice number 2 focuses on the release of emotion, for not all emotion is equal. Differentiation between 'useful' emotion and unhelpful emotion is the skill in this practice. Let me explain.

Man 'uses' emotion to radiate and *test* his reactions. This is his innate ability – a survival strategy, yes, but also a pleasure giving method of discrimination; when he follows his pleasure – his inspiration – he *grows* and develops. *Emotion* is his ability to sense his truth and to make informed and appropriate decisions. A rise in emotions of reticence, warning and doubt will perhaps 'save the life' of man in 'unseen' danger. Likewise, emotions of exuberance, joy and laughter within, will indicate a different path. Far from being a by-product – as commonly thought – to wisdom, they are direct expression of inner wisdom.

But man is not his emotion, and this is the confusion. Emotion is an *expression*, not a 'fact'. Man himself – the core essence of him, or her – is 'neutral'. It is the energies which flow through which create the 'living conditions' within him.

In an attempt to gain worth, man is tempted; not by the flesh or the pleasure, but by the harbouring of emotions. And

302

like an accumulation of sand on a beach, it becomes impossible to identify today's tidal offering from yesterday's.

The tides will not cease, this is the flow of man and of the universe, but what *can* happen, is an appreciation of not the beach, but the land itself.

'Underneath' man's emotions lie his knowledge – the essence of all his wisdom, and experience – the nutrients and 'goodness' of millennia seeped deep into the pores of his being. Awareness of his or her depth – the core of the planet, if you will – begins the process of non-attached observation of the waves on the surface.

A blustery day provides information, as does a calm stillness or any range of movement of the waters in between. It is the awareness that these observations are only information, which allows the awareness itself. Practise not attachment to feeling, but observation of *what the feeling feels like*. In this awareness, man has choice.

FRI 5TH JUNE 2015, LONDON AT 8.15AM, SESSION 137

PRACTICE 3

Practice number 3 relies on instinct. When we follow our instinct – physically or spiritually – we 'gain' in stature. By this, I mean confidence – for that is what stature is.

Instinct is thought primarily by man to be a survival mechanism: *'To get him out of danger'.* Whilst this is indeed useful, it is but one aspect of instinct. There are four main components, or categories (as within, so without), of instinct.

The first benefit of instinct is awareness itself. Without inclination of what to give attention to, there would be no awareness, no observation. Man is bred with an instinct to observe – in order to learn and grow. There is not a day that goes by, for every human being on earth whatever their conscious capacity, to experience growth and learning. Sitting in one's room, staring at four white walls will in itself create awareness. And so there is accumulated learning. Nothing stands still, all is in fluctuation, and as such, man is instinctively giving his awareness.

The second benefit is the absorption of data. The human brain and senses are 'offered' (some might say bombarded) millions, billions, trillions of particles of data. Instinct tells man what he needs to absorb, what is *useful*. Absorption of data is a very different 'function' to awareness. In awareness, we 'hold' the observation in neutrality, or perhaps with colouration of judgement, but nevertheless it is 'held' outside of man's being. Absorption carries a different energy, as the data is turned into information and accepted and integrated by man. This may be 'beneficial' or non-beneficial in outcome, but in either instance, ownership of the data, and its transmutation into information, has occurred.

The third property of instinct is the charitable nature of it. 'Healthy' instinct incorporates the grander scheme of life. It salutes to oneself, but it also in itself, has awareness of the whole – of the rest of humanity. Instinct *itself* carries a profound energy of togetherness, or camaraderie and of connection. When man follows his instinct – even within a 'life or death' moment – he is partaking in and actioning the energy of camaraderie, *'of wanting to be there for all of humanity'*. His experience and reflection will be of his individual survival – and perhaps of his close family – but this is just a reflection of his desire for the survival of the whole. The greater the sense of individual survivorship, the greater desire for the survivorship of mankind as a whole. The understanding of this aspect of instinct would be of benefit to those seeking understanding of others. For within 'selfishness' lies great equanimity.

The fourth benefit to man of instinct, is access to the font of all knowledge. Wisdom lies at the root of all movement. It is the creator of the movement. As man 'taps into' his stream of wisdom, he creates the movement in the organism of life which corresponds to his experience, and by default, to the experiences of others.

Each man's interpretation of wisdom will be different. There are common 'themes' and some might say doctrines, as to what constitutes wisdom, but instinct is man's avenue to his own knowledge of such. Instinct shows man his unique access and *is* the access. This is why man is so spellbound – and at times, distraught – by his or her instinct.

The understanding of one's instinct is the basis of the understanding of oneself. Greater knowledge, greater wisdom, will never cease. As such, man's instincts will cease not either. The creationism of humanity is guaranteed in the same way that the creationism of man is exercised to his or her individual capacity. The refrainment of instinct creates the blockages in flow man witnesses in the exterior world. Observation of how he or she allows his or her own instinct will offer great clarity, and increased understanding. This is the practice of number 3.

TUES 4TH JUNE 2015, LONDON AT 10.15AM, SESSION 138

PRACTICE 4

Practice number 4 is a simple one to adopt and incorporate. It is the integration of the breath into the body.

Many breathe as if air is *separate* from man, with the image of filling the lungs and exhaling from the lungs. Yet man resides *in* air. By dis-allowing this life-force whole-heartedly into his system, man creates a subtle resistance to his life-force.

The lungs act as vacuums for oxygen and other particles but man 'moves' within air itself. (Indeed, it is more complex than this, but of sufficient detail to enable this exercise.) When man consciously allows the air he breathes to infiltrate and travel to all parts of him – to the very essence of his core – he not only nourishes his senses and creates vitality, but he *welcomes* and embraces 'life' itself.

To become *one* with nature and reality, we must breathe as one with nature and reality. To fight the breath is to fight one's truth; and to accept the breath is to accept oneself within the order of oneself and the whole. Such a simple practice, with profound impact.

WED 10TH JUNE 2015, LONDON AT 13.30PM, SESSION 139

PRACTICE 5

Let us take our focus now to the mind, to the space in the cranium where thought 'arises'. Thought *arises* in the head, but is 'generated' in the mental body of man.

'Quietening the mind' is a form of releasing the mental body from the need to 'provide answers'. The 'mind' asks the questions, which the mental body attempts to answer. And so, the vicious cycle.

Man's mental body encompasses him; he thinks with his toes, and his belly button, and his torso – all of him. He is perpetually absorbing, filtering and desiccating awareness in response to the demands and critique of the mind. Man's mind is not tangible in physicality, yet is *known* in presence by all that walk the planet. And yet so little is understood by man of his own mind that he defers to the body to 'deal with it'.

Conscious awareness is the process of stepping into the mix – between the mind and the mental body: between the questions and the answers. Quietening the mind allows the body time to pause, recover ground and forge ahead with the feeling of space. The brain is the engine room of the mental body – as the heart is of the physical body – and so, it will accommodate to the degree to which it is asked.

The brain is capable of increased capacity – in response to the offerings of the mind; but whilst the mind is preoccupied elsewhere (creating self-diagnostic methods of reason and judgement) it cannot request of the brain.

Quietening the mind offers a multitude of effects. Not only does it offer peace to the mental body, but it enables the other organs and powerhouses of the physical body to 'breathe again'. The heart, liver, vital organs receive space as the mind gives permission to 'not provide answers'. This 'turnaround' *is* the freedom the physical body wishes: what man seeks in his seeking of harmony. *Letting go*, so much more than an act of release: also an act of gain, towards the new thought and life of the person.

"But how do I quieten the mind?" you may ask. And so I present practice number 5.

The 'option' to quieten the mind is practice 5. In the awareness that there is the option, or the choice to quieten the mind if so desired, is what enables the choice to be made. The 'answer' is provided 'outside' of the body – and in this single act, the chain of question-answer has been broken. The thought that we can have non-thought is as powerful as the non-thought to the thought itself.

By breaking the chain of thinking-in-order-to-answer the body is able to relax. Whether the mind is 'quietened' or not, the break in the chain creates space, and therefore an 'element' of peace within. The intention towards peace enables the flow to adjust according to the equation being offered. A new chain has been 'formulated' which can be enjoyed at one's leisure. With the break comes the inner connection. And this is always good.

MON 15TH JUNE 2015, LONDON AT 14.00PM, SESSION 140

PRACTICE 6

Transcendence is a form of being which encapsulates a region of 'survival' elusive to common day-to-day practice. And yet man practices transcendence without realising it.

'Moving through' time and space *is* transcendence. Being stuck, isn't. What man may judge as transcendence is merely alignment with his energies and potential. When one is aligned with his or her potential, he or she is in a *state* of transcendence. It is the *potential* which gives rise to the qualifying aspect – not the actuality.

Man has a habit of judging 'actuality' rather than potential. This one outlook, this one moment of pause as one observes 'what has been accumulated' creates an immediate energy of *stuck-ness* and the transcendent energy has been lost…dropped.

The *elusiveness* is not of the state of transcendence itself, but of the ability to observe without judging and comparing.

Comparing what man has or doesn't have, has gained or has lost, is what keeps him stuck in a cycle of material and energetic consumption. The past and the future become the conveyors of blessings and judgements, whilst man himself is left incapacitated and helpless within the grasp of time.

There is a belief that time and space move around man, when in fact it moves *through* man. The 'decision' to make a lifetime of a certain quantity of years, is a decision. *"His life was shortened by…"* is the most lazy and incomprehensible of outlooks: a denial of the beauty and value of the time and space of another.

'Survival' is misconstrued. Man only has *experience*. Life is experience. Moments followed by moments of experience. To judge another's experience as lacking in any way is what causes the elusiveness of transcendence – of the movement of time and space – through man.

Practice number 6 is the awareness of time and space moving through oneself. In mastering the art of present moment awareness, time becomes a clock and space becomes an opportunity. In observing the present-moment experience, past and future are not 'ignored' but *included* within the moment. Time becomes timeless and space becomes formless. The potential appears rather *beautifully,* effortless.

TUES 16TH JUNE 2015, LONDON AT 12.05PM, SESSION 141

PRACTICE 7

Practice number 7 relies on the instinct of 'doing one's best'. Not one's best according to what will please another – but one's best according to what pleases the soul.

Man's ego is predominantly beset to please others and yet is conditioned to protect the self. The instinct to 'do one's best' can capture man's spirit, or drain his spirit.

Cultivation of the awareness of the 'why' of wishing to do one's best will identify the source. But do not be tricked by the first response offered, for the ego will confound you with reasons of an 'obvious' nature as well as those of a deeply emotional one. Persist in asking the question of *why* until you hear the soul's response – the one which causes but the faintest of reactions, yet the deepest of resonations.

Knowing *when* to do one's best is the skill to seek. Much opportunity is wasted by incongruent action at a distempered time. And much time is wasted by confluence of the ego with matters pertaining to the soul. In such instances, refrainment is the action of choice.

'Doing one's best' means, at the root of its meaning: doing when one is *at* his or her best. And for this, the 80/20 rule applies. A rule of nature, its application relevant to all 'physical' action and as such, a requirement in *being at one's best.*

The practice of alignment to one's best – as quantified by the soul, not the ego – ensures 100% capacity. In truth, 100% exists not, for all action and inaction is linked in exchange, but the principle of focus of alignment creating the desired effect is the practice I offer.

The combination of 80% alignment with 20% effort not only ensures effortless and productive output, but the *understanding* between the soul and the ego. Alignment is of the soul energy, effort is of ego energy – and so, both are heard. It is the combination of choice.

Practice towards pleasing the soul rather than the drive of others creates a multitude of effects. The common fear of 'displeasure of the Gods' at the lack of compassion for one's fellow man becomes unfounded as the suggestion from the soul will always include kindness for others. Man's challenge, is to trust this process of cause and effect, and that the cause he or she partakes in will have an unknown effect. But this, a paradigm of a law of nature, is what enables the very peace man seeks.

SUN 21ST JUNE 2015, LONDON AT 17.15PM, SESSION 142

PRACTICE 8

Practice number 8 is one of refrain, not of compulsion, for this is always to be encouraged, but of thoughtlessness.

'Thoughtful action' will always supersede compulsion, but thoughtless action gets in the way of the greater potential and benefit of considered, thoughtful movement. Both instinct and measured action are 'cast aside' by the force of man's lack of attentive connection to both his truth, and the greater truth he stands within.

Quietening the mind enables this truth to be heard. It also enables compulsive instinct *within* this awareness to 'have a voice'. One's expression and voice, never of truth when as a result of thoughtlessness.

It is rare I would advocate restraint, but the circumstance of thoughtlessness requires no less: an obstacle which must be removed in order for truth to be felt.

Removal of thoughtlessness within itself sounds a misnomer: *"How can one remove something which is 'not there'?"* And this is why its presence is so destructive and undesirable. A lack of awareness breeds a greater lack, as the exchanges compound the effect.

The ability to restrain oneself from thoughtlessness is not acquired through *additional* thought, but through the realisation of the thought of thoughtlessness in itself. For thoughtlessness is an energetic force man partakes in – or chooses not to.

Much discussion has been had on the subject of 'consciousness'. As consciousness is 'currently' understood, man believes he has access to, and is part of, a greater, more effluent source of being-ness, and that man *comes to realise this* – or not. There is 'some' truth in this, but not enough to make it a source of prevalence to society: man is quite uncomfortably comfortable in his current state. The thoughtlessness which drives his day does not require a greater complexity in nature. And yet, he is not, on the whole, 'happy'.

Becoming awake to 'consciousness' is the process of adopting restraint for thoughtlessness. Many label the process as adopting compassion, or kindness, or empathy, but in truth it is, at its root level, the practice of adopting restraint.

When man releases moments of thoughtlessness, he discovers beneath the shadows, a sweeter, more fragrant stream of being-ness. This is what mankind alludes to as being the greater force of the universe. But it is not that *practical* or 'obvious' – although it *is* that pleasurable.

Restraint of thoughtlessness enables man to 'touch' the stream which beautifies nature, but it is his role – his aspect of the exchange – to nurture the energy. This he does by paying attention to it, by residing in a greater awareness for what lies beneath man and his fellow men and women.

Through this, the eighth practice towards greater peace and connection, man can begin to gain consideration for the thought that perhaps his thoughts – the very control of his being-ness – are preventing him access to 'a better place'. When harbouring rampant thoughts, one can practice posing the question: *"What is the thought of intent of this thought?"* When the realisation comes – *that there 'is' no intention* – one is awake to being ruled by thoughtlessness.

It is the act of intention which decides the outcome. No intention, no outcome. So if the intention is not to feel *'better'*, peaceful, joyful, productive, and it is not to feel *'worse'*, then it is thought-less.

MON 22ND JUNE 2015, LONDON AT 10.30AM, SESSION 143

PRACTICE 9

When one has begun to awaken to the realisation that not all thoughts are equal in their power, we begin to understand that each thought has a 'value'. It is this value-ness which feeds back to man the *appropriateness* and significance of what he observes from his vantage point between the edges of reason and belief.

'Value' is quantifiable in a way that no other 'reflection' is. Many consider love as the ultimate tangibility of worth. But only in so much as the *value* of the love can be assessed and enjoyed. Man is bound and freed by the degree to which he can enjoy the value of something – and yet this enjoyment is itself dependent upon its value. And so, how to break *into* this cycle of reflection?

Practice number 9 enables this entering. By allowing oneself to consider the meaning of an experience or thought, we can consider its value. And yet, the value must be one's own meaning – not, as commonly displayed, the value of another.

Singular awareness is the practice of fine-tuning our awareness to reflect one's personal, *actual* value. It begins the process of questioning our beliefs and appropriateness of the belief itself. Our edge of reason is in perpetual flow, yet man's beliefs often remain 'fixed'. This in itself creates conflict. By practicing singular awareness, one is immediately *thought-full* and considering one's intention. The enjoyment of the experience can be considered, for in the singularity there is the possibility of appreciation – for appreciation can only be generated from within.

The practice of singular awareness is not as *easy* as it may sound. Man is not conditioned to 'think for himself' whilst operating within the group. But it is a worthwhile practice which leads to the 're-organisation' of values. It is the journey of self-realisation.

TUES 23RD JUNE 2015, LONDON AT 14.40PM, SESSION 144

PRACTICE 10

Owning one's values is practice number 10 – and can only be achieved with the benefit of hindsight. We have to notice the lack – the absence of something – in order to create the demand within. When there is a desire for something, there is the willingness to accept or strive for it – and *then* the 'ownership' of value.

The reflection on *what is missing* is what creates ownership. And so, you might ask, how can one *own* what one does not have?

When it is acknowledged that time and space do not 'exist' as man perceives it, the present opens before him. Noticing a feeling of desire (created by a sense of lack) does not require attachment to past or future. Man has a *habit* of making all desire conditional: *"When I get this, then I'll be happy"; "When she apologizes for what she did then, then I can accept her today."* These conditions trap a man or woman or child in the outcome of what is no more than lack of ownership of his or her emotions. By making the outcome dependent upon the actions of another, he defers ownership and de-values his worth.

In the process, he traps himself further into perceptions of space and time. The clock ticks…

By contrast (and I use this term in jest…) acknowledgement of an inner desire, acknowledging one's worth in relation to the *wish* for something of a personal nature, creates value and feeds man's worth. By acknowledging 'what is missing *today*' man has the opportunity and ability to *put it right*. Conflict moves to acknowledgement, to action, to 'wholeness'. As man takes responsibility for his emotions, he accepts responsibility for his value – and in the process, brings all his pasts and all his futures into the present.

THURS 25TH JUNE 2015, LONDON AT 11.05AM, SESSION 145

PRACTICE 11

Practice 11 relies on using one's intuition – to gain stability within oneself. One can only be stable in the world when stable within. A house produced by unstable materials will weather not a storm. But a house of rigidity will not either. Adaptability, agility and ease are needed to manage the elements, and for man, this comes from within.

Agility comes in response to timely action – being flexible in the moment, as the moment strikes. There is an alignment which allows the movement to happen *instantaneously*.

This alignment comes from connection *'within'* ones intuition. Many practice 'deferring' to intuition; to at times asking themselves – their deeper self – what to do. This is wonderfully empowering and gratifying, for there is the knowledge of one's truth.

But a deeper level – one where a person resides within this intuition – affords even greater depth of awareness of Self. In being *in* one's wisdom, movement has an ethereal fluidity and lack of measure. It becomes effortless as a stability underpins all action and '*in*-action' enabling a freedom of movement. Intuition becomes one's 'base state'.

Tipping into the base state of intuition or self-truth requires nothing more than the desire to trust oneself – to trust that we will know when something does not feel right, does not feel in line with truth. The decision – *the intention* – to trust that one knows when something or someone is not in alignment with one's energetic make-up of the moment is the 'work' of trusting one's intuition. Upon this decision lies the intention, and so the shift has happened.

Transference to one's state of intuition happens in a gradual manner in response to presenting cause and effect. As the awareness grows that decisions are not needed – that life has become effortless – then one settles and absorbs the ability to flow and move with the tides. By relinquishing the posture of defence, one acquires the stance of flow.

<u>MON 29TH JUNE 2015, LONDON AT 8.50AM, SESSION 146</u>

PRACTICE 12

Randomness creates the world man resides in. The opportunity for choice is what sets man apart from other humanistic terms of reference. He has the ability not only to 'see' choice, but to create choice. And it is this differentiation which sets him apart.

Overwhelment occurs when man has a conflict of choice. But a conflict will only occur, not when man has too many items to choose from, but when he is being hindered from *creating* the choice he wishes. An example may be when presented in a store with the benefit of choice. It is not the item before him he needs to choose, but the item he wishes to place his attention to *away from the store*. Man 'presumes' the overwhelment is before him, yet it is *within* him.

Randomness is the field of all available choice – all creative potential. And yet there is always just one choice to be made: the answer to one's framework of reference.

Referring to one's framework 'positions' one within contextual connections of energetic matter. A study of metaphysical inertia will only be relevant to those requiring analysis of quantum theories for the benefit of *their* analysis. In that intention, results will be garnered and *translated* into a new context – relevant to the next person's frame of reference. And so information flows.

The same occurs in all matter. When operating outside of one's personal frame of reference, data is invalid – useless for the purposes of the information-seeker. Overwhelment occurs as awareness that the information being gathered belongs not to one's study but to another. As one's own framework remains 'empty' and neglected, conflict arises. Choosing to adhere to one's unique frame of reference within the option of all choice is not an *easy* challenge. For a challenge it is.

Man mistakes grasping opportunities with creating opportunities. In believing the offering is from *without*, a sense of 'bad judgement' is created in response to an inability to choose; in turn in response to a conflict over frames of reference.

There will always be untold choice and opportunity. Man's growth is in the realisation that he must chose the opportunities which uniquely fuel his soul and being – and that when so doing, he will inadvertently and uncompromisingly create from his or her field of Randomness. The outcome relies on the intention of the choice, not the choice itself.

Practice number 12 is connection with one's' field of Randomness – in cultivating an awareness that as one's conscious thought 'connects' and interacts with the field or sea of potential, it 'brings to life' energetic matter. First awareness, then thought, then outcome. The wonder is in observing the magic of the universe at play within one's hands. By choosing to honour one's frame of reference – whatever that may be – one partakes in the fabric of reality. *This* is what man calls conscious living.

FRI 21ST AUG 2015, LONDON AT 15.20PM, SESSION 147

PRACTICE 13

The 'drama' of one's life can be a valuable source of intelligence – but not to one of natural disposition towards 'dramatic responses'. A response relying on one's instinctual nature carries much weight, but it serves well to question the nature of the instinct.

Man has *instinct* – the deep source of what and who he is – but he also has 'instinctual responses' which may not in themselves relate to his or her instinctual nature. Instinctual nurture is very different from instinctual nature.

Practice 13 is the awareness of the differentiation between instinctual nature and one's instinctual responses. An awareness of the nurtured tendency to self-soothe – however the means – an example of a nurtured reaction to an instinctive feeling. The *true* instinct, soothed beneath the learned instinct. A band-aid to the nurturing of the wound below. And the true instinct: to heal the wound – the *wounded* instinct.

Wounded instinct happens in the absence of self-care. Man self-soothes in the absence of self-care. Self-care is a pro-active energy, dependent upon awareness, worth, self-recognition and a 'totality' of being. One cannot be *well* if one does not care *well* for oneself. And yet man oft neglects his or her care in favour of the care of others.

Nurturing others is a natural instinct. It is something man is predisposed to do – for the benefit of all. And yet how can he care for others if he cannot care for himself?

Observation of one's core instinctual responses in the face of self-care and care of others displays whether man is operating in accordance with his or her natural instinct or not. Lack of care = lack of truth. There is no other means to justify the neglect. Care of Self, unique in its nature to each of us; the means by which we discover our truth, for to honour one's care relies on the approval of the healing – whatever form it takes.

Man's instinct to view 'healing' as the application of a band-aid – *to get him back to where he was* – prevents the opportunity for him to discover his unique means of self-care. For the true self-care required to heal his wounds may take him from the nurture he has developed, to his nature – his instinctual Self.

Practice number 13 is the observation – and implementation – of what necessitates self-care. Without such awareness, man is at the mercy of 'the fixer' – the one who professes answers yet knows not the answer to the question: *"How do I make myself feel better?"* For to feel 'better', one must learn to feel the source of his or her pain or wound. The healing comes from the direction of the intention of wellbeing, and this direction must always come from the person wishing the healing. Man's brother and sister facilitates, loves, cares for, but cannot heal the other. Man inspires wellness, fixes bones, repairs tissue – enables and facilitates the means – but it is man's instinct which creates the 'nature' of wellbeing. As such, man is a co-creator of his fellow brother's wellbeing, but always the creator of his own. Awareness of the differentiation and the prevalence of each will help in identifying the draws on man's thoughts and emotions, for equally, man heals through the healing of others.

SUN 30TH AUG 2015, ALTEA AT 10.15AM, SESSION 148

PRACTICE 14

Practice 14 relies on the sense of individuation to silence the unnecessary confluents of the mind. Man believes he is unique yet professes little in the way of individuation of the Self – he mixes, for the most part, his own wish for connection with his individuality. And yet they differ in resonance.

Connection – to others, and within – requires a desire for interaction: an exchange. Individuation requires by contrast, a 'stance': a stillness. They differ, and yet one enables the other.

Individuation – a term coined to represent a strength of character and self-sufficiency – symbolises an acceptance of both Self, and one's environment. It is all-encompassing and yet it treads lightly. It is a process – never-ending and without aim – and also, in its momentary execution, also a state of awareness, of totality and completeness. It is the means and the method to enable one's execution of not just 'life' but oneself.

The stance of individuation prescribes to the notion of 'aliveness'. It is the connection with and to this *aliveness* which enables the counter-action of considered stillness within awareness. In connecting to the 'pulse' of life – of the universe, not just one's planet – the individualised man, woman or child *resonates* back in his or her own frame of movement. Within both the exchange of stillness *and* the movement, individuation occurs.

A sense of individuation depends upon the ability to silence the mind. A 'busy' mind observes not the intricacies of 'aliveness' within one's surroundings; the presence is lost to the internal chatter of thieves. For the mind steals time from the conscious creator.

Totality in presence gifts man time. He savours the day, the moment, the instant. This feeds his instinctual self, and so creates an ever-lasting'ness which connects him to more than what he perceives. He likes what he sees, for he feels what creates and enables him to experience not just survival, but *aliveness*. His chain of actions – never reactions – allows his individuation to flourish. The power becomes the presence he enjoys as he moves, silently and sweetly, from experience to timeless experience. But behold not the power of such a man, for one cannot see what one does not recognise. Behold instead, the power within.

Individuation supports man's desire for connection, through the intimacy of shared experience. Shared experiences of connection with the aliveness of one's reality enables the reflection of one's power to the other, and so, a deeply pervasive sharing of presence. The individuation of the Self, through one's inner connection to the whole, is what enables this connection at depth. The connection, not 'above' one's awareness, but below and 'within' one's presence. It is the joining of souls within the collective field of aliveness. It is the breath which feeds the soul.

Access to this point of individuation, the access in turn to the whole, occurs within the silenced mind. Using pin-point awareness aids this process. As does awareness of the power of silence – not the silence of no-sound but the ethereal silence of all-sound: of oneself *within* the movement. By locating the pin-point of silence within man, one creates a focus for attention upon one's silence. In connecting with this area of inner power, man enables his power to grow and to consume his actions and thoughts, for it is not the thoughts that silence themselves, but the silence which overlays the thoughts. Like water upon a fire, silence dispels the thought.

WED 2ND SEPT 2015, LONDON AT 11.05AM, SESSION 149

PRACTICE 15

Silence within one's being helps identify one's dispelled emotions. In the absence of the inner fluctuations of emotional tirage comes the observation of what has passed. It is the sense of *something*, something one cannot quite identify, yet in its absence becomes noticeable. Silence intensifies and projects the sound of retreating emotions, and for this reason, becomes addictive.

Addictive attraction to the sound of silence enables one to relax into the feelings of softness and comfort this lack of effortful living brings. In the attraction of the silence – the desire *for* something – we notice not what falls away until it is no longer there. Letting go happens 'by itself'. Life is embrued with a softness which allows for the birth of greatness. From the meek comes the strong, and from the silence chimes the sound of truth.

Truth cannot be deciphered in amongst noise of the mind – it arises from the place of the soul, between the cracks of the senses, responding to the call. It seeks the silence, the place where it can be heard, for it knows that within such pleasure it reflects its gifts and offerings.

Silence enables the soul visibility and presence. It loves movement, action, stillness, dynamism, but it craves the pleasure of silence. In sleep it finds such a repose, but it is within the day – the moments of awake'ness and aliveness that it benefits most.

Practice number 15 is the harbouring of silence for the benefit of the soul. Connection to the feeding of the soul creates greatness – the expression of man's truth. Man's fear of hearing the voice of the soul is what perpetuates his apparent love of busyness, of 'noise' and of tempestuous makings of dramatic scenes – within and without.

The practice of soul-connected-silence strengthens man's resolve to action and displays of self-compassion. In the momentary silence he is awake to himself and his fellow man: awake to the communication.

SAT 5TH SEPT 2015, LONDON AT 8.45AM, SESSION 150

PRACTICE 16

Practice 16 is the cultivation of love. Love *is* silence. Love has no words, and no need. It just is. Love therefore heals the mind of disturbance and ingratiated thought of Self and others. But identifying the source of one's love requires the skill of silence. One leads to the other.

Need, desire, want, emotion, is not love. All useful, all part of one's instinctual nature, but not love. The art is knowing the difference.

Cultivating a practice of the awareness of love is what offers benefit to the soul. The psyche will resist silence, perhaps for its interpretation of love, but perseverance within the silence of love results in the feelings man desires: the *feelings* of love.

Feelings have voice – musical intonations of vast degrees – but it is the feelings of silence man seeks. Love is silence. It is the backdrop which reflects the noise, and so, it permeates all. Love, as silence, is greater than 'what-is', of who man is, yet available at any time, in any moment. This is the unconditionality one refers to.

Man's physical body is silent – in constant movement, yet silent. 'Sound' is created *by* man. Sound is vital, yet not at the expense of silence. The two complement one another.

Knowing, when one sits or rests within silence, one is resting within love is the practice to adopt. The knowing is sufficient to allow the permeation. This is practice number 16.

SUN 6TH SEPT 2015, LONDON AT 10.20AM, SESSION 151

PRACTICE 17

Practice 17 relies on the need for balance. The acquisition of silence enables movement of a different kind – one more gentle, softer, and with grace. Movement as such becomes flowing in nature as one aspect leads to another.

It is the 'aspects' of one's life which influence one's responses and actions. But aspects are none other than perceptual reflections of influential consideration. The 'influence' is within how one regards the aspect. The response or action comes from a stance of balance, or an extreme. There are no other options.

Silence contributes to balance, enables the 'noise' to be integrated or rejected. Silence enables the flow. As day needs night and night needs day. The balance is the resulting contribution from silence *and* noise.

Universal forces work on a system of balance and counter-balance. 'Flow' does the same. The greater the pull in one direction, the greater the release in another. Failure to follow such rules result in a *breaking*: the counter-balance to the lack of balance. It is nature, and it is law.

Acquisition of balance is most readily achieved through *flow*: a state where noise and silence are acknowledged and contained within each moment. Flow contains an openness, an acceptance – a lack of resistance. For a river to flow, there remains but movement after the passing – a continuum of movement from past, future, to present. There is no beginning, and no end, and as such, there is balance.

Balance requires such flow – to not see life and reality in terms of stop and start, here and now, if and but. These expectations of the psyche prevent flow and hinder balance.

Acquisition of balance involves acceptance, openness, trust and willing. It also involves the sense of Self: of individuation, and of participation – a willingness to ride the wave in acknowledgement of the journey. The flow which carries contains the movement. Man's part: to enjoy the participation, whatever the circumstances, for the circumstances – the aspects – create the flow. Aspectual observations – not within themselves, but *because of* themselves – define one's circumstances. Balance, flow, happens when one accepts the chosen river and relinquishes resistance to movement. The art is: within the movement, to accept the movement and yet be not of movement but of the stillness within.

MON 7TH SEPT 2015, LONDON AT 9.00AM, SESSION 152

PRACTICE 18

Differences between silence and stillness can confound, for they are different, yet contain elements of similarity and distinction. Both 'elevate' one to a place of greater vision and also ground one to deeper resonance, but within these movements are differences.

Silence envelops, stillness pervades. Both work 'together' yet one does not need the other – as silence requires noise and stillness requires movement.

Silence and stillness together enable compounded effect and create a loveliness within the exchange. It is the desired effect of practices such as meditation and transcendence. It is not however exclusive to a practice, but available at any time; within *noise*, within *movement* and within all aspects of *life*.

Adopting a resonance with the combination of stillness and inner silence allows the envelopment and pervading of this force and connection with greatness: greatness within and the greatness without. It affords a connection which protects and provides, and, whilst powerful in delivery, elicits a softness and gentleness which raises the question: *"What is power?"*

Practice 18 is the recognition of this combination within one's day – the moment on the way to work, when about one's tasks, upon waking, perhaps in meditation. The recognition allows the furthering and the greatness to flow.

TUES 8TH SEPT 2015, LONDON AT 8.50AM, SESSION 153

PRACTICE 19

Recognition of the combination of silence and stillness begins the process, but it is the frequency with which one recognises which aids the development. This awareness though, if in practice, prohibits the very act of awareness of oneself in such a manner. All reflection changes.

The alignment of stillness and silence (within noise and movement) takes one to the place of neutrality – of gratitude and purity. It is a 'letting go' of the handrails – and so, in this letting go, freedom from confluent thoughts occurs. How can one be aware, whilst not aware?

Recognition of this alignment happens on a level which differs from conscious awareness. First unconscious awareness, followed by conscious awareness, superseded by deep knowing. In the silence and stillness is one's truth. When in truth, one needs not awareness to recognise the state: one just is.

Practice 19 is the art of letting go into stillness and silence. Time has no relevance in such matter, and so, do not monitor the time *achieved* but the depth of enjoyment. To enjoy, *deeply en-joy*, for just a second is much more valuable than to contribute effort.

Letting go and enjoyment go hand in hand. The man, woman or child who proffers enjoyment will realise this skill; without effort. Effort diffuses joy and ridicules the soul, for within the soul's resonance is but the wish for joy.

Truth creates meaning, not effort. Trust creates ability, not effort. Enjoyment creates desire, not belief. Man's fortitude: misplaced when placed upon effortful living, for effort denies the heart and the soul of man.

Silence, stillness, when heard inspire man to his purpose – a purpose which will always benefit his fellow man. Through silence, not noise, he locates his voice. When the silence is deep enough, he becomes ready to share his voice, for now he is in communication with himself. He can proceed.

FRI 11TH SEPT 2015, LONDON AT 17.50PM, SESSION 154

PRACTICE 20

All these practices, all 19 of them, are in the direction of a quietening of the mind and a deepening of inner connection. They intentionalize a quietude and a depth to connection with one's soul. They also – as the practice deepens – create a greater connection with the divinity within one, and the divinity which emanates out and connects with the greater essence of man: his fellow man.

In the connection gained within, one will always witness an equidistant connection without – not of 'numbers' and reach of communication, but of depth and resonance. It is a frequency which radiates at a signal different to one which man typically adopts within a 'noisy' mind. The 'radiation' occurs from the *body* of man, through his vibrational sensory field. It is a vibration one cannot 'see' visually, but can see within a person: the man or woman who emanates a discreet confidence, knowing and ease of being. It is highly attractive to observe, and highly 'attractive' in practicality.

One attracts according to one's vibrational match: like attract like – this is understood. But what is little understood is *how* this occurs, and this is what I wish to share.

Practice number 20 is the final practice in this series; it is the one which when employed, 'sweeps-up' and *neutralises* all previous practices. It is the raising of the vibration to a level which renders purposeless any attempt to 'return to base', to 'be of old' and to attempt direction of ego. It is a 'packaging' and 'releasing' of all past karma and all past history, and in its execution it serves to render without need all those who surrender to the experience. In the nothing, a new reality appears, a vision of a reality which in one's superseded awareness one partakes within and yet is not of. It is an opening to a vision not seen by eyes, but understood by the soul of man and is what one can only describe as heaven on earth. It is the blending of the sublime within man with the sublime within his fellow man; of all men.

Like attracts like is a gravitational force within the fields of conscious dimensions – dimensions which will never be witnessed within current confined 'logical' thinking, but are apparent within dimensional thinking which relies on not infrastructures of plausibility but on the elements of *implausibility*. By looking at what *does not* 'make sense' one finds the answer to what man questions but dare not ask.

Plausibility is constraint and ignorance of mind. The mind *knows* better – the operator of the mind, man, is at whose feet responsibility lies for the ignorance. Imagine having a computer which knows every formula and eventuality, and yet one refuses to allow the emergence of such data! This is the activity of man in his busy little mind – a mind so capable it astounds! Man seeks what he knows, what *makes sense* and what he can 'rely' on. Yet this reliance is weak in the face of the unknown and in the face of gravitational force. In 'maintaining' strands of logic, man *keeps his world together* yet destroys the opportunity to *rise to the challenge* of a greater vibrational understanding of himself and the divine congruence of 'what-is'. In 'keeping himself together' he creates the tension which attracts greater reflections of such reality.

The cosmos is an exchange. It pulls together, or it pushes apart. Depending on the point of viewing is the outcome of such dynamics. Man, in general, 'pulls together' and so the cosmos 'pushes apart' – it is the gravitational dimension which enables the balance. Within such balance, the place of neutrality and of ascension. Man, whilst connecting with the *implausibility* of the least understood, believes the existence of gravitational forces to be the reflection of existence: the 'plausibility' within his reality. But nature astounds and nurture can deceive: the implausibility, that man *creates* gravitational force, perhaps 'a step too far' for the confined mind to grasp?

Those that understand a different reality understand that inverse 'logic' offers such *sense*. Life is a mirror, and man's reflection can confuse the sensitive of heart and the unwilling of adventure. But it is in the willingness to face the courage to question that which appears beyond the comprehension of man that understanding emerges. The mirror reflects what one wishes to see, for like attracts like, but it is the force which maintains the mirror and maintains man which provides the *energy* to allow the exchange. In the exchange between man and his mirror – his perceptual reflection of what he *chooses* to see – he gains the awareness needed to locate this aspect within him.

Man has evolved over millennia of time and space – the emergence through the mergence. The 'transition' to a vibrational level which permits a vision beyond the measures of comprehension is what will enable the life-creating resonance of the human race. It is a mergence of levels of understanding, which in the capture of their understanding proffer a greater depth of freedom, of belonging and of love. The joy which awaits beholds the beauty of the journey. In taking his first step, man guarantees his partaking. And in letting go, he activates his presence. Man is God.

The End

Reflections

A PERSONAL COMMUNICATION, MON 10TH OCT 2016:

Mr P: *"…people, Delilah, don't understand love. They feel lots, suppress lots, but don't know how to be frank in the face of their love and needs. We all my dear, need love. Just few acknowledge this in its purest form, for as I discussed in the book, we have it misconstrued within our whys. We, Delilah, are our whys, but we operate in the energy of love. But energy management – the battle-field of the planet – is where people play out their misconstrued ideas of love. Our reason, unforsaken in the face of one's beliefs. Our reason my dear, is love. This is the power of healing and of transformation. This is what is happening to you right now – the unveiling of love for yourself – and yes, this will, at times, be pain-ful. It is the balance."*

It is with the deepest of gratitude and love I thank my friends and family.
Without their care and support, this book would not have been possible.

In particular, I thank my son. Little does he know how much he inspires and teaches me.

Most of all, I thank life itself; for the love and connection, the contrast and the compassion, the humour and joy it brings.

www.DelilahSullivan.com

69423105R00192

Made in the USA
Columbia, SC
20 April 2017